THE NEW LOOK-IT-UP BOOK

BOAT MAN'S HAND BOOK

EMERGENCIES ▶

SAFETY ▶

SEAMANSHIP ▶

PILOTING ▶

WEATHER ▶

ELECTRONICS ▶

RACING ▶

AMENITIES ▶

SOURCES ▶

GOVERNMENT ▶

TABLES ▶

MAINTENANCE ▶

YOUR BOAT ▶

Compiled & Edited by Tom Bottomley

MOTOR BOATING & SAILING BOOKS
P.O. Box 2316, New York, N.Y. 10019

CONTENTS

EMERGENCIES

SAFETY

SEAMANSHIP

PILOTING &
NAVIGATION

WEATHER

ELECTRONICS

RACING

AMENITIES &
DIVERSIONS

INFORMATION
SOURCES

GOVERNMENT
REQUIREMENTS

USEFUL
TABLES

MAINTENANCE

PERSONAL BOAT
INFORMATION

OLLOW THE ARROWS

o find desired information quickly, place your thumb
t the arrow for the appropriate section, and flip
hrough the pages to the matching tabbed page edges
n the book.

For John A. Bottomley

Library of Congress catalog card number
76-172013

ISBN 0-910990-06-9

MOTOR BOATING & SAILING BOOKS
224 W. 57th St.
New York, N.Y. 10019

John R. Whiting—Business Manager
Editor—Thomas R. Bottomley

Composition, printing, and bind-
ing by The Haddon Craftsmen,
Inc., Scranton, Pa.

1.
EMERGENCIES

Safe boating practices minimize the danger of accidents afloat; indeed, recreational boating is one of the safest of all participant sports. However, the prudent skipper should know what to do in an emergency. Study this section; have your wife or other regular crew members study it so the right steps will be taken if you are not present, or are incapacitated. Make regular "man overboard" and "fire" drills a part of your safety routine.

MAN OVERBOARD

Here are steps to follow if someone falls out of, or off, your boat:

1. *Post a lookout.* It is imperative that the person in the water be kept in sight at all times, or at least the spot where he was last seen. Designate a specific crewman to do nothing but act as this lookout. At night, keep a search or flash light on the person.

2. *Throw over a personal flotation device.* Throw the man overboard a life ring, buoyant cushion, or other buoyant device, even though he may be a strong swimmer. A water-activated strobe light attached to a life ring is extremely effective at night.

3. *Don't let anyone jump in the water to help,* except in the case of a small child or elderly or handicapped adult. In such case, be sure the rescuer takes a life ring or other buoyant device with him.

4. *Maneuver to return* to the spot where the person fell overboard. Determine *in advance* whether turning to port or starboard is fastest. Stopping and backing down may be the fastest for some boats, but this should be done *only* in daylight, and *only* when the person in the water can be seen clearly. *Never* back down over the spot where a person went down! If you are alone, note your compass heading, and turn back 180 degrees on the reciprocal heading. Otherwise follow the signals of your lookout. Sailboat operators should carry out "man overboard" drills from a variety of headings in respect to the wind, in order to minimize confusion and loss of time in a real emergency.

5. *Use additional markers.* In some circumstances, particularly at night, it may be helpful to throw over additional buoyant objects to ensure that the path back to the victim can be traced.

6. *Maneuver for the pick up.* In some cases, you can approach from windward of the victim, and let the boat drift down toward him, providing a lee. In most cases, however, it is best to approach from leeward in order to avoid having your boat blow right over the victim. Just slight amounts of power will be needed to keep your boat under control. A sailboat should approach nearly on the wind so that it can luff up to stop headway when the victim is reached. In any case, stop the boat a short distance from the victim, and throw him a light line, such as a ski tow rope, that floats. It is less hazardous than trying to maneuver your boat right up to him.

7. *Get the victim on board.* If necessary, have a man who is physically able ready to go into the water to assist the victim. This crewman should take a light safety line with him. A transom boarding platform is a help in getting the victim aboard, or a boarding ladder can be rigged. A line with a large loop, tied with a bowline, may be hung over the side to provide a foot-hold or handhold. Be sure the propeller is stopped whenever there is a person in the water near the stern of the boat.

8. *Call for help if necessary.* If the victim is not rescued imme-diately, get on the radio with the urgent communications sig-nal "Pan" to summon assistance from the Coast Guard, marine police, and nearby boats. Continue the search until the victim is located, or you are released by a competent authority.

EXPLOSIONS AND FIRES

Fires on a boat are serious, but usually they can be brought under control if you act quickly, and your boat is properly equipped with the required portable or fixed extinguisher systems.

Explosions

1. In the case of an explosion, be ready to go over the side. Grab a personal flotation device. Federal law requires that your PFDs be readily accessible.

2. When clear of danger, check about and account for all those who were aboard. Render such assistance as you can to anyone burned, injured, or without a buoyant device. Keep everyone together to facilitate rescue.

Fires

1. If possible, apply the extinguishing agent by:
   a. Using a fire extinguisher,
   b. Discharging a fixed smothering system, or
   c. Applying water to wood or materials of that type.
2. If practical, jettison burning materials.
3. Reduce the air supply to the fire by:
   a. Maneuvering the vessel to reduce the effect of wind. It is generally recommended that the boat be turned into the wind, as the fire is usually aft; this allows persons on board not needed for fighting the fire to assemble on the bow.

    b. Closing hatches, ports, vents, doors, etc. if the fire is in an area where this action will be effective.

4. Make preparation for abandoning your boat:
    a. Put on lifesaving devices, and
    b. Signal for assistance by radio or any other means available.

LEAKS AND DAMAGE CONTROL

The circumstances of suddenly taking on water are so varied as to permit only the most generalized advance planning, but in most cases the following steps to be taken by the skipper, may be effective:

1. Immediately switch on all bilge pumps. The risk of harm to the pumps by running them dry is far less than that of having water in the bilge get a head start. Turn them off as soon as you are sure they are not needed.

2. Assign members of the crew to operate manual bilge pumps, as necessary.

3. Assign a member of the crew to inspect for leaks, to pull up floor boards and check the bilges, if necessary.

4. If the boat is taking on water, turn helm over to another crew member, and take charge of the damage control actions. In most cases, boat should be slowed or stopped to minimize inflow of water; in some cases a hole may be kept above water by remaining on plane.

5. If regular pumps, manual and electric, do not handle influx of water, stop your engine, shut the water intake seacock, transfer the water intake to the bilge, and restart the engine so its water pump is also drawing water from the bilge. Note: there must be enough water flowing in bilge to meet engine's cooling needs, and caution must be exercised to prevent debris from being sucked into the cooling system.

6. If possible, cover the hole from the outside with canvas, bunk sheets, towels, or any other material available. Lash or nail it in place. It may be possible to nail boards over the hole, or a piece of tin from a can, to reduce leakage. On fiberglass or aluminum hulls, clinch the nails over from inside to prevent the patch from falling away from the hull. The object is to restrict water flow to an amount that can be handled by your pumps.

7. Call the Coast Guard for assistance if you have a radiotelephone, or display one or more of the distress signals described in Table 1–1.

DISTRESS SIGNALS

Accepted forms of distress signals have been written into the various Rules of the Road or related Pilot Rules. They are listed in Table 1–1. An additional signal, developed in Canada, is illustrated in Fig. 101.

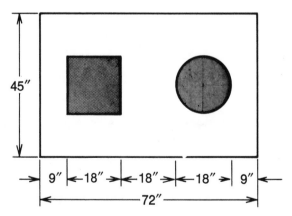

Fig. 101 Distress signal developed in Canada is a rectangle of fluorescent orange-red cloth on which are marked a black square and circle. Note dimensions shown.

Table 1-1

DISTRESS SIGNALS

	Rules of the Road or Pilot Rules			
Distress Signal	Inland	Great Lakes	Western Rivers	Inter-national
Continuous sounding with any fog-signal apparatus	D/N	D/N	D/N	X
Firing of a gun or other explosive signal	D/N	D/N(2)	D/N(2)	X(2)
Flames on the vessel (as from a burning tar or oil barrel, etc.)	N	N	N	X
A signal consisting of a square flag having either above or below it a ball or some object resembling a ball			D	D	X
Slowly and repeatedly raising and lowering arms outstretched to each side	D	D	D	X
Rockets or shells, throwing stars of any color or description, fired one at a time at short intervals		N	D/N	X
The International Code signal of distress indicated by NC			D	X
The signal SOS sent in the Morse Code (. . . − − − . . .) sent by any means				X
The spoken word "Mayday" by radiotelephone				X
A rocket parachute flare or a hand flare showing a red light				X
A smoke signal giving off a volume of orange colored smoke				X

The above signals can be used singly or in any combination.

Notes 1—D = Day use; N = Night use;
D/N = Day or night use;
X—IntRR do not specify in
terms of day or night use.
2—fired at intervals of about
one minutes

RADIOTELEPHONE DISTRESS PROCEDURE

1. If radio is so equipped, activate the Radiotelephone Alarm Signal.
2. Give the distress signal "Mayday" three times.
3. Give your boat's name and call sign, three times.
4. Give particulars of your boat's position (latitude and longitude, if in the open sea, or true bearing and distance in miles from a known geographical position).

5. Give the nature of the distress, the kind of assistance required, the number of persons aboard, and any other information that would facilitate rescue.

FIRST AID

INJURY OR AILMENT	TREATMENT
Burns	Treat for shock. Relieve pain and prevent contamination. Avoid greasy ointments.
Convulsions	Seek medical aid. Restrain patient from self-injury.
Cuts	Place thick gauze pad over wound, bandage snugly with adhesive strips. Minor cuts—wash with soap and water, dry, and dress as above.
Electrocution	Apply mouth-to- mouth resuscitation. Treat for shock.
Fainting	Lower patient's head, loosen clothing, sprinkle face lightly with cold water. If patient does not respond, summon medical aid immediately. Keep person warm.
Fever	Apply cold head compresses. Rub body with mixture of 50% alcohol and water. Keep patient in bunk or bed, have him take aspirin, hot tea.
Fractures	Seek medical aid. Keep patient lying down and warm. Do not move if spine or skull fractures are suspected. If patient must be moved, immobilize broken limbs with splints.
Heat exhaustion	Shade patient, have him lie down with head low. Wrap in blanket; give cup of strong coffee or tea. Seek medical aid.

Jellyfish,	Rinse area with fresh water, wash with
Man-of-war, etc.	soap (green germicidal soap if possible),
stings	apply household ammonia.
Seasickness	Stay in fresh air if possible, breathe deeply. Move, stay busy. If vomiting, take liquids as soon as possible afterwards.
Shock	Patient should lie down and remain quiet. Keep him warm, but not perspiring. Raise feet if he feels faint; raise chest and head slightly if breathing is difficult.
Sunburn	Relieve discomfort from mild burn with olive oil or petroleum jelly. If burn is severe or victim feels sick, seek medical aid, and treat as for regular burn.
Sunstroke	Have person lie down with head elevated. Loosen clothing, keep in shade. Give no stimulants, and seek medical aid.

Based on Chris-Craft "Boatman's Guide: First Aid"

See "Boating Safety" section for information on first aid kits and their contents.

ACCIDENTS

In the case of collision, accident, or other casualty, the federal law requires the operator, if and so far as he can do so without serious danger to his own vessel or persons aboard, to render such assistance as may be necessary and practicable to other persons affected by the incident in order to save them from danger as a result thereof. The operator must also give his name and address, and the identification of his vessel, to any person injured and to the owner of any property damaged.

Whenever death results from a boating accident, a written report must be submitted within 48 hours of the accident, to the

Coast Guard Officer in Charge, Marine Inspection, nearest to the place where the accident occurred.

If the accident results in injuries in which the victim is incapacitated for more than 72 hours, or physical damage to property in excess of $100, the report must be submitted within five days of the incident. Many states require a report to be submitted to a state official, as well as to the Coast Guard.

Written reports to the Coast Guard should include the following:

1. The numbers and/or names of vessels involved.
2. The locality where the accident occurred.
3. The time and date when the accident occurred.
4. Weather and sea conditions at the time of the accident.
5. The name, address, age, and boat operating experience of the operator of the reporting vessel.
6. The names and addresses of operators of other vessels involved.
7. The names and addresses of the owners of vessels or property involved.
8. The names and addresses of any person or persons injured or killed.
9. The nature and extent of injury to any person or persons.
10. A description of damage to property (including vessels) and estimated cost of repairs.
11. A description of the accident (including opinions as to the causes).
12. The length, propulsion, horsepower, fuel, and construction of the reporting vessel.
13. Names and addresses of known witnesses.

Artificial Respiration

Every boatman should have a working knowledge of the principles of artificial respiration. When the need for it arises, there is no time to search for instructions nor to study each step while, at the same time, attempting to apply the treatment. A boatman who has familiarized himself in advance with one of the accepted methods is more likely to work with calm assurance, saving precious minutes that could mean the difference between success and failure. Through the courtesy of The American National Red Cross, we reproduce below the simplified illustrated methods they advocate. In recent years the mouth-to-mouth method, illustrated in steps 1 to 5, has come into widespread use. Recognizing, however, that some rescuers cannot or will not apply this method, the Red Cross includes instructions for the older manual chest pressure—arm lift (Silvester) and back pressure—arm lift (Holger Nielsen) methods. Study carefully the additional instructions at the bottom of the page applicable to all methods.

If victim is not breathing, begin some form of artificial respiration at once. Wipe out quickly any foreign matter visible in the mouth, using your fingers or a cloth wrapped around your fingers.

MOUTH-TO-MOUTH (MOUTH-TO-NOSE) METHOD

Tilt victim's head back. (Fig. 1). Pull or push the jaw into a jutting-out position. (Fig. 2).

If victim is a small child, place your mouth tightly over his mouth and nose and blow gently into his lungs about 20 times a minute. If victim is an adult (see Fig. 3), cover the mouth with your mouth, pinch his nostrils shut, and blow vigorously about 12 times a minute.

If unable to get air into lungs of victim, and if head and jaw positions are correct, suspect foreign matter in throat. To remove it, suspend a small child momentarily by the ankles or place child in position shown in Fig. 4, and slap sharply between shoulder blades.

If the victim is adult, place in position shown in Fig. 5, and use same procedure.

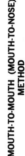

MANUAL METHODS OF ARTIFICIAL RESPIRATION

Rescuers who cannot, or will not, use mouth-to-mouth or mouth-to-nose technique should use a manual method.

THE CHEST PRESSURE-ARM LIFT (SILVESTER) METHOD

Place the victim in a face-up position and put something under his shoulders to raise them and allow the head to drop backward.

Kneel at the victim's head, grasp his wrists, cross them, and press them over the lower chest (Fig. 6). This should cause air to flow out.

Immediately release this pressure and pull the arms outward and upward over his head and backward as far as possible (Fig. 7). This should cause air to rush in.

Repeat this cycle about 12 times per minute, checking the mouth frequently for obstructions.

If a second rescuer is available, have him hold the victim's head so that the jaw is jutting out (Fig. 8). The helper should be alert to detect the presence of any stomach contents in the mouth and keep the mouth as clean as possible at all times.

THE BACK PRESSURE-ARM LIFT (HOLGER NIELSEN) METHOD

Place the victim face-down, bend his elbows and place his hands one upon the other, turn his head slightly to one side and extend it as far as possible, making sure that the chin is jutting out. Kneel at the head of the victim. Place your hands on the flat of the victim's back so that the palms lie just below an imaginary line running between the armpits (Fig. 9).

Rock forward until the arms are approximately vertical and allow the weight of the upper part of your body to exert steady, even pressure downward upon the hands (Fig. 10).

Immediately draw his arms upward and toward you, applying enough lift to feel resistance and tension at his shoulders (Fig. 11). Then lower the arms to the ground. Repeat this cycle about 12 times per minute, checking the mouth frequently for obstruction.

If a second rescuer is available, have him hold the victim's head so that the jaw continues to jut out (Fig. 12). The helper should be alert to detect any stomach contents in the mouth and keep the mouth as clean as possible at all times.

RELATED INFORMATION FOR ALL METHODS

If vomiting occurs, quickly turn the victim on his side, wipe out the mouth, and then reposition him.

When a victim is revived, keep him as quiet as possible until he is breathing regularly. Keep him from becoming chilled and otherwise treat him for shock. Continue artificial respiration until the victim begins to breathe for himself or a physician pronounces him dead or he appears to be dead beyond any doubt.

Because respiratory and other disturbances may develop as an aftermath, a doctor's care is necessary during the recovery period.

2.
SAFETY

Boating safety requires carrying equipment to be used in an emergency, as well as operating precautions to prevent emergencies. Here are your basic requirements:

TOOLS AND PARTS

1. Tools for on-board repairs should include:
   Set of combination open-end/box wrenches in 7/16, 1/2, 9/16, 5/8, 11/16, and 3/4 inch sizes.
   10" open-end adjustable wrench.
   Screwdriver assortment, including one for Phillips heads.
   Pair of slip-joint (ordinary) pliers.
   Pair of sharp diagonal-cutting pliers.
   Vice-grip or locking plier-wrench.
2. On-board spare parts:
   Vee-belt for each size used on engine(s), matched belt pairs, if such are used.
   Water pump impeller (for inboard engines)
   Set of spark plugs

Fuel pump and strainer, fuel filter elements if separate filters are installed.

Distributor cap, rotor arm, condenser, breaker point set.

At least two spares for each type fuse used aboard the boat.

FIRST AID KIT

The container for your first aid kit should be plastic; avoid a metal that could rust, or cardboard that could soak up moisture. Seal it with tape to keep it moisture-tight, but do not lock it. The kit should contain both the following simple instruments, and consumable supplies:

1. *Instruments*

Scissors, small and sharp. If there is room for two pairs, one should be of the blunt-end surgical type.

Packet of single-edge razor blades.

Tweezers, small, pointed. Tips must meet exactly to pick up small objects.

Safety pins, assorted sizes.

Thermometer, inexpensive oral-rectal type, in a case.

Tourniquet.

Eye-washing cup, small, metal.

Cross Venti-breather device to aid in mouth-to-mouth resuscitation.

Hot water bottle.

Ice bag.

2. *Supplies. Within reasonable limits, substitutions can be made* to reflect local availability, personal preferences.

Bandages, 1″, 2″, and 4″ sterile gauze squares, individually wrapped. Bandage rolls, 1″ and 2″. Band Aids or equivalent, assorted size, plus "butterfly closures."

Triangular bandage, 40″, for use as sling or major compress.

Elastic bandage, 3″ width, for sprains or splints.

Adhesive tape, waterproof, 1″ and 2″ by 5 or 10 yards.

Absorbent cotton, standard size roll.

Applicators, cotton-tipped individual swabs, such as Q-tips.

Antiseptic liquid, such as tincture of iodine or merthiolate.

Petroleum jelly, small jar.

Antiseptic ointment, 1 oz. tube of Bacitracin or Polysporin, or as recommended by your doctor.

Nupercainal ointment, 1 oz. tube.

Pain killer, aspirin or related compounds.

Sleeping pills, Seconal or equivalent as prescribed by your doctor.

Antibiotics, for use *only* if there will be a delay in reaching a doctor and infection appears serious. Use Achromycin, Erythromycin, or similar drug as prescribed by your doctor.

Ophthalmic (eye) ointment, small tube of butyn sulfphate with metaphen.

Antihistamine, Pyrabenzamine tablets, or as prescribed by your doctor.

Ammonia inhalants.

Seasickness remedy, Dramamine, Marezine, Bonamine, or Bonine tablets or suppositories.

Anti-acid preparation, liquid or tablet.

Anti-diarrhea drug, 3 oz. bottle of Paregoric (prescription required) or 8 oz. bottle of Kaopectate.

First aid manual.

FIRE EXTINGUISHERS

The type and number of fire extinguishers required for boats of each class are shown in Table 10–2. (See "Government Requirements" Section). In choosing those for your boat, you will find the following information valuable:

Classes of Fires

Fires are classified into three categories:

Class A—fires in ordinary combustible materials such as wood, paper, cloth, etc., where the "quenching-cooling" effect of quantities of water or solutions containing large percentages of water is most effective in reducing the temperature of the burning material below the ignition temperature.

Class B—fires in flammable petroleum products or other flammable liquids, greases, etc., where the "blanketing-smothering" effect of oxygen-excluding media is most effective.

Class C—fires involving electrical equipment where the electrical conductivity of the extinguishing media is of first importance.

Fire Extinguishers

Fire extinguishers are classified on the same "A", "B", "C" system as are fires. Some types of extinguishers, however, have a suitability greater than their basic classification. Extinguishers required by law on boats are in the "B" category, but a carbon-dioxide or dry-chemical extinguisher will also have value in fighting an electrical ("C") fire. On the other hand, a foam-type "B" extinguisher is effective on ordinary Class "A" fires but is *not* safe on Class "C" electrical fires. Boatmen should remember that for typical Class "A" fires in wood, paper, or bedding, the popular dry-chemical extinguishers are *not* as suitable as an ordinary bucket of water.

Fire extinguishers should be distributed around the boat in relation to potential hazards. One should also be near the boat's control station where it can be grabbed quickly by the helmsman. Another should be mounted near the skipper's bunk so that he can roll out at night with it in his hand. Other locations include the galley (but remember that water is best on a stove alcohol fire!) and any other compartment at some distance from the location of other extinguishers. Fire extinguishers should be mounted where they are clearly visible to all on board as they move about the boat.

It is important to keep in mind that the small extinguishers usually carried on boats normally discharge the extinguishing agent for only *eight to 12 seconds,* and then are empty.

SAFETY

BILGE VENTILATION

The "proper and efficient" ventilation of boat bilges was established as a requirement by the Motorboat Act of 1940 for all boats employing volatile fuels (gasoline) with certain limited exceptions. These are:

(1) Boats constructed before the effective date of the Act, 25 April 1940.

(2) Boats of "open" construction.

Open Construction Defined

The Coast Guard has prepared a set of specifications to guide the boat owner as to whether his craft meets the definition of "open construction." To qualify for exemption from the bilge ventilation regulations, the boat must meet *all* of the following conditions.

(1) As a minimum, engine and fuel tank compartments must have 15 square inches of open area directly exposed to the atmosphere for each cubic foot of *net* compartment volume. (Net volume is found by determining total volume and then subtracting the volume occupied by the engine, tanks, other accessories, etc.)

(2) Fuel and engine compartments must have at least one square inch of open area per cubic foot within one inch of the compartment bilge level, or floor, so that vapors (which are heavier than air) can drain out into open areas.

(3) There must be no long or narrow unventilated spaces accessible from the engine or fuel tank compartments into which a fire could spread, unless the space meets requirements of item 4 below.

(4) Long, narrow compartments, such as side panels, if joining engine or fuel tank compartments and not serving as ducts, must have at least 15 square inches of open area per cubic foot through frequent openings along the compartment's full length.

Diesel fuel does not come within the Coast Guard's definition of a "volatile" fuel, and thus bilge ventilation legal requirements are not applicable. It is, however, a sensible step to provide essentially the same ventilation system for your boat even if it is diesel-powered.

VENTILATION FUNDAMENTALS

If a boat will entrap fumes, i.e., it is not an "open" boat, it is required to have at least two ventilator ducts fitted with cowls at their openings to the atmosphere.

The ventilators, ducts, and cowls must be installed so that they provide for efficient removal of explosive or flammable gases from bilges of *each* engine and fuel tank compartment. Intake ducting must be installed to extend from the cowls to at least midway to the bilge or at least below the level of the carburetor air intake. Exhaust ducting must be installed to extend from the lower portion of the bilge to the cowls in the open atmosphere. Ducts should not be installed so low in the bilge that they could become obstructed by a normal accumulation of bilge water.

Cowls attached to intake and exhaust ducts should be located and trimmed for maximum effectiveness, and so as to prevent recirculation of fumes through the bilges.

ACCEPTABLE VENTILATION SYSTEMS

No foolproof ventilation system has been developed. The efficiency of various shaped cowls and ducts, the size and location of components, the capacity of mechanical blowers, and the choice of materials are all related to safety. There is no such thing as a ventilation system "approved by the Coast Guard." There has been, however, a great deal of study and thought, some testing, and years of experience upon which to base requirements. These have led to the conclusion that, as a *minimum,* fresh air must be ducted into *each* engine and fuel tank compartment, and dangerous fumes ducted out of the craft.

To create a flow through the ducting system, at least when underway or when there is a wind, cowls (scoops) or other fittings of equal effectiveness are needed on all ducts. A wind-actuated rotary exhauster or mechanical blower is considered equivalent to a cowl on an exhaust duct.

Ducts Required

Ducts are a necessary part of the ventilation system. For safety and long life, ducts should be made of nonferrous, galvanized ferrous, or sturdy high-temperature-resistant non-metallic materials. Ducts should be routed clear of, and protected from, contact with hot engine surfaces.

Mechanical Blowers

To provide a positive means of exhausting vapors when there is little or no movement of air, and especially before starting engines when risk of explosion is greatest, mechanical blowers are *recommended* for engine spaces. This is not, however, a legal requirement.

It is suggested that ducting separate from the natural ventilation system be installed for mechanical blowers. Exhaust blowers should be of the sealed or arcless type, and, if located within the compartment being ventilated, be positioned as high as possible. Blower fan blades or impellers should be non-sparking; if installed in the exhaust duct of the natural ventilation system, they should not interfere with functioning of the duct as a natural ventilator.

Exterior terminations of separate power exhaust ducts may be fitted with flush louvered fittings instead of cowls.

Positioning of Cowls

Normally, the intake cowl will face forward in an area of free airflow underway, and the exhaust cowl will face aft where a suction effect can be expected.

The two cowls, or sets of cowls, should be located with respect to each other, horizontally and/or vertically, so as to prevent return of fumes removed from any space to the same or any other space. Intake cowls should be positioned to avoid pick-up of vapors from fueling operations.

Air for Carburetors

Openings into the engine compartment for entry of air to the carburetor are in addition to requirements of the ventilation system.

Size of Ducts

Ventilation must be adequate for the size and design of the craft. There should be no constriction in the ducting system that is smaller than the minimum cross-sectional area required for reasonable efficiency. Where a stated size of duct is not available, the next *larger* size should be used.

Small motorboats. To determine the minimum cross-sectional area of the cowls and ducts for motorboats having small engine

Table 2-1   **VENTILATION REQUIREMENTS**

Net volume (cu. ft.)	One intake and one exhaust system — Minimum inside diameter for each (inches)	Area (sq. in.)	Two intake and two exhaust systems — Minimum inside diameter for each (inches)
Up to 8	2	3	....
12	2½	5	....
17	3	7	....
23	3½	10	2½
30	4	13	3
39	4½	16	3
48	5	20	3

NOTE.—Determine gross compartment volume, then determine the volume of tanks, engine and other items in that compartment. The difference is the net compartment volume.

and/or fuel tank compartments, see Table 2–1, which is based on *net* compartment volume (as previously defined).

Cruisers and larger boats. For most cruisers and other large motorboats, Table 2–2, which is based on the craft's beam, is a practical guide for determination of the minimum size of ducts and cowls.

GENERAL SAFETY PRECAUTIONS

Ventilation systems are *not* designed to remove vapors in large quantities such as might be caused by breaks in fuel lines, leaking tanks, or dripping carburetors. If gas odors are detected, repairs are generally needed.

Before starting the engine, especially on calm days and on boats without a power ventilation system, the engine compartment should be opened to dissipate any vapors that may be present.

Table 2-2   TWO INTAKE AND TWO EXHAUST SYSTEMS

Vessel beam (feet)	Minimum inside diameter for each duct (inches)	Area (square inches)
7	3	7
8	3¼	8
9	3½	9
10	3½	10
11	3¾	11
12	4	12
13	4¼	13
14	4¼	14
15	4½	15
16	4½	16
17	4½	17
18	5	18
19	5	19

The smaller the compartment, the quicker an explosive mixture of gasoline vapors can develop.

Regardless of the ventilation system installed, always open hatches and use your nose to detect any gasoline odors. Even the slightest trace should warn you to search for the cause and to ventilate the compartment thoroughly before pressing the starter switch.

FUELING PRECAUTIONS

Certain precautions must be carefully and completely observed every time a boat is fueled with gasoline. Step by step, these are:

Before Fueling

1. Make sure that the boat is securely made fast to the fueling pier. Fuel before darkness, if possible.
2. Stop engines, motors, fans, and other devices capable of producing a spark. Open the master switch if the electrical system has one. Put out all galley fires and open flames.
3. Close all ports, windows, doors, and hatches so that fumes cannot blow aboard and below.
4. Disembark all passengers and any crew members not needed for the fueling operation.
5. Prohibit all smoking on board and in the vicinity.
6. Have a filled fire extinguisher close at hand.
7. Measure the fuel in the tanks and do not order more than the tank will hold. Allow for expansion.

While Fueling

8. Keep nozzle or can spout in contact with the fill opening to guard against static sparks.
9. Do not spill gasoline.
10. Do not overfill. The practice of filling until fuel flows from the vents is highly dangerous.
11. For outboards, remove portable tanks, and fill on shore.

After Fueling

12. Close fill openings.

13. Wipe up any spilled gasoline; dispose of wipe-up rags ashore.

14. Open all ports, windows, doors, and hatches; turn on bilge power exhaust blower. Ventilate boat this way at *least* five minutes.

15. Sniff low down in tank and engine compartments. *If any odor of gasoline is present, do not start engines.*

16. Be prepared to cast off lines as soon as engine starts; get clear of pier quickly.

LIGHTNING PROTECTION

One seldom hears of a boat, power or sail, being struck by lightning, yet cases have been reported. A skipper can add to both his physical safety and his peace of mind by obtaining some basic information and taking a few precautionary actions.

Protective Principles

A grounded conductor, or lightning protective mast, will generally divert to itself direct lightning strokes which might otherwise fall within a cone-shaped space, the apex of which is the top of the conductor or mast and the base a circle at the water's surface having a radius approximately twice the conductor's height. Probability of protection is considered to be 99.0% within this 60° angle as shown in fig. 201. Probability of protection can be increased to 99.9% if mast height is raised so that the cone apex angle is reduced to 45°.

To provide an adequately grounded conductor or protective mast, the entire circuit from the masthead to the ground (water) connection should have a conductivity equivalent to a #8 gauge wire. The path to ground followed by the conductor should be essentially straight, with no sharp bends.

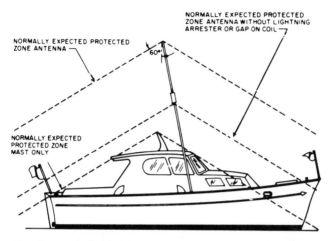

NORMALLY EXPECTED PROTECTED
ZONE ANTENNA WITHOUT LIGHTNING
ARRESTER OR GAP ON COIL

NORMALLY EXPECTED PROTECTED
ZONE ANTENNA

60°

NORMALLY EXPECTED
PROTECTED ZONE
MAST ONLY

SAFETY

Fig. 201   Under certain conditions, a grounded radio
antenna can provide a "cone of protection" from lightning strikes for a boat and its occupants. (From A.B.Y.C.
Safety Standards)

If there are metal objects of considerable size within a few
feet of the grounding conductor, there will be a strong tendency
for sparks or side flashes to jump from the grounding conductor
to the metal object at the nearest point. To prevent such possibly
damaging flashes, an interconnecting conductor should be provided at all likely places.

Large metallic objects within the hull or superstructure of a
boat should be interconnected with the lightning protective system to prevent a dangerous rise of voltage due to a lightning flash.

Protective Measures

For power boats, a radio antenna may serve as a lightning or
protective mast provided it is equipped with a transmitting-type
lightning arrester or means for grounding during electrical storms,
and that the antenna height is sufficient to provide an adequate
cone of protection for the length of the craft. Antennas with loading coils are considered to end at a point immediately *below the*

coil unless the coil has a suitable gap for bypassing lightning current. The size of the grounding conductor, interconnection, and grounding of metallic masses should be in accordance with principles noted above.

Sailboats with metallic standing rigging will be adequately protected provided that all rigging is grounded and a proper cone of protection exists. Interconnection and grounding of metallic masses should be done as on power boats.

Metal objects situated wholly on a boat's exterior should be connected to the grounding conductor at their upper or nearest end. Metal objects within the boat may be connected to the lightning protective system directly or through the bonding system for underwater metal parts.

Metal objects that project through cabin tops, decks, etc., should be bonded to the nearest lightning conductor at the point where the object emerges from the boat and again at its lowest extreme end within the boat. Spotlights and other objects projecting through cabin tops should be solidly grounded regardless of the cone of protection.

A ground connection for lightning protection may consist of any metal surface, normally submerged, which has an area of at least one square foot. Propellers and metallic rudder surfaces may be used for this purpose; the radio ground plate is more than adequate. A steel hull itself constitutes a good ground connection.

Protection for Personnel

As the basic purpose of lightning protection is safety of personnel, the following precautions should be taken by the crew and guests.

Individuals should remain inside a closed boat as much as practicable during an electrical storm.

Persons should avoid making contact with any items connected to a lightning protective conductor, and especially in such a way as to bridge between two parts of the grounding system.

No one should be in the water during a lightning storm.

WATER SKIING

Water skiing, one of the most popular sports related to boating, does present problems in safety afloat. The following guides should do much to reduce hazards:

1. Allow no one who is not qualified as a basic swimmer to engage in water skiing. A ski belt or vest is intended to keep a stunned or unconscious skier afloat.

2. Ski only in safe areas, out of channels and away from other boats. Some bodies of water will have areas designated for this sport, with skiing prohibited elsewhere.

3. Install a wide-angle rear-view mirror, or take along a second person to act as lookout. This will permit watching the skier *and* the waters ahead. Some state laws require this mirror, or a second person in the boat, or both.

4. Make sure the skier wears the proper lifesaving device.

5. If the skier falls, approach him from the lee side; stop your motor before taking him aboard.

6. In taking the skier on board, be careful not to swamp the boat. On smaller boats, it is usually safer to take a person aboard at the stern.

Skiing Signals

The following set of signals is recommended by the American Water Ski Association; see fig. 202. Make sure that the skier, boat operator, and safety observer all know and understand these signals:

Faster—Palm of one hand pointing upward.

Slower—Palm pointing downward.

Speed O.K.—arm upraised with thumb and finger joined to form a circle.

Right Turn—arm outstretched pointing to the right.

Left Turn—arm outstretched pointing to the left.

Return to Drop-off Area—arm at 45° from body pointing down to water and swinging.

Cut Motor—finger drawn across throat.

Stop—hand up, palm forward, policeman style.

Skier O.K. after Fall—hands clenched together overhead.

Pick Me Up, or Fallen Skier, Watch Out—one ski extended vertically out of water.

Fig. 202 This simple set of hand signals will allow adequate communication from the skier to the operator or observer on the towing boat. All must be thoroughly familiar with the full set of signals if maximum safety is to be achieved.

(From the **USCG** Recreational Boating Guide)

SAFETY

FASTER

SLOWER

SPEED O.K.

RIGHT TURN

LEFT TURN

BACK TO DROP-OFF AREA

CUT MOTOR

STOP

SKIER O.K. AFTER FALL

PICK ME UP OR
FALLEN SKIER — WATCH OUT

3.

SEAMANSHIP

Obviously, it takes more than a study of these pages to become a seasoned skipper. Given here are the things you *should* know, the minimum arts of good seamanship. Here are the most common and useful knots and splices, basic anchoring techniques, docking techniques, and lock and bridge procedures.

To supplement this information, every boatman—whether new to the sport or with years of experience—can benefit from classes in piloting and seamanship given free by the U. S. Power Squadrons, the U. S. Coast Guard Auxiliary, and the American Red Cross. (Addresses are given in the "Organizations" section of the Boatman's Handbook.)

KNOTS, SPLICES

Illustrated here are eight knots that every boatman should know. They represent just a few of the many that were developed for shipboard use during the age of the square-riggers, but they are all that are needed on the average pleasure boat.

Also presented are the eye splice, short splice, and long splice. Because the eye splice is used for so many applications, it is shown as made with double-braided nylon line as well as standard three-strand rope. The method illustrated is that developed by Samson Cordage Works.

Fig. 301 Overhand knot is used to keep the end of a line from unlaying. This knot jams, and may become almost impossible to untie.

Fig. 302 The figure eight knot can be used as a "stopper" to prevent a line from running through a sheave. It does not jam, and can be untied easily.

Fig. 303. The square or reef knot is used for tying light lines of the same size together, for tying awning stops, reef points, and similar uses. It can jam after being stressed heavily, and become difficult to untie.

Fig. 304. The bowline is a knot second only in usefulness to the square knot. It will not slip, does not

pinch or kink the rope as much as some other knots, and it does not jam or become difficult to untie. By tying a bowline with a small loop, and passing the line through the loop, a running bowline is obtained. This is an excellent form of running noose. Bowlines are used wherever a secure loop or running nose is needed in the end of a line, such as one to be secured to a bollard. They also may be used in securing lines to anchors.

Fig. 305 The clove hitch is used for making a line fast temporarily to a pile or bollard.

Fig. 306 Two half hitches

are used for making a line fast to a bollard, pile, timber, or stanchion. Note that the knot consists of a turn around the fixed object, and a clove hitch around the standing part of the line.

Fig. 307 Fisherman's bend, or anchor bend, is handy for making fast to a buoy or spar, or to the ring of an anchor.

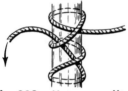

Fig. 308 Use a rolling hitch to bend a line to a spar or rope. Close the turns up tight and take

the strain on the arrow-tipped end.

Fig. 309 Correct method of making fast to a cleat: the half hitch which completes the fastening is taken with the free part of the line. The line then can be freed without taking up slack in the standing part.

Fig. 310. Common incorrect method of making fast to a cleat: the half hitch is taken with the standing part of the line, and the line cannot be freed unless it is possible to take up slack on the standing part.

EYE SPLICE

1. Start by unlaying the strands about 6″ to 1′ or more, or 6 to 10 turns of lay, depending on rope size. Whip the ends of each strand. With synthetic line, it's helpful to use masking or friction tape around the unlaid strands every 4″ to 6″, to help hold the "turn" in the strand.

2. Form a loop in the rope by laying the end back along the standing part. Hold the standing part away from you in the left hand, loop toward you. The stranded end can be worked with the right hand.

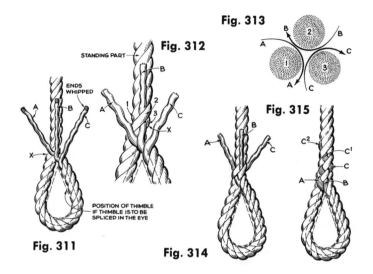

Fig. 313

Fig. 312

STANDING PART

ENDS
WHIPPED

Fig. 315

POSITION OF THIMBLE
IF THIMBLE IS TO BE
SPLICED IN THE EYE

Fig. 311

Fig. 314

3. The size of loop is determined by Point X, fig. 311, where the opened strands are first tucked under the standing part of the rope. If splice is to go around a thimble, the rope is laid snugly in the thimble groove and Point X will be at the tapered end of the thimble. The thimble may be taped or tied in place until the splice is finished.

4. Lay the three opened strands across the standing part as shown in fig. 311 so the center strand B lies over and directly along the standing part. Left-hand strand A leads off to the left; right hand strand C to the right of the standing part.

5. Tuck ends of strands A, B, and C under the strands of the standing part; see fig. 312. Start with center strand B. Select the topmost strand (2) of the standing part near Point X, and tuck B under it. Haul it up snug, but not so tight as to distort the natural lay of all strands. Tuck is made from right to left, against the lay of the standing part.

6. Tuck strand A under strand (1), which lies to the left of strand (2). Tuck strand C under strand (3), which lies to the right of strand (2). Tuck from right to left in every case. The greatest risk of a wrong start is in the first tuck of strand C. It must go under (3) from right to left; refer to fig. 313. If the first three tucks are correct, splice will look as shown in fig. 314.

7. Complete splice by making at least two additional tucks with each strand, in rotation, in manila line, and at least four additional tucks in synthetic line. As each tuck is made, be sure it passes from right to left under one strand of the standing part, then over the next one above it. This is shown in fig. 315. Note C, C^1, and C^2, the same strand as it appears after successive tucks.

The eye splice with double-braided synthetic line is illustrated and described in figs. 316–323 and their captions.

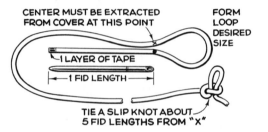

Fig. 316 Tightly tape end with one layer of tape. Mark a big dot one fid length from end of line. From the dot, form a loop the size of the eye you want, and mark with an X as shown.

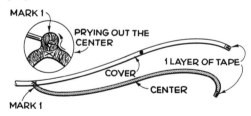

Fig. 317 Bend line sharply at X, and spread strands apart firmly to make opening so center can be pried out. Mark one big line on center where it comes out (this is Mark #1), and use your fingers to pull all the center out of the cover from X to the end. Pull on paper tape inside center until it breaks back at slip knot; you need to get rid of it so you can splice. Put a layer of tape on end of center.

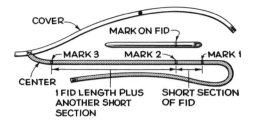

Fig. 318 Pull out more of the center. From Mark #1 measure a distance equal to the short section of the fid, and mark two heavy lines (this is Mark #2). Mark #3 is three heavy lines at a distance of one fid length plus one short section of fid from Mark #2.

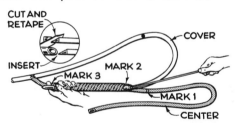

Fig. 319 Insert fid into center at Mark #2, and slide it lengthwise through "tunnel" until point sticks out at Mark #3.

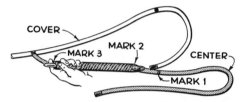

Fig. 320 Cut across taped end of cover to form a point, and re-tape tightly with one layer of tape. Jam this point into open end of the fid. Jam pusher into fid behind the tape. Hold center gently at Mark #3, and push both fid and cover through the center until dot almost disappears at Mark #2.

Fig 321 Note how center tail must travel through cover. It must go in close to dot, and come out through opening at X. On large eyes several passes may be necessary for fid to reach X. When this occurs simply reinsert fid at exact place it comes out and continue to X. To start, insert fid in cover at dot and slide it through tunnel to X. Form tapered point on center tail, jam it into open end of fid, and push fid and center through the cover. After fid

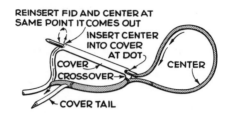

comes out at X, pull all center tail through cover until tight, then pull cover tail tight.

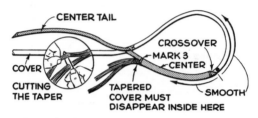

Fig. 322   Unravel cover tail braid all the way to Mark #3, and cut off groups of strands at staggered intervals to form a tapered end. Hold loop at crossover in one hand, and firmly smooth both sides of loop away from crossover. Do this until the tapered tail section completely disappears inside Mark #3.

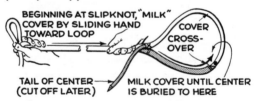

Fig. 323   Hold rope at slipknot, and gently begin to "milk" or slide the cover slack toward the loop. You'll see the center begin to disappear into the cover. Go back to the knot, and continue sliding cover more and more firmly until all center and the crossover are buried inside the cover.

SHORT SPLICE

A short splice is used where two ropes are to be permanently joined, provided they do not have to pass through the sheave

hole, swallow, or throat of a block. When a rope must pass
through a block, a long splice must be made.

1. Unlay the strands of both rope ends for a short distance, as
   described for the eye splice. Whip the ends, or fuse them if
   synthetic line is used, and seize the ropes to prevent the
   strands from unlaying too far.

2. Bring the ends of the ropes together so that the strands of one
   lie alternately between the strands of the other, as shown in
   fig. 324. Tie all the strands of one rope temporarily to the
   other; see fig. 325 (some boatmen eliminate this step, as it is
   not essential).

3. Remove the seizing from one rope, and tuck in the strands
   from the other, just as if it were an eye splice, working from
   right to left with each strand passing over and under the
   strands of the other rope.

4. Remove the temporary seizing from the other rope, and repeat
   the above process with the other strands. Splice should appear
   as shown in fig. 326.

5. Short splice, and eye splice, can be tapered by cutting out
   yarns from the strands after the necessary full tucks have been
   made. Never cut end strands off too close to the standing part
   of the rope; a heavy strain may allow them to work out.

6. A second method of making the splice is to start as in fig. 324,
   and then tie pairs of strands from opposite ends in an overhand knot; see fig. 327. This in effect, makes the first tuck.

Fig. 324

Fig. 326

Fig. 325

Fig. 327

ANCHORS AND ANCHORING

ANCHOR TYPES

Danforth

This is a lightweight anchor with long, sharp flukes designed so that heavy strains bury the anchor completely. It tends to work down through soft bottoms to firmer holding ground below, burying part of the rode as well as the anchor itself. Anchor has a round rod at the crown end to prevent the anchor from rolling or rotating. See Fig. 328.

Danforth Utility (Northill)

The Northill resembles the old kedge type anchor, in that it is a "hooking" type. The stock, however, is at the same end as the arms, and it can be folded against the shank for stowage. Anchor is particularly efficient in sand and mud, and has performed well on rocky bottoms.

Plow (CQR)

This is another anchor that tends to bury itself completely, and in form resembles the farmer's plowshare. When lowered, it first lies on its side on the bottom. When a pull is put on the rode, it rights itself, driving the point of the plow into the bottom; additional strain on the rode buries the anchor completely. Because the shank pivots, this anchor tends to remain buried even when the angle of pull is changed by wind or current, but it breaks out easily with a vertical pull.

Kedges

A kedge is the traditional anchor, with arms, flukes, and stocks as distinguished from modern stockless types. Holding power depends more on anchor weight than design. Shoulders on the

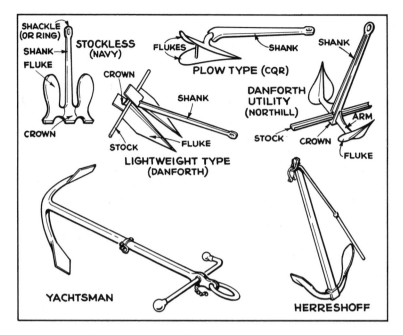

Fig. 328

flukes are nearly square, and invite fouling the rode as a vessel swings. Dull bills make it difficult to bite in hard bottoms.

Yachtsman and Herreshoff

These evolved from the kedges, and feature changes in the size and shape of fluke relative to the arm. Flukes are diamond-shaped to reduce risk of fouling, and sharpened bills permit better penetration of the bottom. These are not burying-type anchors, and serve best on rocky bottoms. Retrieval, using a trip line (See fig. 329), is not too difficult if the anchor is snagged.

Navy

These stockless anchors are fine for large ships, but depend on weight more than design for holding power. Those "suitable" for a small boat would be too heavy for practical use.

SEAMANSHIP

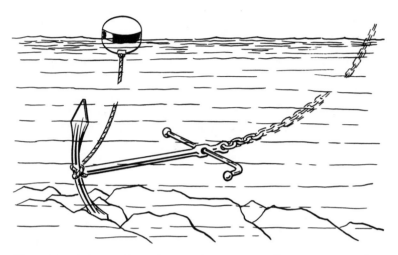

Fig. 329   A buoyed trip line to the crown will permit an anchor fouled in rocky bottom to be hauled up fluke first.

Sea-Claw

An improved version of the navy type, with round stock at the crown, is more suitable for use on pleasure boats than the navy anchor.

Grapnels

These are stockless anchors with five curved, sharp-billed claw-like prongs at the crown end of the shank. They are not used to anchor a boat in position. By dragging one back and forth over the bottom, the boatman can grapple for a piece of equipment lost overboard.

BASIC ANCHORING TECHNIQUE

1. Enough anchor line (rode) for the selected anchorage should be coiled on forward deck so as to run freely and without kinking or fouling. Make sure it is properly secured to the anchor, and that the bitter end is secured.

2. Having selected a suitable spot, run in slowly. Use ranges ashore, buoys, or landmarks; later these will aid in determining if you are holding or dragging, especially if the marks are visible at night.

3. Give rocks, shoals, reefs, or other boats as wide a berth as possible. Your boat may swing in a full circle while at anchor.

4. As you approach spot where anchor is to be lowered, head up against wind or current, as needed, to hold your boat on the heading it will assume when anchored. Check other boats of your type that are at anchor in the area.

5. In a motorboat or auxiliary under power, bring the bow up slowly to the point where the anchor is to be lowered. Check the headway by putting the boat into reverse, if necessary. Just as the boat gathers sternway, lower—do not drop—the anchor until it hits bottom, crown first. Do not stand in the coils of the anchor line on deck.

6. With the anchor on the bottom and the boat reversing slowly, pay out the rode, preferably with a turn around a bitt, as the boat takes it. When a scope (see fig. 330) of 7:1 or 8:1 is reached, snub the line by holding it on the bitt: the anchor

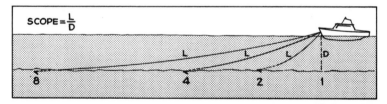

Fig. 330 Scope is the ratio of length of rode (L) to depth of water (D), plus allowance for height of bow above water. At (1) length of rode equals the depth. At (2) rode length is twice the depth; at (4) four times the depth. Note how the angle between rode and bottom decreases. At (8) the scope is 8:1 and the short length of chain at the anchor lies flat on the bottom.

should take a quick, sure bite into the bottom. Snubbing too soon may cause the anchor to drag. Once the anchor is set, the line can be shortened somewhat if the anchorage is crowded and such a scope would be excessive.

7. In setting a lightweight burial-type anchor, particularly on soft mud bottoms where the anchor can sink and skid, snub the rode briefly when a scope of 2:1 is reached to start the points to dig in properly, then back down until full scope has been paid out.

8. When the proper scope has been attained, apply a back-down load in excess of any that may be anticipated from wind or current. Check your ranges to see if the anchor is dragging.

9. Make the anchor rode fast, and shut off the boat's engine(s).

Anchoring without Power

1. When under sail, approach your anchorage with the wind abeam so you can spill the wind from your sail to slow the boat down, or trim in to gain more headway. Make the approach under mainsail only.

2. When you reach the point where the anchor is to be lowered, you should just have steerageway, but no more. Shoot the bow directly into the wind, let the sheet run, and drop the sail. As the boat loses headway, her bow will fall off and the boat will begin to drift to leeward. Now lower your anchor.

3. As the boat drifts back, pay out scope. Occasionally give a few jerks on the line; this helps to set the anchor. Hand-test the line by pulling it. Your anchor will be holding when the boat is drawn toward it as you pull on the line. Pay out the usual scope of 7:1 or 8:1.

Rocky Bottoms

If the bottom is foul or rocky in the area where you must anchor, it is advisable to rig a buoyed trip line, as shown in fig. 330. Make a light line fast to the crown; the line should be long enough to reach the surface, where it is buoyed with any con-

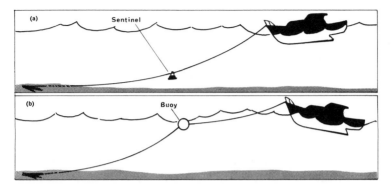

Fig. 331 Two methods of increasing anchor efficiency in rough weather. See text for advantages and disadvantages of each.

venient float. Be sure to allow for rise in tide. If the anchor does not come free with a normal pull on the rode, haul in on the trip line, and the anchor will be freed, crown first.

Anchor Dragging

1. If it appears that your anchor is dragging, pay out more scope, with an occasional sharp pull to help give the anchor a new bite. If you are dragging badly, take a turn around a bitt and snub the line occasionally. If the anchor is not holding by the time you have paid out a scope of 10:1, haul it back aboard and try again—preferably with a larger anchor.

2. If you do not have a larger (storm) anchor, you can add a sentinel to the anchor line (fig. 331). This is simply a weight sent more than half way down the rode. It lowers the angle of pull on the anchor, and puts a sag in the line that must be straightened out before a load is thrown on the anchor.

3. An alternative to the sentinel is a buoy on the anchor line. This carries the vertical load in the anchoring system, and limits the basic load on the boat to that required to hold the boat in position. The buoy permits the boat's bow to rise up easily over wave crests, rather than being pulled down into them, increasing the loads on both anchor and rode.

GETTING UNDER WAY

When you are ready to *weigh anchor* and get under way, run
up to the anchor slowly under power, so that the line can be
taken in easily without hauling the boat up to it. Ordinarily the
anchor will break out readily when the line stands vertically.

As the line comes in, it can be whipped up and down to free
it of any grass or weed it may have picked up. This clears the line
before it comes on deck. If the anchor is not too heavy, mud can
be washed off by swinging it back and forth near the surface as it
leaves the water. With care, the line can be snubbed around a
bitt and the anchor allowed to wash off as the boat gathers way,
preferably astern. Two things must be watched: don't allow the
flukes to hit the topsides, and be careful that water flowing past
the anchor doesn't get too good a hold and take it out of your
hands.

Manila, if used, must be coiled loosely on deck and allowed to
dry thoroughly before stowing below. When the anchor is on
deck, the stock (if there is one) can be folded and the anchor
lashed down securely in its chocks.

PERMANENT MOORINGS

Permanent moorings, as distinguished from ordinary ground
tackle in daily use, consist of the gear used when boats are to be
left unattended for long periods, at yacht club anchorages, for
example. The traditional system has often consisted of a mushroom anchor, chain from the anchor to a buoy and a pennant of
stainless steel or nylon from the buoy to a light pick-up float at
the pennant's end. See fig. 332.

Mushroom anchors, especially the type with a heavy bulb cast
in the shank, have been able through suction to develop great
holding power under ideal conditions if they are allowed time
enough to bury deep in bottoms that will permit such burying.

Ideally, scope for the mooring anchor should be five to seven times the depth of the water, but this often means a swinging radius of several hundred feet. In crowded anchorages this is impossible. The recommended standards shown in Table 3–1 were prepared by the Manhasset Bay Yacht Club of Port Washington, N.Y., to meet average conditions.

SEAMANSHIP

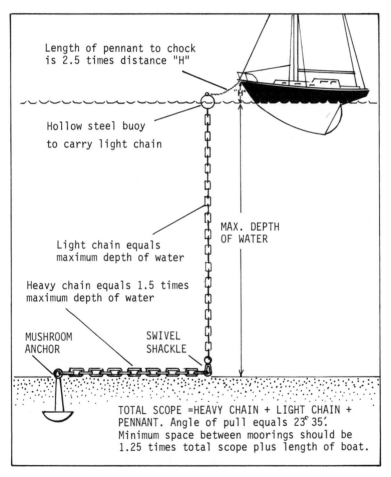

Length of pennant to chock is 2.5 times distance "H"

Hollow steel buoy to carry light chain

MAX. DEPTH OF WATER

Light chain equals maximum depth of water

Heavy chain equals 1.5 times maximum depth of water

MUSHROOM ANCHOR

SWIVEL SHACKLE

TOTAL SCOPE =HEAVY CHAIN + LIGHT CHAIN + PENNANT. Angle of pull equals 23° 35'. Minimum space between moorings should be 1.25 times total scope plus length of boat.

Fig. 332

Table 3-1

ANCHOR WEIGHT* (pounds)

BOAT LENGTH (Maximum)	Lunch hook	Working anchor	Storm anchor
20′	**4** (10)	**5** (20)	**12** (40)
30′	**5** (15)	**12** (30)	**18** (60)
40′	**12** (20)	**18** (40)	**28** (80)

*Bold-face figures based on modern lightweight burial-type anchors of efficient design. Figures in parentheses show how weights would be increased, using a formula of ½, 1 lb. and 2 lbs. per foot for certain kedges.

Mooring Buoys

To comply with new uniform state waterway regulations (applicable on waters under state control), mooring buoys should be white with a horizontal blue band. Buoys used in any mooring system should be of a type that transmits strain directly through chain or rod. See fig. 333. Buoys perform a useful function in removing much of the vertical load, the pennant is under a more nearly horizontal load, and the boat's bow is freer to lift to heavy seas.

Fig. 333 A plastic foam buoy. Note how the strain is transmitted by a solid rod that runs through the buoy.

Table 3-2

SUGGESTED RODE AND ANCHOR SIZES*

For Storm Anchor (Winds up to 60 knots)

L.O.A.	BEAM SAIL	BEAM POWER	RODE NYLON	RODE CHAIN	ANCHOR NORTHILL	STANDARD	HI-TENSILE
10'	4'	4'	100'-¼"	3'-³⁄₁₆"	12 lb. (6-R)	8-S	5-H
15'	5'	5'	125'-¼"	3'-³⁄₁₆"	12 lb. (6-R)	8-S	5-H
20'	6'	7'	150'-⅜"	4'-¼"	27 lb. (12-R)	13-S	12-H
25'	6'	8'	200'-⅜"	4'-¼"	27 lb. (12-R)	22-S	12-H
30'	7'	10'	250'-⁷⁄₁₆"	5'-⁵⁄₁₆"	46 lb. (20-R)	22-S	20-H
35'	8'	12'	300'-½"	6'-⅜"	46 lb. (20-R)	40-S	35-H
40'	10'	14'	400'-⅝"	8'-⁷⁄₁₆"	80 lb. (30-R)	65-S	60-H
50'	12'	16'	500'-⅝"	8'-⁷⁄₁₆"	105 lb. (50-R)	130-S	60-H
60'	14'	19'	500'-¾"	8'-½"	105 lb. (50-R)	180-S	90-H

For Working Anchor (Winds up to 30 knots)

L.O.A.	BEAM SAIL	BEAM POWER	RODE NYLON	RODE CHAIN	ANCHOR NORTHILL	STANDARD	HI-TENSILE
10'	4'	4'	80'-¼"	3'-³⁄₁₆"	6 lb. (3-R)	4-S	5-H
15'	5'	5'	100'-¼"	3'-³⁄₁₆"	6 lb. (3-R)	8-S	5-H
20'	6'	7'	120'-¼"	3'-³⁄₁₆"	12 lb. (6-R)	8-S	5-H
25'	6'	8'	150'-⅜"	3'-³⁄₁₆"	12 lb. (6-R)	8-S	5-H
30'	7'	10'	180'-⅜"	4'-¼"	27 lb. (12-R)	13-S	12-H
35'	8'	12'	200'-⅜"	4'-¼"	27 lb. (12-R)	22-S	12-H
40'	10'	14'	250'-⁷⁄₁₆"	5'-⁵⁄₁₆"	46 lb. (20-R)	22-S	20-H
50'	12'	16'	300'-½"	6'-⅜"	46 lb. (20-R)	40-S	35-H
60'	14'	19'	300'-½"	6'-⅜"	80 lb. (30-R)	65-S	35-H

For Lunch Hook

L.O.A.	BEAM SAIL	BEAM POWER	RODE NYLON	RODE CHAIN	ANCHOR NORTHILL	STANDARD	HI-TENSILE
10'	4'	4'	70'-¼"	3'-³⁄₁₆"	6 lb. (3-R)	2½-S	5-H
15'	5'	5'	80'-¼"	3'-³⁄₁₆"	6 lb. (3-R)	2½-S	5-H
20'	6'	7'	90'-¼"	3'-³⁄₁₆"	6 lb. (3-R)	2½-S	5-H
25'	6'	8'	100'-¼"	3'-³⁄₁₆"	6 lb. (3-R)	4-S	5-H
30'	7'	10'	125'-¼"	3'-³⁄₁₆"	6 lb. (3-R)	4-S	5-H
35'	8'	12'	150'-¼"	3'-³⁄₁₆"	12 lb. (6-R)	4-S	5-H
40'	10'	14'	175'-⅜"	4'-¼"	12 lb. (6-R)	8-S	5-H
50'	12'	16'	200'-⅜"	4'-¼"	12 lb. (6-R)	8-S	12-H
60'	14'	19'	200'-⅜"	4'-¼"	27 lb. (12-R)	13-S	12-H

*Suggested sizes assume fair holding ground, scope of at least 7-to-1 and moderate shelter from heavy seas.

PLOW ANCHORS—Woolsey, manufacturer of the Plowright anchor, makes the following recommendations for winds up to 30 knots: for *working anchors*, 10'-21', 6 lbs.—22'-32', 12 lbs.—32'-36', 18 lbs.—36'-39', 22 lbs.—39'-44', 35 lbs. For *lunch hooks*, they advise stepping down one size. For *storm anchors*, up one size.

KEDGES—Holding powers vary widely with the type. Best to consult manufacturer for individual recommendations.

TABLE 3-3   SUGGESTIONS FOR PERMANENT YACHT MOORINGS
For Wind Velocities Up to 75 M.P.H.

Boat Length Overall	Mushroom Anchor (Min. Wt.)	Heavy Chain Length (Feet)	Heavy Chain Diameter (Inches)	Light Chain Length (Feet)	Light Chain Diameter (Inches)	Length (Minim.) (Feet)	Pennant Diameter (Inches) Manila	Pennant Diameter (Inches) Nylon	Pennant Diameter (Inches) Stainless Steel	Total Scope (Chocks to Mushroom) (Feet)
—FOR MOTOR BOATS—										
25	225	30	$7/8$	20	$3/8$	20	1	$7/8$	$9/32$	70
35	300	35	1	20	$7/16$	20	$1\frac{1}{4}$	1	$11/32$	75
45	400	40	1	20	$1/2$	20	$1\frac{1}{2}$	$1\frac{1}{4}$	$3/8$	80
55	500	50	1	20	$9/16$	20	2	$1\frac{1}{2}$	$7/16$	90
—FOR RACING TYPE SAILBOATS—										
25	125	30	$5/8$	20	$5/16$	20	1	$7/8$	$9/32$	70
35	200	30	$3/4$	20	$3/8$	20	$1\frac{1}{4}$	1	$11/32$	70
45	325	35	1	20	$7/16$	20	$1\frac{1}{2}$	$1\frac{1}{4}$	$3/8$	75
55	450	45	1	20	$9/16$	20	2	$1\frac{1}{2}$	$7/16$	85
—FOR CRUISING TYPE SAILBOATS—										
25	175	30	$3/4$	20	$5/16$	20	1	$7/8$	$9/32$	70
35	250	30	1	20	$3/8$	20	$1\frac{1}{4}$	1	$11/32$	70
45	400	40	1	20	$7/16$	20	$1\frac{1}{2}$	$1\frac{1}{4}$	$3/8$	80
55	550	55	1	20	$9/16$	20	2	$1\frac{1}{2}$	$7/16$	95

DOCKING

To handle a boat, or a ship, you must first *know* it. Know *what it will do, how fast it will do it,* and *in what space.* No article or text can give you this knowledge—it can come only from actual experience and practice. But attention can be drawn to certain basics which will enable you to get much more from experience. Some of the more important of these. . . .

A. *The propeller controls the direction of a boat when docking, almost as much as the rudder.*

A vessel with a propeller that turns in a clockwise direction when viewed from astern with the engine turning ahead (called a right-handed vessel) is the most common. This vessel's bow will usually swing to port slowly when going ahead, even with the rudder amidships, *but* the stern will swing rather sharply to port when the vessel is going astern, often regardless of where the rudder is. For left-handed vessels the effects are reversed.

B. *This "turning effect" of the propeller is much more pronounced when going astern.*

Since much of a rudder's effect comes from the wash of the propeller rushing past it, if the engine is reversed this wash will be directed in a direction *away* from the rudder and much of the effect of the helm is lost. The propeller takes over in a pronounced fashion.

C. *Brief spurts of engine power may be used to turn the bow or stern of the vessel as desired, without getting the boat under way.*

With the rudder to starboard, a brief spurt of the engine (throttle is opened momentarily) will swing the bow to starboard *but*, if the engine is cut off before the vessel gathers way, most of the power of the engine will have gone into turning the vessel rather than getting it moving through the water. The heavier the boat, the more this is so. Don't be afraid to gun your engine briefly to gain maneuverability. A boat's pretty heavy and won't shoot ahead the moment power is applied.

D. *The wind, tide, and current can often be as much help in docking as the engines and helm.*

Nature will often dock your boat for you, if given half a chance. Why waste gas and temper fighting her? A good policy many times is "Ride with the current."

Now to the actual processes of docking. These are presented in outline form to make it easier to grasp details without wading through a lot of text. The word "wind" will be used to cover whichever factor has the most effect on the vessel at the moment, whether it is actually the wind, or whether it may be tide or current. In calm or still water almost any of the methods outlined will work equally well. Boats are shown port side to the docks; for the reverse condition, simply reverse the rudder orders, but maintain the same engine speeds and directions.

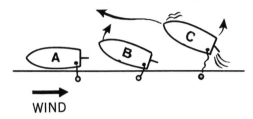

WIND

Fig. 334 Leaving a dock, boat alongside dock, wind ahead: A. Single up to one stern line, no power, no rudder. B. Let wind swing bow out, or push bow out with boat hook. C. With bow out 15 or 20 degrees, swing stern clear by using hard left rudder (right rudder if dock is to starboard) and brief spurts of power. Let stern line go when boat is a few feet from the dock, and go ahead slowly. Steer away from the dock with slight rudder.

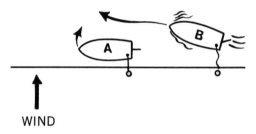

WIND

Fig. 335 Leaving a dock, boat alongside dock, wind off the dock: A. Single up to one stern line and let the wind swing the bow out. B. Ease off on the stern line until clear of the dock. Let go the line, and go ahead slowly. Steer away from the dock with slight rudder.

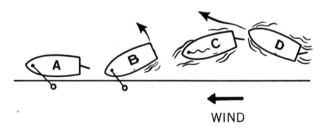

WIND

Fig. 336 Leaving a dock, boat alongside dock, wind astern: A. Single up to bow spring line. B. Let wind swing the stern out or use the engine in brief spurts with hard left rudder (right rudder if moored starboard side to dock). C. Reverse engine and back off slowly; cast off line. D. When well clear of dock, go ahead slowly and use slight rudder to steer away from the dock.

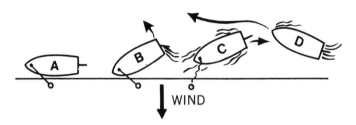

Fig. 337 Leaving a dock, boat alongside dock, wind on the dock: A. Single up to bow spring line led well aft. B. Use spurts of power ahead to bring stern out, using hard left rudder (right rudder if dock is to starboard). C. Use engine in reverse to back away from dock, cast off bow spring. D. When well clear, go ahead with engine, and steer clear of the dock.

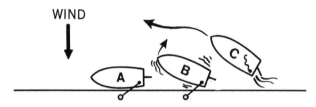

Fig. 338 Leaving a dock, boat alongside dock, wind on the dock: A. Single up to single stern spring line. B. Use half to full power astern to swing bow out, no rudder. C. Use rudder half left (half right if dock is to starboard) and engine slow ahead to bring stern out. Cast off line, and go ahead slowly using slight rudder to steer clear of dock.

Fig. 339 Leaving a slip: A. Single up to single stern line, long enough to reach from stern cleat to a point forward about ⅔ the length of the boat. Make outboard end of line fast to outer end of the slip. B. Go astern slowly until line is taut, then swing rudder hard left. Boat's stern will swing to port under full control.

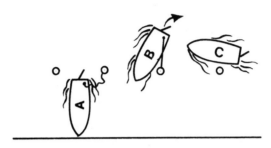

C. Cast off when clear, go ahead, give a slight kick of left rudder to swing stern out, then use slight right rudder to steer clear.

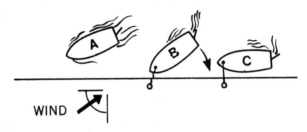

WIND

Fig. 340 Docking, wind off the dock or ahead: A. Approach slowly at an angle of 30 to 40 degrees to the dock. B. Put engine in reverse to halt boat with bow about one foot from dock, get bow line ashore. C. With hard right rudder, use spurts of power ahead to bring stern in to dock. C. Tie up.

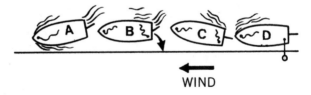

WIND

Fig. 341 Docking, wind astern: A. Approach closely to dock, at an angle of 10 to 15 degrees. B. When one or two feet from dock, use right rudder and brief spurt of power to start stern swinging toward dock. C. As soon as stern starts to swing in (boat parallel to dock), reverse engine to stop boat. D. Get stern line ashore, and let wind bring bow in to dock. Tie up.

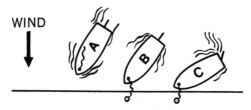

Fig. 342   Docking, wind on the dock: A. Approach at a steep angle of about 60 to 80 degrees. B. Reverse engine to stop boat about a foot from dock; ease boat off with boathook if possible; get bow line ashore. C. Let wind bring stern in, using engine in reverse and hard right rudder for braking action. Tie up.

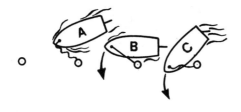

Fig. 343   Entering a slip, wind anywhere but astern: A. Approach slowly, roughly parallel to end of slip. Pass a line to the pile or cleat nearest your approach. B. Reverse engine to slow the approach and stop the boat just short of the far piling, with the line taut. C. Put rudder hard left and use spurt of power to swing boat into slip, using the pile as a pivot. Ease into slip and tie up.

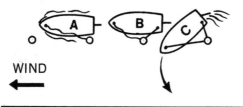

Fig. 344   Entering a slip, wind astern: A. Approach as in Fig. 343, but use enough power to stop boat completely after passing the bow line. B. Pass a stern line to the same pile or cleat. C. Haul

both lines taut and use engine, wind, and rudder to ease boat
around and into the slip. Tie up.

DAMS AND LOCKS

Dams on our inland waterways, without locks, would restrict
river cruising to the individual pools and prevent through navigation except to small vessels light enough to be portaged around
the dams. Locks, in conjunction with the dams, provide the means
for boats to move from level to level. Locks vary in size but since
they must invariably handle commercial traffic, their limiting
dimensions offer no restriction to the movement of pleasure craft.

Locks are practically water-tight chambers with gates at each
end. Valves are provided to admit water as required. When a
vessel is about to be locked upstream to a higher level, the upstream gate is closed, the downstream gate opened, and the water
stands at the lower level. The vessel enters the lock through the
open gates at the lower end, the gates close behind her, and
water is valved in until the chamber is full to the upstream level.
Now the upstream gate is opened, and the boat is free to resume
her course upstream. Locking down is naturally the reverse of
this procedure.

Signals are provided for vessels approaching a lock (commonly
a long and a short blast) answered by signals from the lock
tender. The river boatman should familiarize himself with the
special signals applicable to the particular waterway he is using.

On the Ohio, vessels sound a long and a short blast on the
whistle from a distance of not more than one mile from the lock.
On the New York State Barge Canal, they signal with three
distinct blasts. When approaching a lock, boats must wait for the
lockmaster's signal before entering. When bound downstream,
stay in the clear at least 400 feet upstream from the end of the
guide wall leading along the bank into the lock. Approach
through the buoyed channel directly toward the lock and keep

clear of spillway sections of the dam. Be particularly careful not to obstruct the movement of any large commercial craft that may be leaving the lock. When bound upstream, keep well clear of the turbulent water invariably found below a dam.

On the Mississippi, signs are painted on the river face of the guide wall warning small craft not to pass a given point until signalled by the lock attendant. Near this sign a signal cord is placed. Small craft may use this to alert lock attendants, in lieu of signals used on other waters.

Traffic signal lights at the Ohio locks resemble those you find on the highway—red, amber and green, vertically arranged. Flashing red warns: do not enter, stand clear. Flashing amber signifies: approach, but under full control. Flashing green gives you the all-clear signal to enter. (On N. Y. State Canals, a fixed green light gives clearance to enter; fixed red requires the vessel to wait. U. S. and commercial vessels take precedence; pleasure boats may be locked through with commercial craft if a safe distance may be maintained between them.)

Where locks are in pairs (landward and riverward) the lockmaster on the Ohio may also use an air horn, the significance of his blasts as follows: 1 long, enter landward lock; 2 long, enter riverward lock; 1 short, leave landward lock; 2 short, leave riverward lock.

The Secretary of the Army has established an order of priority with respect to the handling of traffic at locks, giving precedence in this order: 1, U. S. military craft; 2, mail boats; 3, commercial passenger craft; 4, commercial tows; 5, commercial fishermen; and 6, pleasure boats. This means that small pleasure craft may sometimes have to wait to be locked through with other vessels. In deciding on an order of precedence, the lockmaster also takes into account whether vessels of the same class are arriving at landward or riverward locks, and whether they are bound upstream or downstream.

The concrete walls of locks are usually rough and dirty. Consequently a boat will need adequate fender protection. Ordinary cylindrical fenders will pick up dirt and roll on the wall to smear the topsides. Fender boards, consisting of a plank (2-by-6 perhaps, several feet long) suspended horizontally outside the usual fenders, work well amidships or aft where sides are reasonably straight. Bags of hay have the same objection as cylindrical fenders, except on heavily flared bows at the edge of deck where they flatten down and work pretty well. Auto tires wrapped with burlap would be ideal except that their use is illegal in some canals. As you can't be sure which side of a lock you'll be using, it's wise to fender both sides.

Another essential in locking is adequate line. How heavy it is to be depends on the size of boat; how long depends on the depth of the locks. Good ½″ manila or ⅜″ nylon or Dacron are generally adequate for average sized cruisers. In general, each line (bow and stern) will have to be at least twice as long as the depth of the lock. The object of this is to permit your running the bight of a line around a bollard on the top of the lock wall, using it double. Then, on the lower level, when you're ready to cast off, you can haul the line in without assistance from above. At Little Falls, N. Y., the drop is roughly 40 feet, so 100 feet is not too much for the length of each of the two lock lines in such cases.

Ladders are often recessed into lock walls and on some canals small boats can follow the ladder up, rung by rung, with boat hook or lock lines. On the Ohio, boats are requested not to use the ladders. In addition to big bollards along the top of the lock walls, some locks have other recessed posts at intervals in the walls in vertical line. Locking up, lines can be cleared successively from lower posts and transferred to higher ones within reach. In other locks, floating mooring hooks move up and down to follow the pool levels.

Rising or falling, stand by your lock lines at all times and tend them carefully. This requires a hand forward and another aft, though with only two aboard the helmsman could handle the after line. One of the most dangerous practices is to make fast to a bollard above and then secure to a bitt or cleat on deck. If the level drops, your boat is "hung," with risk of serious damage.

Entering and leaving locks, it's always imperative to throttle down and keep the boat under complete control. This is especially true when locking through with other boats. Sometimes, on fleet cruises, it will be necessary to tie up two abreast at each lock wall. This is entirely feasible as long as all boats are intelligently handled.

Occasionally one hears cautions concerning the possibility of a boat's being tossed about as water boils into locks from the open valves. Actually, lock tenders on our inland waters are careful to control this flow, and there is little cause for apprehension on this score. With a light boat, however, some thought should be given to placement in a lock when passing through with large commercial craft. A light hull, directly astern of a powerful tug, can take quite a tossing around when her big wheel starts to throw the water astern.

There are various kinds of locks, all of which accomplish the same end of effecting a change of level. Gates may swing or roll back and in cases are hoisted in vertical lift, permitting traffic to pass through under the gate. On the Trent Waterway in Canada, a hydraulic lock lifts the boat in a water-filled chamber and in another instance a marine railway actually hauls the boat out to get her up over a hill. Through passage on a waterway like the Trent, then, is obviously limited to vessels within the capacity of the ways to haul. At Troy, N. Y., a Federally operated time lock opens only at slated intervals—on the hour—occasionally causing a slight delay in lockage.

Lock permits, once necessary for pleasure boats, are no longer required to navigate the New York State Barge Canal. On Western Rivers, no special permission or clearance is required for passage through the locks. There are regulations to be observed, however, and copies of these should be obtained from Army Engineer Offices at Chicago or St. Louis.

SEAMANSHIP

INTERNATIONAL FLAGS AND PENNANTS

ALPHABET FLAGS			NUMERAL
			PENNANTS
Alfa *Diver Down; Keep Clear*	**K**ilo *Desire to Communicate*	**U**niform *Standing into Danger*	1
Bravo *Dangerous Cargo*	**L**ima *Stop Instantly*	**V**ictor *Require Assistance*	2
Charlie *Yes*	**M**ike *I Am Stopped*	**W**his- key *Require Medical Assistance*	3
Delta *Keep Clear*	**N**ovem- ber *No*	**X**ray *Stop Your Intention*	4
Echo *Altering Course to Starboard*	**O**scar *Man Overboard*	**Y**ankee *Am Dragging Anchor*	5
Foxtrot *Disabled*	**P**apa *About to Sail*	**Z**ulu *Require a Tug*	6
Golf *Want a Pilot*	**Q**uebec *Request Pratique*	REPEATERS 1st Repeat	7
Hotel *Pilot on Board*	**R**omeo	2nd Repeat	8
India *Altering Course to Port*	**S**ierra *Engines Going Astern*	3rd Repeat	9
Juliett *On Fire; Keep Clear*	**T**ango *Keep Clear of Me*	CODE *and* Answering Pennant (Decimal Point)	0

WHITE   BLUE   RED   YELLOW   BLACK

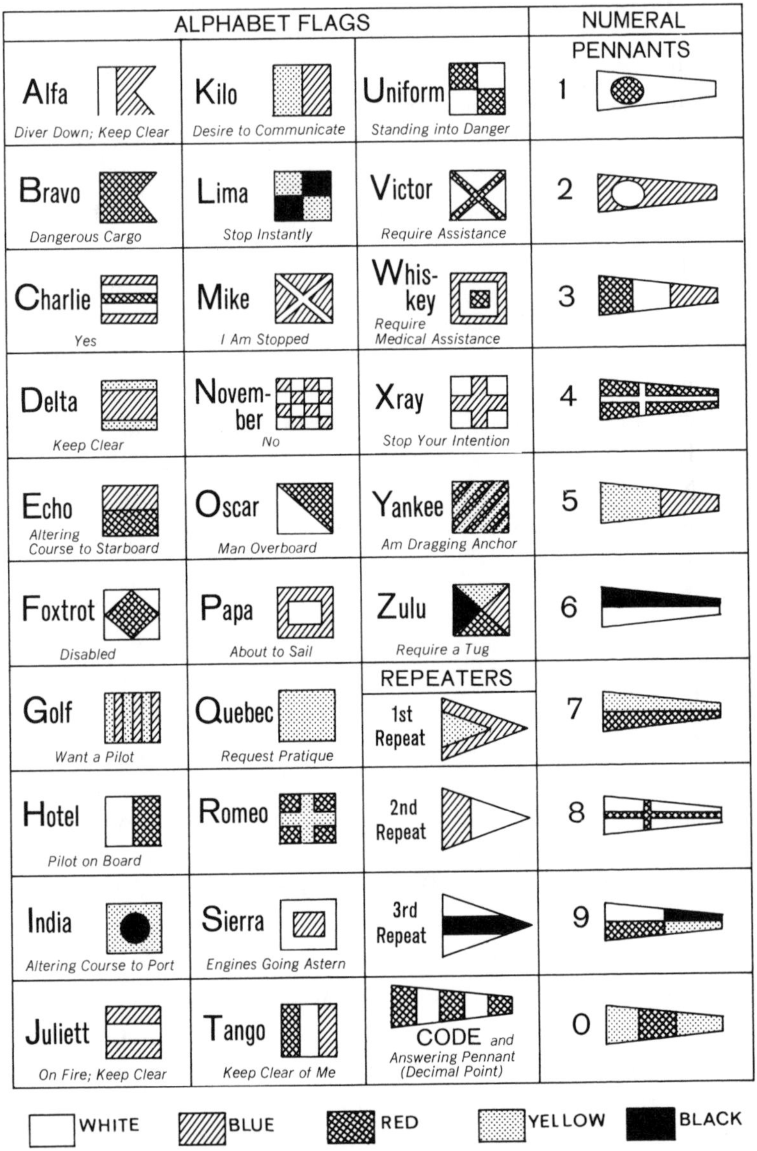

Fig. 345 International Flags and Pennants.

INTERNATIONAL FLAGS AND PENNANTS

Alphabet and numeral pennants are illustrated in fig. 345, and the manner in which they should be used is shown in fig. 346. Note the meanings given to the individual flags; learn to recognize at least those that convey an emergency message, such as "V" and "W." You should also know the multiple-flag emergency signals, and if you race a sailboat, you'll need to know the signals used in races and regattas.

Emergency Signals

In addition to the single-flag emergency signals, the following multiple-flag emergency messages may be displayed:

A E   I must abandon my vessel.
A N   I need a doctor.
C B 4   I require immediate assistance; I am aground.
C B 5   I require immediate assistance; I am drifting.
C B 6   I require immediate assistance; I am on fire.
C B 7   I require immediate assistance; I have sprung a leak.
K Q 1   I am ready to be taken in tow.
N C   I am in distress and require immediate assistance.
Z L   Your signal has been received but not understood.

Racing Signals

D   Do you assent to postponing the race until later in the day?
E   Do you assent to calling the race off for the day?
T   Send club launch.
W   Permission to leave squadron is requested.
X   Permission to proceed at will is requested.
Y   Leave all marks to starboard.
Z   Leave all marks to port.
A I   Finish—This yacht will take time at finish.
A J   Finish—Will you take time at finish?
A K   Finish—Yachts will take their own time at finish.

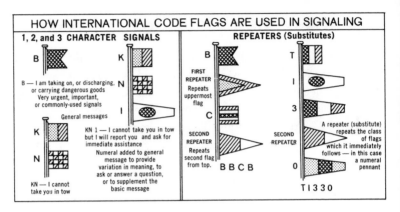

Fig. 346

A N   Race Committee—Is Committee on board committee boat?
A O   Race Committee—Report is ready.
A P   Race Committee—Report on board this vessel at ....
A Q   Race Committee—Do you agree to race tomorrow?
A V   Start—Race will be sailed on ....
A W   Start—Race will be sailed today at ....
A X   Start—Race will be sailed tomorrow at ....
A Y   Start—When will race be started?

Naval Oceanographic Office publication H.O.102 lists meanings for all standard flag signals. Also given are specific rules for signaling by flag, flashing light, sound, and radio.

4.
PILOTING & NAVIGATION

RULES OF THE ROAD

There are four sets of "Rules of the Road" in effect at the current time. These are the International Rules, Inland Rules, Great Lakes Rules, and Western Rivers Rules. Each requires specific signals and actions for certain meeting and overtaking situations, and specific lighting arrangements for recreational boats and commercial vessels of various classifications.

Fortunately for the boatman, his lighting requirements and right-of-way requirements are the same under Inland, Great Lakes, and Western Rivers rules, and many boats on Inland waters have the option of using light arrangements that conform to the International Rules. Coast Guard pamphlets are available that completely cover each set of rules (see the Government Publications listing in the Organizations section). Detailed explanations of light requirements and right-of-way situations are given in Chapters 4 and 5 of Chapman's *Piloting, Seamanship and Small Boat Handling*, published by *Motor Boating & Sailing Books*.

The wise boatman will have a thorough knowledge of the rules that apply to all types of boats and ships operating in his home waters, but briefly listed here are major requirements that always apply.

Meeting Head-On

When meeting a boat head-on, keep to the right. Show that you intend to do so by swinging the bow of your boat in that direction, even more than necessary. The proper signal is one short blast from either boat, to be answered by one blast from the other. A "short blast" is one second.

If a boat is coming towards you head on, but is so far to your right that the boats will pass at a safe distance, both can maintain course. One boat may signal his intention to do so with two blasts of his horn. The other boat should answer with the same signal.

Danger Zone

Your boat's "danger zone" is the area from dead ahead to two points abaft the starboard beam. Two points equal 22½ degrees. A boat in your danger zone has the right away, if coming toward you. Your boat is the burdened vessel and must alter course, slow down, or stop if necessary, to avoid collision. The privileged vessel may sound one blast in his horn; if so you must answer with one blast.

Overtaking

The boat being overtaken is the privileged vessel, and should hold course and speed. The overtaking boat is the burdened vessel, and must keep clear until it is well forward of the privileged vessel, and no danger of collision exists. A boat is overtaking another when it is approaching from within the angle formed by lines two points (22½ degrees) abaft the beam of the privileged vessel, on either side.

If the overtaking boat plans to pass to the left of the privileged vessel (leaving it to starboard), a signal of two blasts is given, and is answered by the same signal. If the overtaking vessel plans to leave the privileged vessel to port, a signal of one blast is given, and is answered by the same signal.

Crossed Signals

In head-on meeting situations, either vessel can signal first; in overtaking situations, the burdened vessel signals first, to indicate on which side she desires to pass. In crossing situations the privileged vessel signals first. In any case, the second vessel answers with the *same* signal to show that the intent of the first boat is understood. If the skipper of the second vessel believes the action signaled by the first boat will lead to a collision, or is in any other way dangerous, he should sound the *danger* signal of four or more short blasts. *Never* answer a two-blast signal with one blast, or a one blast signal with two blasts.

General Prudential Rule

Each set of rules has its "General Prudential Rule" or equivalent that makes it mandatory for the *privileged* vessel to alter course, slow down, stop, or take such other action as may be necessary to avoid a collision, if a collision might result should she hold her course and speed.

Rules Jurisdictions

International Rules apply to all vessels operating on the "high seas" outside specific boundary lines that are shown on coastal charts at entrances to harbors, rivers, bays, etc. Along many coastal stretches, International Rules apply right up to the shore except for minor coves and other indentations. Great Lakes Rules apply on the Great Lakes and their tributaries as far east as Montreal; Western Rivers Rules apply on the Mississippi River, all the tributaries emptying into it, and all *their* tributaries. Also included is that part of the Atchafalaya River above its junction with the Plaquemine-Morgan alternate waterway, and the Red River of the North.

CHARACTERISTIC LIGHT PHASES

Illustration	Symbols and meaning		
	Lights which do not change color	Lights which show color variations	Phase description
	F.=Fixed	Alt.=Alternating	A continuous light. (steady)
	F. Fl.=Fixed and flashing	Alt. F. Fl.=Alternating fixed and flashing	A fixed light varied at regular intervals by a flash of greater brilliance.
	F. Gp. Fl.=Fixed and group flashing.	Alt. F. Gp. Fl.=Alternating fixed and group flashing.	A fixed light varied at regular intervals by groups of 2 or more flashes of greater brilliance.
	Fl.=Flashing	Alt. Fl.=Alternating flashing.	Showing a single flash at regular intervals, the duration of light always being less than the duration of darkness.
	Gp. Fl.=Group flashing.	Alt. Gp. Fl.=Alternating group flashing.	Showing at regular intervals groups of 2 or more flashes
	Gp. Fl. (1+2)=Composite group flashing.	. . . .	Light flashes are combined in alternate groups of different numbers
	Mo. (A)=Morse Code.	. . . .	Light in which flashes of different duration are grouped in such a manner as to produce a Morse character or characters.
	Qk. Fl.=Quick Flashing.	. . . .	Shows not less than 60 flashes per minute.
	I. Qk. Fl.=Interrupted quick flashing.	. . . .	Shows quick flashes for about 4 seconds, followed by a dark period of about 4 seconds
	E. Int.=Equal interval. (Isophase)	. . . .	Light with all durations of light and darkness equal
	Occ.=Occulting.	Alt. Occ.=Alternating occulting	A light totally eclipsed at regular intervals, the duration of light always greater than the duration of darkness
	Gp. Occ.=Group Occulting.	. . . .	A light with a group of 2 or more eclipses at regular intervals
	Gp. Occ. (2+3)=Composite group occulting.	. . . .	A light in which the occultations are combined in alternate groups of different numbers

LIGHTED BUOYS

The following information is excerpted from Volume 1 of the Coast Guard Light List CG-158 (Atlantic Coast), and it applies to all navigable waters of the United States.

Light Color Characteristics

Red lights on buoys are used only on red buoys or red and black horizontally-banded buoys with the topmost band red. Green lights on buoys are used only on the black buoys or black and red horizontally banded buoys with the topmost band black. White lights on buoys are used on any color buoy. No special significance is attached to a white light on a buoy, the purpose of the buoy being indicated by its color, number, or its light phase characteristic.

Light Phase Characteristics

(a) Lights on red buoys or black buoys, if not fixed, will always be regularly flashing or regularly occulting. For ordinary purposes the frequency of flashes will not be more than 30 per minute (slow flashing). For purposes when it is desired that lights have a distinct cautionary significance, as at sharp turns or sudden constrictions in the channel, or to mark wrecks or dangerous obstructions, the frequency of flashes will not be less than 60 per minute (quick flashing).

(b) Lights on red and black horizontally banded buoys will always show a series of quick flashes interrupted by eclipses about eight times per minute (interrupted quick flashing).

(c) Lights on black and white vertically striped buoys will always show a white Morse Code "A" (Short-Long) flash, this combination recurring at the rate of about eight times per minute. See Fig. 401.

Fig. 401 Characteristic Light Phases

PILOTING

PRIMARY SEACOAST LIGHTS

If you do any extended cruising, you should know how to identify all major and secondary light structures (or ships) in your cruising area. Light lists published by the Coast Guard are available that give the following information for each light: Name, character and period of light; location; height of structure above water; description of structure, vessel, or buoy; and special characteristics. (See the Government Publications listing, Section IX).

The excerpt and drawing, figs. 402, 403, illustrate a typical major light and its description. The light number in this case is of little significance. The structure is identified as Galveston Jetty Light, with a light that flashes alternately white and red on a 10-second cycle: a four-tenths second white flash, four and six-tenths second interval, four-tenths second red flash, and four and six-tenths second interval. It is located on the south jetty at Latitude 29° 19.7 and Longitude 94° 41.5 and its light is 91 feet above sea level. The white light is of 250,000 candlepower; the red light is 140,000 candlepower, and in normal visibility it can be seen from a distance of 15 miles. The description is self-

(1)	(2)	(3)	(4)	(5)	(6)		(7)
	Name	Location	Light or day-beacon	Candle-power	Structure, vessel, or buoy		
No.	Character and period of light	Latitude, N. Longitude, W.	above water		Top of lantern above ground	Established. Moved or rebuilt	Radiobeacon, fog signal, sectors and remarks
	(Duration in Italics)	Deg. Min. Deg. Min.	Feet	Miles seen, in Italics	Feet	Year	
EIGHTH DISTRICT		TEXAS					
7482 6466 14034	GALVESTON JETTY LIGHT Alt. Fl. W. & R., 10ˢ 0. 4ˢW fl., 4. 6ˢec. 0. 4ˢR fl., 4. 6ˢec. Resident Personnel.	On south jetty, near east end. 29 19.7 94 41.5	91	W. 250,000 R. 140,000 15	Cream-colored cylindrical brick tower with black pilasters, on skeleton structure.	1916	RADIOBEACON: Antenna 70 feet 278° from light tower. See p. XVII for method of operation. HORN; diaphragm; 1 blast ev 20ˢ(2ˢbl). Special Radio Direction Finder Calibration Service, see p. XIX.

Fig. 402 Excerpt from the Light List Vol. II (Atlantic and Gulf Coasts) describes Galveston Jetty Light illustrated in Fig. 403.

Fig. 403 Galveston Jetty Light.

explanatory. It has a radio beacon, with antenna located 70 feet away from the light tower at a true bearing of 278°; A description of its use by boatmen is given on page XVII of the Light List. The fog signal is generated by a diaphragm horn, and it is a single two-second blast given every 20 seconds. A special direction finder calibration service is available, and a description of its operation is given on page XIX of the Light List.

BOUNDARY LINES OF INLAND WATERS

Within the areas subject to the jurisdiction of the federal government there is a sub-category known as "inland waters." By an Act of Congress of 1895, with subsequent amendments, authority was established for the prescribing of boundary lines dividing the "high seas" from rivers, bays, sounds, harbors, etc. These boundaries are of primary importance in connection with the Rules of the Road.

Federal waters inshore of these boundary lines are subject to the Inland Rules of the Road and the Inland Pilot Rules, except for certain interior areas where other laws and regulations known as the Great Lakes Rules and the Western Rivers Rules are in effect. Offshore of the boundary lines, the International Rules of the Road (the full name of which is the International Regulations for the Prevention of Collision at Sea) are effective. It should be noted that the International Rules have been adopted by the United States and are legally applicable to all vessels in U.S. national waters *within* the three-mile limit of national sovereignty, as well as to U.S. vessels on the high seas.

Delineation of Boundary Lines

The International-Inland boundary lines are drawn at all major entrances to harbors, rivers, bays, etc., roughly parallel with the general trend of the shoreline. The lines are established with respect to aids to navigation—lighthouses, lightships, buoys—for ease of identification. Boatmen in waters where such boundaries exist should be familiar with them.

Following are boundary lines, as described in *CG-169, Rules of the Road,* published by the Coast Guard and corrected to August, 1972. These boundaries are subject to change, and the daily Federal Register, available at many libraries, can be checked for such modifications.

82.1   General Basis and Purpose of Boundary Lines

Under section 2 of the act of February 19, 1895, as amended (28 Stat. 672, 33 U.S.C. 151), the regulations in this part are prescribed to establish the lines dividing the high seas from rivers, harbors, and inland waters in accordance with the intent of the statute and to obtain its correct and uniform administration. The waters inshore of the lines described in this part are "inland waters," and upon them the Inland Rules and Pilot Rules made in pursuance thereof apply. The waters outside of the lines described in this part are the high seas and upon them the Inter-

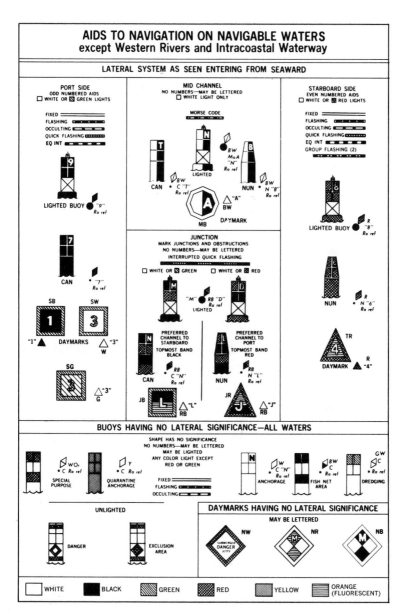

Fig. 404

national Rules apply. The regulations in this part do not apply to the Great Lakes or their connecting and tributary waters.

82.2   General Rules for Inland Waters

At all buoyed entrances from seaward to bays, sounds, rivers, or other estuaries for which specific lines are not prescribed in this part, the waters inshore of a line approximately parallel with the general trend of the shore, drawn through the outermost buoy or other aid to navigation of any system of aids, are inland waters, and upon them the Inland Rules and Pilot Rules made in pursuance thereof apply, except that Pilot Rules for Western Rivers apply to the Red River of the North, the Mississippi River and its tributaries above Huey P. Long Bridge, and that part of the Atchafalaya River above its junction with the Plaquemine-Morgan City alternate waterway.

Atlantic Coast

82.5   All Harbors on the Coast of Maine, New Hampshire, and Massachusetts between West Quoddy Head, Maine, and Cape Ann Light, Mass.

A line drawn from Sail Rock Lighted Whistle Buoy 1 to the southeasternmost extremity of Long Point, Maine, to the southeasternmost extremity of Western Head; thence to the southeasternmost extremity of Old Man; thence to the southernmost extremity of Double Shot Islands; thence to Libby Island Light; thence to Moose Peak Light; thence to the eastern extremity of Little Pond Head. A line drawn from the southern extremity of Pond Point, Great Wass Island, to the southernmost point of Crumple Island; thence to Petit Manan Light; thence to Mount Desert Light; thence to Martinicus Rock Light; thence to Monhegan Island Light; thence to Seguin Light; thence to Portland Lightship; thence to Boon Island Light; thence to Cape Ann Lighted Whistle Buoy 2.

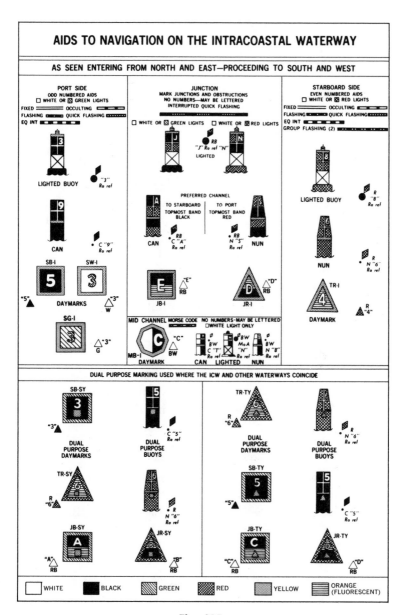

PILOTING

Fig. 405

82.10   Massachusetts Bay

A line drawn from Cape Ann Lighted Whistle Buoy 2 to Boston Lightship; thence to Cape Cod Light.

82.15   Nantucket Sound, Vineyard Sound, Buzzard's Bay, Narragansett Bay, Block Island Sound, and easterly entrance to Long Island Sound

A line drawn from Chatham Light to Pollock Rip Lightship; thence to Great Round Shoal Channel Entrance Lighted Whistle Buoy GRS; thence to Sankaty Head Light. A line drawn from the westernmost extremity of Smith Point, Nantucket Island, to No Mans Land Lighted Whistle Buoy 2; thence to Gay Head Light; thence to Block Island Southeast Light; thence to Montauk Point Light on the easterly end of Long Island, N.Y.

82.20   New York Harbor

A line drawn from East Rockaway Inlet Breakwater Light to Ambrose Light; thence to Highlands Light (north tower).

82.25   Delaware Bay and tributaries

A line drawn from Cape May East Jetty Light to Cape May Harbor Inlet Lighted Bell Buoy 2CM; thence to South Shoal Lighted Bell Buoy 4; thence to the northernmost extremity of Cape Henlopen.

82.30   Chesapeake Bay and Tributaries

A line drawn from Cape Henry Light to Cape Henry Buoy 1; thence to Chesapeake Bay Entrance Lighted Bell Buoy CBC; thence to North Chesapeake Entrance Lighted Gong Buoy NCD; thence to Cape Charles Light.

82.35   Charleston Harbor

A line drawn from Charleston Light on Sullivan's Island to Charleston Lighted Whistle Buoy 2C; thence to Folly Island loran tower.

PILOTING

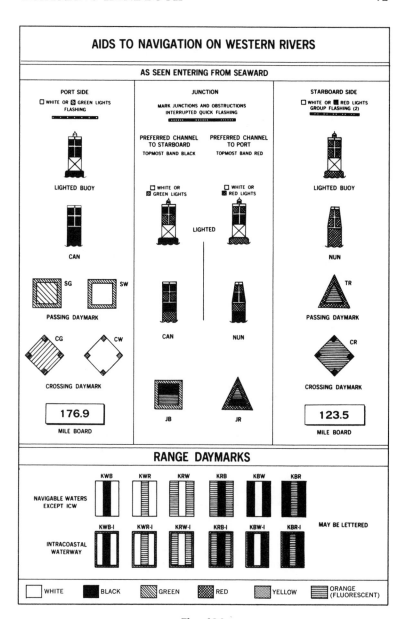

Fig. 406

82.40   Savannah Harbor

A line drawn from the southwesternmost extremity of Braddock Point to Tybee Lighted Whistle Buoy T; thence to the southernmost point of Savannah Beach, bearing approximately 278° True.

82.45   St. Simon Sound, St. Andrew Sound, and Cumberland Sound

A line drawn from the tower located 1,700 yards, bearing 068° true from St. Simons Light to St. Simons Lighted Whistle Buoy St. S; thence to St. Andrew Sound Outer Entrance Buoy; thence to St. Marys Entrance Lighted Whistle Buoy STM; thence to Amelia Island Light.

82.50   St. Johns River, Fla.

A line drawn from the east end of the north jetty to the east end of the south jetty.

82.55   Florida Reefs and Keys from Miami to Marquesas Keys

A line drawn from the east end of the north jetty at the entrance to Miami Harbor, to Miami Lighted Whistle Buoy M; thence to Fowey Rocks Light; thence to Pacific Reef Light; thence to Carysfort Reef Light; thence to Molasses Reef Light; thence to Alligator Reef Light; thence to Tennessee Reef Light; thence to Sombrero Key Light; thence to American Shoal Light; thence to Key West Entrance Lighted Whistle Buoy; thence to Sand Key Light; thence to Cosgrove Shoal Light; thence to westernmost extremity of Marquesas Keys.

Gulf Coast

82.60   Florida Keys from Marquesas to Cape Sable

A line drawn from the northwesternmost extremity of Marquesas Keys to Northwest Channel Entrance Lighted Bell Buoy 1; thence to the southernmost extremity of East Cape, Cape Sable.

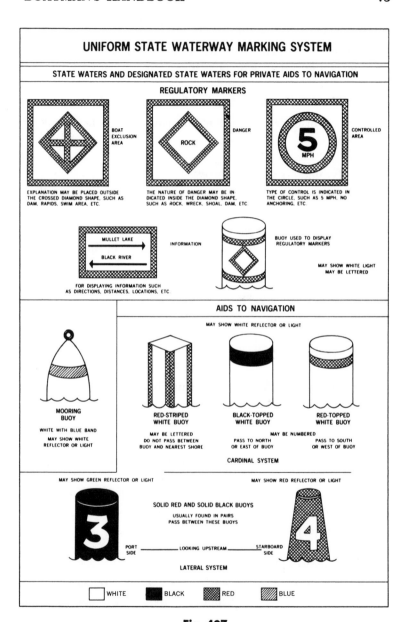

UNIFORM STATE WATERWAY MARKING SYSTEM

STATE WATERS AND DESIGNATED STATE WATERS FOR PRIVATE AIDS TO NAVIGATION

REGULATORY MARKERS

BOAT EXCLUSION AREA

EXPLANATION MAY BE PLACED OUTSIDE THE CROSSED DIAMOND SHAPE, SUCH AS DAM, RAPIDS, SWIM AREA, ETC.

DANGER

ROCK

THE NATURE OF DANGER MAY BE INDICATED INSIDE THE DIAMOND SHAPE, SUCH AS ROCK, WRECK, SHOAL, DAM, ETC.

CONTROLLED AREA

5 MPH

TYPE OF CONTROL IS INDICATED IN THE CIRCLE, SUCH AS 5 MPH, NO ANCHORING, ETC.

MULLET LAKE

BLACK RIVER

INFORMATION

FOR DISPLAYING INFORMATION SUCH AS DIRECTIONS, DISTANCES, LOCATIONS, ETC.

BUOY USED TO DISPLAY REGULATORY MARKERS

MAY SHOW WHITE LIGHT
MAY BE LETTERED

AIDS TO NAVIGATION

MAY SHOW WHITE REFLECTOR OR LIGHT

MOORING BUOY

WHITE WITH BLUE BAND
MAY SHOW WHITE REFLECTOR OR LIGHT

RED-STRIPED WHITE BUOY

MAY BE LETTERED
DO NOT PASS BETWEEN BUOY AND NEAREST SHORE

BLACK-TOPPED WHITE BUOY

PASS TO NORTH OR EAST OF BUOY

RED-TOPPED WHITE BUOY

MAY BE NUMBERED

PASS TO SOUTH OR WEST OF BUOY

CARDINAL SYSTEM

MAY SHOW GREEN REFLECTOR OR LIGHT

MAY SHOW RED REFLECTOR OR LIGHT

3

SOLID RED AND SOLID BLACK BUOYS

USUALLY FOUND IN PAIRS
PASS BETWEEN THESE BUOYS

PORT SIDE ——— LOOKING UPSTREAM ——— STARBOARD SIDE

4

LATERAL SYSTEM

☐ WHITE   ■ BLACK   ▨ RED   ▨ BLUE

Fig. 407

82.65   San Carlos Bay and Tributaries

A line drawn from the northwesternmost point of Estero Island to Caloosa Lighted Bell Buoy 2; thence to Sanibel Island Light.

82.70   Charlotte Harbor, Fla., and Tributaries

Eastward of Charlotte Harbor Entrance Lighted Bell Buoy off Boca Grande.

82.80   Tampa Bay and tributaries

A line drawn from the southernmost extremity of Long Key, Fla., to Tampa Bay Lighted Whistle Buoy; thence to Southwest Channel Entrance Lighted Bell Buoy 1; thence to the shore on the northwest side of Anna Maria Key, bearing approximately 109° true.

82.89   Apalachee Bay, Fla.

Those waters lying north of a line drawn from Lighthouse Point on St. James Island to Gamble Point on the east side of the entrance to the Aucilla River, Fla.

82.95   Mobile Bay, Ala., to Mississippi Passes, La.

Starting from a point which is located 1 mile, 90° true, from Mobile Point Light, a line drawn to Mobile Entrance Lighted Whistle Buoy 1; thence to Ship Island Light; thence to Chandeleur Light; thence in a curved line following the general trend of the seaward, highwater shore lines of the Chandeleur Islands to the southwesternmost extremity of Errol Shoal (lat. 29°35.8′ N., long. 89°00.8′ W.); thence to a point 5.1 miles, 107° true, from Pass a Loutre Daybeacon.

82.100   Mississippi River

The Pilot Rules for Western Rivers are to be followed in the Mississippi River and its tributaries above the Huey P. Long Bridge.

CANADA

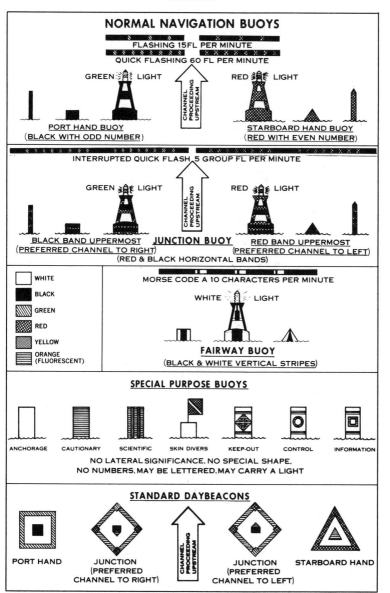

AIDS TO NAVIGATION, DEPARTMENT OF TRANSPORT

Fig. 408

82.103   Mississippi Passes, La., to Sabine Pass, Tex.

A line drawn from a point 5.1 miles, 107° true, from Pass a Loutre Daybeacon to South Pass Lighted Whistle Buoy 2; thence to Southwest Pass Entrance Midchannel Lighted Whistle Buoy; thence to Ship Shoal Daybeacon; thence to Calcasieu Channel Lighted Whistle Buoy 20; thence to Sabine Bank Channel Lighted Bell Buoy 18.

82.106   Sabine Pass, Tex., to Galveston, Tex.

A line drawn from Sabine Pass Lighted Whistle Buoy 1 to Galveston Bay Entrance Channel Lighted Whistle Buoy 1.

82.11   Galveston, Tex., to Brazos River, Tex.

A line drawn from Galveston Bay Entrance Channel Lighted Whistle Buoy 1 to Freeport Entrance Lighted Bell Buoy 1.

82.116   Brazos River, Tex., to the Rio Grande, Tex.

A line drawn from Freeport Entrance Lighted Whistle Buoy 1 to a point 4,350 yards, 118° true, from Matagorda Light; thence to Aransas Pass Lighted Whistle Buoy AP; thence to a position 10.5 miles, 90° true, from the north end of Lopeno Island (27°00.1′ N. latitude, 97°15.5′ W. longitude); thence to Brazos Santiago Entrance Lighted Whistle Buoy 1.

Pacific Coast

82.120   Juan de Fuca Strait, Wash., and Puget Sound

A line drawn from the northernmost point of Angeles Point to Hein Bank Lighted Bell Buoy; thence to Lime Kiln Light; thence to Kellett Bluff Light; thence to Turn Point Light on Stuart Island; thence to westernmost extremity of Skipjack Island; thence to Patos Island Light; thence to Point Roberts Light.

82.122   Grays Harbor

A line drawn from Grays Harbor Bar Range Rear Light to Grays Harbor Entrance Lighted Whistle Buoy 3; thence to

Grays Harbor Entrance Lighted Whistle Buoy 2; thence to Grays Harbor Light.

82.125   Columbia River Entrance

A line drawn from the west end of the north jetty (above water) to Columbia River South Jetty Bell Buoy 2SJ.

82.127   Crescent City Harbor

A line drawn from Crescent City Outer Breakwater to the highest point in the center of Whaler Island.

82.129   Arcata—Humboldt Bay

A line drawn from the outer end of Humboldt Bay North Jetty to the outer end of Humboldt Bay South Jetty.

82.131   Bodega and Tomales Bays

A line drawn from the northwestern tip of Tomales Point to Tomales Point Lighted Horn Buoy 2; thence to Bodega Harbor Approach Lighted Gong Buoy BA; thence to the southernmost extremity of Bodega Head.

82.133   San Francisco Harbor

A straight line from Point Bonita Light drawn through Mile Rocks Light to the shore.

82.135   Santa Cruz Harbor

A line drawn from Santa Cruz Light to the southernmost projection of Soquel Point.

82.137   Moss Landing Harbor

A line drawn from the west end of Moss Landing Harbor North Breakwater to the west end of the pier located 0.3 mile to the south of Moss Landing Harbor North Breakwater.

82.139   Monterey Harbor

A line drawn from Monterey Harbor Breakwater Light to Mon-

PILOTING

terey Harbor Anchorage Buoy B; thence to Monterey Harbor Anchorage Buoy A; thence to the north end of Monterey Municipal
Wharf 2.

82.141   Estero—Morro Bay

A line drawn from the outer end of Morro Bay Entrance East
Breakwater to Morro Bay Entrance Lighted Bell Buoy 1; thence
to Morro Bay West Breakwater Light.

82.143   San Luis Obispo Bay

A line drawn from the outer end of Whaler Island Breakwater
to the southernmost tip of Fossil Point.

82.144   Ventura Marina

(a) A line drawn from the south end of the detached breakwater to Ventura Marina Light 4.

(b) A line drawn 080° true from the north end of the detached
breakwater to shore.

82.145   San Pedro Bay

A line drawn from Los Angeles Light to Los Angeles Main
Channel Entrance Light 2; a line drawn from Long Beach Light
to Long Beach Channel Entrance Light 2; a line drawn from
Long Beach Breakwater East End Light to Anaheim Bay East
Jetty Light 5; thence to Anaheim Bay West Jetty Light 6.

82.147   Santa Barbara Harbor

A line drawn from Stearns Wharf Light 4 to Santa Barbara
Harbor Lighted Bell Buoy 1; thence to Santa Barbara Harbor
Breakwater Light.

82.149   Port Hueneme

A line drawn from Port Hueneme West Jetty Light 1 to the
southwest end of Port Hueneme East Jetty.

82.151   Marina del Rey

A line from Marina Del Rey Detached Breakwater Light 1 to

shore, in the direction 060° true; a line from Marina Del Rey Detached Breakwater North Light 2 to shore, in the direction 060°
true.

82.153 Redondo Harbor

A line drawn from Redondo Beach East Jetty Light 2 to Redondo Beach West Jetty Light 3.

82.155 Newport Bay

A line drawn from Newport Bay East Jetty Light 4 to Newport
West Jetty Light 3.

82.157 San Diego Harbor

A line drawn from the southerly tower of the Coronado Hotel
to San Diego Channel Lighted Bell Buoy 5; thence to Point Loma
Light.

82.159 Isthmus Cove (Santa Catalina Island)

A line drawn from the northernmost point of Lion Head to
the north tangent of Bird Rock Island; thence to the northernmost point of Blue Cavern Point.

82.161 Avalon Bay (Santa Catalina Island)

A line drawn from White Rock to the northernmost point of
Abalone Point.

Hawaii

82.175 Mamala Bay

A line drawn from Barbers Point Light to Diamond Head
Light.

Puerto Rico and Virgin Islands

82.200 Bahia de San Juan

A line drawn from the northwesternmost extremity of Punta

del Moro to Puerto San Juan Lighted Buoy 1; thence to Puerto San Juan Lighted Buoy 2; thence to the northernmost extremity of Isla de Cabras.

82.205   Puerto Arecibo

A line drawn from the westernmost extremity of the breakwater through Puerto Arecibo Buoy 1; thence through Puerto Arecibo Buoy 2; thence to shore in line with the Church tower in Arecibo.

82.210   Bahia de Mayaguez

A line drawn from the southernmost extremity of Punta Algarrobo to Bahia de Mayaguez Entrance Lighted Buoy 3; thence to Bahia de Mayaguez Entrance Lighted Buoy 4; thence to the northwesternmost extremity of Punta Guanajibo.

82.215   Bahia de Guanica

A line drawn from the easternmost extremity of Punta Brea through Bahia de Guanica Lighted Buoy 6; thence to the westernmost extremity of Punta Jacinto.

82.220   Bahia de Guayanilla

A line drawn from the southernmost extremity of Punta Ventana through Bahia de Guayanilla Entrance Lighted Buoy 2; thence to the southeasternmost extremity of Punta Guayanilla.

82.225   Bahia de Ponce

A line drawn from the southeasternmost extremity of Punta Cuchara through Bahia de Ponce Lighted Buoy 1; thence to Bahia de Ponce Lighted Buoy 2; thence to the southwesternmost extremity of Punta Cabullon.

82.230   Bahia de Jobos

A line drawn from Punta Arenas through Bahia de Jobos Light; thence to Bahia de Jobos entrance Lighted Buoy 2; thence to the southernmost extremity of Cayo Morrillo; thence to the southernmost extremity of Cayos de Pajaros.

82.235   St. Thomas Harbor, St. Thomas

A line drawn from the southernmost extremity of Red Point through West Gregerie Channel Buoy 1; thence to West Gregerie Channel Lighted Buoy 2; thence to the southernmost extremity of Flamingo Point; thence to St. Thomas Harbor Entrance Lighted Buoy 2; thence to Green Cay.

82.240   Christiansted Harbor, Island of St. Croix, Virgin Islands

A line drawn from Shoy Point to Christiansted Harbor Channel Lighted Buoy 1; thence to stack at Little Princess northwestward of leper settlement.

82.245   Sonda de Vieques

A line drawn from the easternmost extremity of Punta Yeguas, Puerto Rico, to a point 1 mile due south of Puerto Ferro Light; thence eastward in a straight line to a point 1 mile southeast of Punta Este Light, Vieques; thence in a straight line to the easternmost extremity of Punta del Este, Isla Culebrita. A line from the northernmost extremity of Cayo Nordeste to Piedra Stevens Lighted Buoy 1; thence to Las Cucarachas Light; thence to Cabo San Juan Light.

Alaska

82.275   Bays, Sounds, Straits and Inlets on the coast of southeastern Alaska between Cape Spencer Light and Sitklan Island.

A line drawn from Cape Spencer Light due south to a point of intersection which is due west of the southernmost extremity of Cape Cross; thence to Cape Edgecumbe Light; thence through Cape Bartolome Light and extended to a point of intersection which is due west of Cape Muzon Light; thence due east to Cape Muzon Light; thence to a point which is 1 mile, 180° true, from Cape Chacon Light; thence to Barren Island Light; thence to Lord Rock Light; thence to the southernmost extremity of Garnet Point, Kanagunut Island; thence to the southeasternmost extremity of Island Point, Sitklan Island. A line drawn from the northeasternmost extremity of Point Mansfield, Sitklan Island 040° true, to where it intersects the mainland.

PILOTING

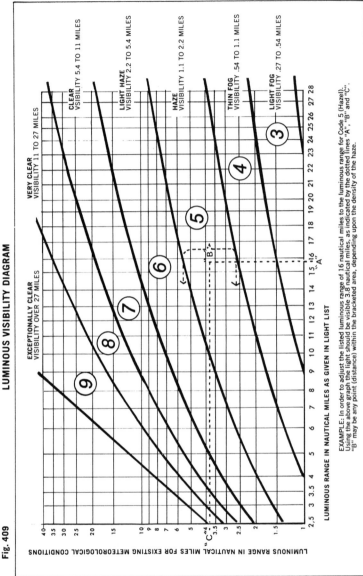

Fig. 409

LUMINOUS VISIBILITY DIAGRAM

LUMINOUS RANGE IN NAUTICAL MILES FOR EXISTING METEOROLOGICAL CONDITIONS

LUMINOUS RANGE IN NAUTICAL MILES AS GIVEN IN LIGHT LIST

EXCEPTIONALLY CLEAR
VISIBILITY OVER 27 MILES

VERY CLEAR
VISIBILITY 11 TO 27 MILES

CLEAR
VISIBILITY 5.4 TO 11 MILES

LIGHT HAZE
VISIBILITY 2.2 TO 5.4 MILES

HAZE
VISIBILITY 1.1 TO 2.2 MILES

THIN FOG
VISIBILITY .54 TO 1.1 MILES

LIGHT FOG
VISIBILITY .27 TO .54 MILES

EXAMPLE: In order to adjust the listed luminous range of 16 nautical miles to the luminous range for Code 5 (Haze), Using the above graph the light should be visible 3.8 nautical miles, as indicated by the dotted lines "A", "B" and "C". "B" may be any point (distance) within the bracketed area, depending upon the density of the haze.

TIME AND TIME SIGNALS

Correct time is a necessity to the offshore yachtsman who must use celestial navigation to plot his course and determine his position. For coastal and inland piloting, the time signal given each hour by most normal AM or FM broadcast stations is accurate enough. In most localities ashore, it is possible to dial a time service operated by the phone company for reasonably accurate time information.

The most reliable time signals are those generated by the U. S. Naval Observatory. Signals based on Naval Observatory time are broadcast by the Bureau of Standards stations WWV in Fort Collins, Colo., and WWVH in Hawaii. Details are given in the following excerpts from the General Information section that appears in each *U. S. Coast Pilot.*

In addition to these, reliable signals are broadcast on 3.330, 14.67, and 7.335 MHz by the Dominion Conservatory, Ottawa, Canada. This is a continuous service, with information given in both French and English.

Time Signals

The United States system of broadcasting time signals begins at 55 minutes 0 seconds of some hour and continues for 5 minutes. Signals are transmitted on every second of this period except the 29th of each minute, the 51st of the first minute, the 52d of the second minute, the 53d of the third minute, the 54th of the fourth minute, the last 4 seconds of the first 4 minutes, and the last 9 seconds of the last minute. The hour signal is a 1.3-second dash, which is much longer than the others.

In all cases the beginnings of the dashes indicate the beginnings of the seconds, and the ends of the dashes are without significance. The number of dashes sounded in the group at the end of any minute indicates the number of minutes of the signal yet to be sent. In case of signal failure or error, the signal is repeated 1 hour later.

The *United States Naval Observatory* at Washington, D.C., is the origin of all Government time signals broadcast in the United States and its possessions. The time signals are broadcast by Navy Radio Station NSS in Washington on the following frequencies: 162 kHz (replaced by 121.95 kHz from 1400 to 2000 on Thursdays), 5870 kHz, 9425 kHz, 13575 kHz, 17050.4 kHz, and 23650 kHz; the hours of transmission are 0155-0200, 0555-0600, 0755-0800, 1155-1200, 1355-1400, 1755-1800, and 2355-0000 *Greenwich Mean Time.*

The *National Bureau of Standards,* in cooperation with the Naval Observatory, broadcasts time signals from its radio station WWV near Fort Collins, Colorado, on radio frequencies of 2.5, 5, 10, 15, and 25 megahertz. The service is continuous, day and night. This insures reliable coverage of the United States and useful coverage of many other parts of the world. The services include standard radio frequencies, standard audio frequencies, standard musical pitch, standard time intervals, time signals, UT2 corrections, radio propagation forecasts, and geophysical alerts.

Each hour is divided into one-minute slots; each minute (except the first) begins with an 0.8-second tone of 1000 Hz at WWV or 1200 Hz at WWVH. The first minute in each hour begins with an 0.8-second tone of 1500 Hz at both stations. The minute slots are divided into a 45-second segment and two 7.5-second segments: on alternate minutes the 45-second segment contains either a standard tone or an announcement.

The announcement slots are available to Government agencies for their own purposes. Those not used by NBS or other agencies will be filled by another standard tone. To prevent interference in those parts of the world which receive both WWV and WWVH, one station's announcements are scheduled to coincide with the other's tones, and vice versa.

The first 7.5-second segment following the 45-second period is used by WWVH to announce Greenwich Mean Time, while WWV is silent. The second 7.5-second segment is used by WWV to announce the time, while WWVH is silent. WWVH uses a feminine voice, and WWV a masculine.

Special Publication 236 describes in detail the standard frequency and time service of the National Bureau of Standards. Single copies may be obtained upon request from the National Bureau of Standards, Boulder, Colorado 80302. Quantities may be obtained from the Superintendent of Documents, U.S. Government Printing Office, Washington, D.C. 20402 at 15 cents per copy.

PILOTING

Time Zones

Time all over the world is based on the O° meridian which passes through Greenwich, England. Starting from the O° meridian, the earth is divided up into 12 time zones eastwards and 12 zones westwards, each consisting of 15° of the total 360° (36:15 = 24) or—in time—one hour. (The 180° meridian forms the International Date Line being both +12 hours and −12 hours from the O° meridian.) Each time zone is equally divided by its meridian. This means that the time boundary lines are 7.5° east and west of the zone meridian. There are, however, deviations from the time according to this system and official local time. The Benelux countries, France and Spain are located in the O-zone with Western European Time but—in practice—these countries use Central European time. Similar conditions prevail in other areas such as Argentina, Chile, Mexico and the Pacific coast in Canada. This does not affect astronomical navigation since all calculations are based on standard time in the form of Greenwich Time.

How to Use a Watch as a Compass

In an emergency, you can get an approximate compass reading from a clock or watch, if the sun is visible and the timepiece is reasonably accurate. Hold the clock or watch so the face is up, and point the *hour* hand in the direction of the sun. South will be midway between the hour hand and the numeral 12.

Table 4-1
A Comparison of International, Inland, Great Lakes and Western River Rules

Fog Signals — To be given by day or night, in fog or thick weather, such as mist or falling snow, or heavy rain storms

	International Rules	Inland Rules	Great Lakes Rules	Western River Rules
How signals are given when under way	Steam vessels:—Whistle; Sailing vessels and Vessels towed:—Fog horn	Same as International	Steam vessel:—Whistle; Sailing vessel (not in tow): Fog horn (See special cases below)	Steam vessel:—Whistle or siren; Sailing vessel:—Fog horn
Fog signal equipment required (For Motor Boats, see special regulations below)	Power-driven vessels:—Whistle sounded by steam, or substitute for steam; fog horn (mechanical); bell; Sailing vessels (20 gross tons or over):—Fog horn and bell	Same as International	Steam vessels:—Whistle, sounded by steam or substitute for steam, audible 2 miles; bell; Sailing vessels:—Fog horn and bell	Steam vessels:—Whistle or siren; bell; Sailing vessels:—Fog horn (Sailing vessels over 20 gross tons also carry a bell)
Steam (power-driven) vessel under way (See Fig. 53)	1 prolonged blast at intervals of not more than 2 minutes	1 prolonged blast at intervals of not more than 1 minute	3 blasts at intervals of not more than 1 minute (except when towing raft)	3 blasts at intervals of not more than 1 minute (2 of equal length, last one longer)
Steam (power-driven) vessel under way but stopped and having no way on (See Fig. 55)	2 prolonged blasts (1 second between) at intervals of not more than 2 minutes	Not mentioned	Not mentioned	Not mentioned
Sailing vessels under way (See Figures 60, 61, 62)	Starboard tack, 1 blast; Port tack, 2 blasts in succession; Wind abaft the beam, 3 blasts in succession; Intervals in each case not more than 1 minute	Same as International	If not in tow, same as International	Same as steam vessel, but uses fog horn
Vessels at anchor or not under way (See Figures 56, 58)	Ring bell rapidly for 5 seconds at intervals of not more than 1 minute*; Vessel aground in addition to anchor signal, gives 3 strokes on bell, before and after	Same as International **	At anchor or aground, ring bell rapidly 3 to 5 seconds at 2-minute intervals. In addition, every 3 minutes, sound signal on whistle or horn—1 short, 2 long, 1 short blasts in quick succession.	Same as International **
Vessels at anchor or not under way (over 350 ft.)	In addition to bell in forepart of vessel sound gong in after part at intervals of not more than 1 minute*	Not mentioned	Not mentioned	Not mentioned

Situation	International	Inland	Great Lakes	Western Rivers
Vessels towing or towed (See Figures 57, 59)	Vessels when towing, laying or picking up a submarine cable or navigation mark, or under way but not under command or unable to maneuver:— 1 prolonged blast (on whistle) followed by 2 short blasts, at intervals of not more than 1 minute. Vessel towed gives 1 prolonged blast, followed by 3 short, on whistle or fog horn	1 prolonged blast (on whistle) followed by 2 short blasts, at intervals of not more than 1 minute. Vessel towed may give same signal (on fog horn)	Steamer towing raft:—Sounds at intervals of not more than 1 minute, a screeching or Modoc whistle for 3 to 5 seconds. Vessel towed:—At intervals of 1 minute strikes bell four times (twice in quick succession, followed by a little longer interval, then twice in quick succession again.)	Vessel towing sounds 3 distinct blasts of equal length at intervals of not more than 1 minute
Small craft or craft not otherwise provided for	Vessels of less than 40 feet, rowboats, and seaplanes on the water, if they do not give regular signals prescribed above, make some other efficient sound signal at intervals of not more than 1 minute (On small seagoing vessels, gong may be used instead of bell)	Rafts and other watercraft not provided for above navigating by hand, power, horse power, or river current, sound 1 blast of fog horn or equivalent signal at intervals of not more than 1 minute	Vessels under 10 registered tons, if they do not give regular signals prescribed above, make some other efficient sound signal at intervals of not more than 1 minute. Produce boats, fishing boats, rafts, or other watercraft navigating by hand power or river current, or anchored or moored in or near channel or fairway, not in port, sound fog horn or equivalent signal at intervals of not more than 1 minute	Not mentioned
Vessels engaged in fishing (but not with trolling lines) (See Figure 54)	1 prolonged blast followed by 2 short blasts at 1 minute intervals (whistle if power-driven; fog horn if sail). Vessels fishing with trolling lines and under way sound the same fog signals as vessels not fishing	Not mentioned	Not mentioned	Not mentioned
Speed in fog or thick weather	Moderate speed, with regard to circumstances and conditions. Power-driven vessel hearing, forward of beam, fog signal of vessel, position of which is not ascertained, must stop and then navigate with caution until danger of collision is past	Same as International	Moderate speed. Steam vessel hearing, from direction not more than 4 points from right ahead, fog signal of another vessel, must reduce speed to bare steerageway, then navigate with caution until vessels have passed.	Moderate speed. Steam vessel hearing, forward of beam, fog signal of another vessel, must reduce speed to bare steerageway, then navigate with caution till vessels have passed

Note: A prolonged blast means a blast of 4 to 6 seconds duration.

FOG SIGNAL EQUIPMENT FOR MOTOR BOATS

Whistle: Motor boats, under way, give their fog signals on the whistle, not on a fog horn. Boats of Class 1, 16-26'; Class 2, 26'-40'; and Class 3, 40-65' carry an "efficient" whistle or other sound-producing mechanical appliance. With respect to motor boats, a blast of at least 2 seconds is considered a prolonged blast. A mouth whistle capable of producing a 2-second blast that can be heard at least ½ mile, on Class 1 only. However, an efficient electric or air horn is preferable, especially on boats with deckhouses. On Classes 2 and 3, whistle must be audible 1 mile. On Class 3, it must be power-operated; on Class 2, hand or power.

Bell: Class 2 and Class 3 carry an efficient bell.

Fog Horn: NOT required on MOTOR boats.

Exemptions: Outboard Motor Boats competing in a race previously arranged and announced or tuning up for such a race are exempt from carrying the above equipment. All boats of Class A, under 16', are also exempt.

* International Rules now authorize, in addition to bell signals at anchor, a warning signal of three blasts (1 short, 1 prolonged, 1 short)

**On Island Waters and Western Rivers, vessels under 65 feet in length and nondescript craft like barges, scows, etc., need not give fog signal when at anchor in special anchorage areas.

Compass Deviation Card

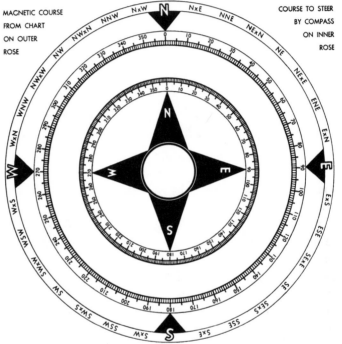

MAGNETIC COURSE
FROM CHART
ON OUTER
ROSE

COURSE TO STEER
BY COMPASS
ON INNER
ROSE

YACHT _____   OWNER _____

PORT _____   DATE _____

Read only MAGNETIC courses on the OUTER rose; only COMPASS courses on the inner one. For each compass heading (inner rose) apply the known deviation and draw a line from that degree or point to the corresponding magnetic heading (outer rose).

TO FIND THE COMPASS COURSE: Locate the magnetic course on the outer rose. Follow the lines to the inner rose and read the compass course.

TO CONVERT COMPASS COURSE TO MAGNETIC COURSE: Locate the compass course on the inner rose. Follow the lines to the outer one and read the magnetic course.

DO NOT CONVERT BEARINGS with this card. To do this find first the deviation for the boat's heading when the bearing was taken. Apply this deviation to the bearing.

5.
WEATHER

WEATHER MAP

The weather map provides a bird's-eye view of the weather over a large area. With its many figures, symbols and lines, the map at first appears to be puzzling. But with a little study of these markings and an understanding of their meaning, the map becomes a picture that gives you a good idea of what's in store.

Some boatmen may receive the weekly compilations of daily weather maps mailed to subscribers by the National Weather Service, Washington, D.C. Most, however, must depend upon newspaper maps for their information. These are drawn from Weather Service master weather charts. Four times each day, the Weather Service in Washington prepares and analyzes surface and upper air weather charts for the entire Northern Hemisphere.

On surface charts, weather data are plotted as received every six hours from more than 750 reporting stations in North America, more than 200 ships at sea, and 1500 stations in other countries. Each station reports the amount of sky covered by cloud, direction and speed of wind, visibility distance in miles, present weather, weather during the last three hours, sea level barometric pressure, air temperature, kinds of low, middle and high clouds,

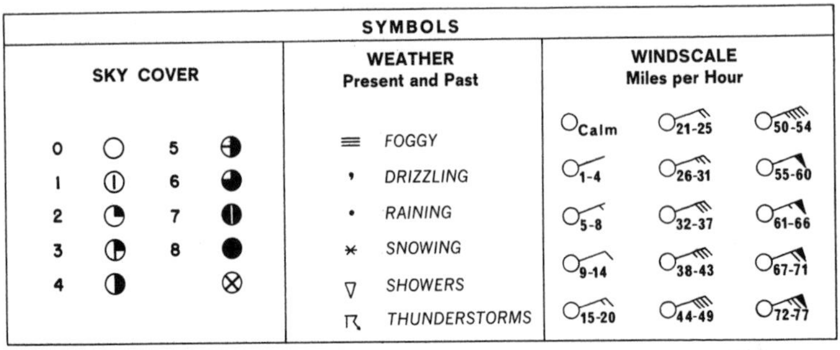

Fig. 501   Weather symbols.

dew-point temperature, character and amount of pressure change in the last three hours, and the character, duration and amount of rainfall in the last six hours. Many of these stations also furnish twelve-hour reports of pressure, temperature, moisture and wind conditions for several levels of upper air. Thus, the central weatherman with his daily surface and several upper air charts has a detailed picture of the weather occurring at the same time over the entire Northern Hemisphere. These charts are used in issuing the daily weather forecasts and warnings of approaching storms.

Over 150 *symbols* are used in entering data on weather maps. Although you may never need know what all the symbols mean, nor have occasion to plot them on a weather map, a knowledge of those most often used will help you to understand and interpret the daily maps appearing in newspapers. See fig. 501.

The Station Model

Fig. 502 shows the *"station model,"* a system weathermen the world over developed for entering data on weather maps. It presents a "model" or picture of the weather at a station, using symbols and numbers, which can be understood in any language. Not only the symbols and numbers but their positions around the station circle tell what each item means.

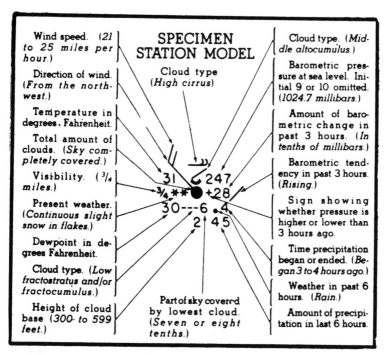

Fig. 502 Station model.

For example, starting with the "station circle" itself (the black dot in the middle)—the fact that this circle is solid black indicates that the sky is completely covered with clouds here.

Let's go counterclockwise around the station circle to examine and understand what's shown. Take the wind first. The symbol indicates a pretty windy day, the wind being from the northwest at 21 to 25 mph. The wind arrows always "fly" with the wind.

Next is temperature in degrees Fahrenheit. As you can see, it was relatively cold, the thermometer registering only 31°.

Since we know the sky was completely overcast, the next two markings—Visibility and Present Weather—begin to give us a picture of conditions at the station. It was a nasty day with a stiff, cold wind blowing light snow all over the place.

Precipitation Symbols

A word about precipitation symbols is in order here. Fig. 501 shows the symbols used to indicate different forms of precipitation—drizzle, rain, snow, etc. Increasing precipitation is indicated by more than one symbol being plotted, the range being from one to four identical symbols.

In fig. 502 the use of the two stars (or asterisks) tells you that it is snowing continuously but lightly at this station. If there had been three stars the snow would have been moderate to heavy. Now, if the *shower* symbol (a triangle) had been shown instead of the star it would have carried a star symbol above it to indicate that the showers were *snow* showers. If the showers were *rain* the shower symbol would have carried a dot (the rain symbol) above it.

Hail is indicated by a small triangle (inverted shower symbol)

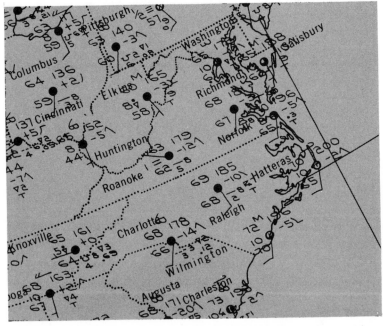

Fig. 503 Section from a National Weather Service surface chart.

above the thunderstorm symbol. Fog is represented by three horizontal lines.

Other symbols around the station circle in fig. 502 are interesting and important to weathermen and anyone wishing to use the information. They are worth studying but since most of them do not appear on the abbreviated maps appearing in newspapers we won't go into a detailed description here. Fig. 502 does provide a brief explanation of each.

Fig. 503 shows a small portion of a Weather Service surface chart with data plotted for several stations. By referring to figs. 501 and 502 you can tell what the weather conditions at any given station are. Let's take Raleigh, N. C. as a case in point:

You can see that the sky is completely overcast, the wind is south, at 9 to 14 mph, the temperature is 69°F., the dew point is 68°, the numeral 2 indicates the clouds are low, the letter T says that precipitation in the past 6 hours was very slight, T standing for "Trace," the barometer has fallen 1.0 millibar during the past 3 hours, there were thunderstorms at the station during the

Inches	Millibars	Inches	Millibars
28.44	963	29.77	1008
28.53	966	29.86	1011
28.62	969	29.94	1014
28.70	972	30.03	1017
28.79	975	30.12	1020
28.88	978	30.21	1023
28.97	981	30.30	1026
29.06	984	30.39	1029
29.15	987	30.48	1032
29.24	990	30.56	1035
29.32	993	30.65	1038
29.41	996	30.74	1041
29.50	999	30.83	1044
29.59	1002	30.92	1047
29.68	1005	31.01	1050

Fig. 504 Conversion table for a weather map's millibars.

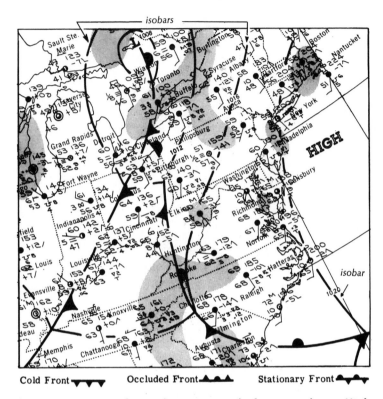

Cold Front ▼▼▼   Occluded Front ▲▲▲   Stationary Front ▲▼▲▼

Fig. 505 Section of weather map with fronts, isobars, Highs, Lows, and direction of fronts plotted on it.

past 6 hours, and the pressure is 1018.5 millibars or 30.08 inches of mercury.

Fig. 504 provides a conversion table for changing millibars to inches and vice versa.

Isobars and Fronts

When data from all stations are entered on the map, the weatherman draws black lines, called *isobars*. These are lines drawn through points having the same ("iso-" means equal) barometric pressure. For example, a 1020 millibar (30.12 inches) isobar is a

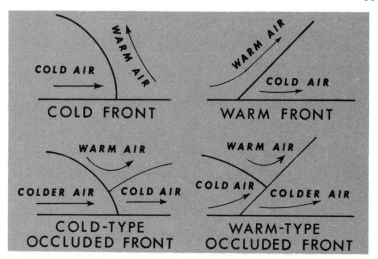

Fig. 506 Diagrams indicate action of cold and warm fronts and show how their interaction form occluded fronts.

WEATHER

line drawn through all points having a barometric pressure of 1020 millibars. Additional isobars are drawn for every four millibar intervals. The purpose of the isobars is to position the centers of low and high pressure—the familiar "LOWS" and "HIGHS" which govern our weather. The centers of high pressures are marked "H" or "High" and the low pressures are marked "L" or "Low." It is the movement of these HIGHS and LOWS which enables the weatherman to forecast weather, taking into consideration, of course, the various data supplied by the weather stations.

The heavier lines in fig. 505 are drawn to indicate *"fronts"*—the boundaries between different air streams. Triangles and half circles are attached to these heavier lines pointing in the direction in which the fronts are moving. The triangle indicates a *"cold front,"* the half circle a *"warm front."* (See also fig. 506.)

A front which is not moving, one which is *"stationary,"* is shown by attaching triangles on one side of the line and half circles on the opposite side. An *"occluded front"* is indicated by attaching

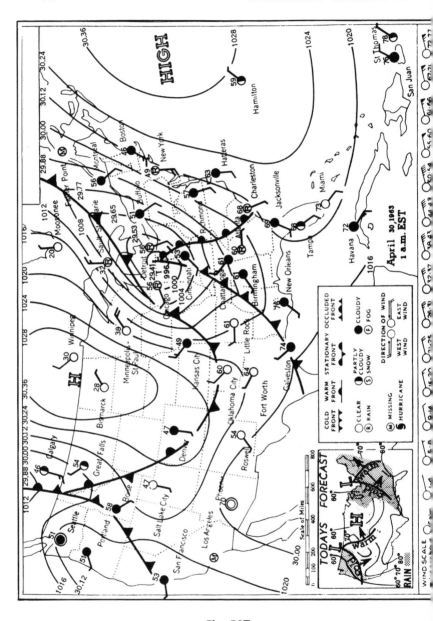

Fig. 507

both triangles and half circles to one side of the line. Fronts and their significance will be explained later.

Newspaper Weather Map

Because of their reduced size, it is impossible to include on newspaper maps all of the data usually entered on a map prepared at a National Weather Service office. To permit easier reading, only sky covered by cloud or other forms of present weather, wind direction and speed, and air temperature are plotted for each station. Barometric pressure at each station is omitted because it can be estimated for any place from the nearest isobar. Incidentally, on some weather maps, isobars may be drawn for 3 millibar intervals; for example, 996, 999, 1002, etc., rather than the 4 millibar intervals. Some maps show isobars marked at one end with the millibar pressure and at the other end in inches. Symbols used for entry of all this information, including those for types of fronts, are usually shown in the margin of newspaper maps. See fig. 507.

Morning newspapers usually contain the weather map prepared from data collected the evening before, while afternoon editions publish the early morning chart. The time is noted on the newspaper chart.

STORM SIGNAL DISPLAYS

Small Craft Advisory: One red pennant displayed by day and a red light above a white light at night to indicate winds up to 38 mph (33 knots) and/or sea conditions dangerous to small craft operations are forecast for the area. See fig. 508.

Gale Warning: Two red pennants displayed by day and a white light above a red light at night to indicate winds ranging from 39 to 54 mph (34 to 47 knots) are forecast.

Storm Warning: A single square red flag with black center displayed by day and two red lights at night indicate winds 48 knots

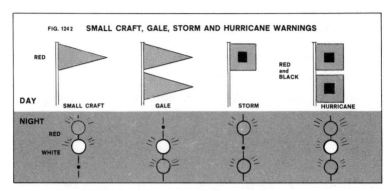

Fig. 508

(55 mph) and above (*no matter how high the velocity*) are fore-cast for the area. NOTE—If winds are associated with a tropical cyclone (hurricane) the *storm warning* display indicates forecast winds of 48 to 63 knots (55 to 73 mph). The *hurricane warning* is displayed only in connection with a tropical cyclone (hurri-cane).

Hurricane Warning: Two square red flags with black centers displayed by day and a white light between two red lights at night to indicate that winds 75 mph (64 knots) and above are forecast for the area.

WEATHER INFORMATION

Storm warnings and storm advisories issued by the National Weather Service are broadcast by designated United States Naval and Coast Guard radio stations. A large number of commercial radio stations also broadcast storm warnings, although at some-what irregular intervals.

The display of storm warning signals from lightships is now authorized. These signals consist of the standard Weather Ser-vice flag hoists, displayed by day in the same manner as from shore stations. No night signals are displayed by lightships, and the day storm flags are displayed only while the lightship is on station, not while proceding to or from station.

National Weather Service Broadcasts

The latest forecasts, weather observations from both the National Weather Service and U.S. Coast Guard stations, and emergency weather warning bulletins, are broadcast on stations operated by the National Weather Service. Since frequencies used are

Table 5-1

DETERMINATION OF WIND SPEED BY SEA CONDITION

Knots	Descriptive	Sea Conditions	Wind force (Beaufort)	Probable wave height (in ft.)
0-1	Calm	Sea smooth and mirror-like.	0	—
1-3	Light air	Scale-like ripples without foam crests.	1	¼
4-6	Light breeze	Small, short wavelets; crests have a glassy appearance and do not break.	2	½
7-10	Gentle breeze	Large wavelets; some crests begin to break; foam of glassy appearance. Occasional white foam crests.	3	2
11-16	Moderate breeze	Small waves, becoming longer; fairly frequent white foam crests.	4	4
17-21	Fresh breeze	Moderate waves, taking a more pronounced long form; many white foam crests; there may be some spray.	5	6
22-27	Strong breeze	Large waves begin to form; white foam crests are more extensive everywhere; there may be some spray.	6	10
28-33	Near gale	Sea heaps up and white foam from breaking waves begins to be blown in streaks along the direction of the wind; spindrift begins.	7	14
34-40	Gale	Moderately high waves of greater length; edges of crests break into spindrift; foam is blown in well-marked streaks along the direction of the wind.	8	18
41-47	Strong gale	High waves; dense streaks of foam along the direction of the wind; crests of waves begin to topple, tumble, and roll over; spray may reduce visibility.	9	23
48-55	Storm	Very high waves with long overhanging crests. The resulting foam in great patches is blown in dense white streaks along the direction of the wind. On the whole, the surface of the sea is white in appearance. The tumbling of the sea becomes heavy and shock-like. Visibility is reduced.	10	29
56-63	Violent Storm	Exceptionally high waves that may obscure small and medium-sized ships. The sea is completely covered with long white patches of foam lying along the direction of the wind. Everywhere the edges of the wave crests are blown into froth. Visibility reduced.	11	37
64-71	Hurricane	The air is filled with foam and spray. Sea completely white with driving spray; visibility very much reduced.	12	45

(Courtesy U.S. Weather Bureau)

WEATHER

Table 5-2

TRUE FORCE AND DIRECTION OF THE WIND FROM ITS APPARENT FORCE AND DIRECTION ON A BOAT UNDER WAY

	APPARENT WIND VELOCITY (Knots)	SPEED OF BOAT							
		5 Knots		10 Knots		15 Knots		20 Knots	
		TRUE WIND		TRUE WIND		TRUE WIND		TRUE WIND	
		Points off Bow	Velocity Knots	Points off Bow	Velocity Knots	Points off Bow	Velocity Knots	Points off Bow	Veloci Knots
I. APPARENT WIND DIRECTION IS DEAD AHEAD	Calm	D. As.	5 K.	D. As.	10 K.	D. As.	15 K.	D. As.	20 K
	4 K.	D. As.	1 K.	D. As.	6 K.	D. As.	11 K.	D. As.	16 K
	8 K.	D. Ah.	3 K.	D. As.	2 K.	D. As.	7 K.	D. As.	12 K
	12 K.	D. Ah.	7 K.	D. Ah.	2 K.	D. As.	3 K.	D. As.	8 K
	16 K.	D. Ah.	11 K.	D. Ah.	6 K.	D. Ah.	1 K.	D. As.	4 K
	22 K.	D. Ah.	17 K.	D. Ah.	12 K.	D. Ah.	7 K.	D. Ah.	2 K
	30 K.	D. Ah.	25 K.	D. Ah.	20 K.	D. Ah.	15 K.	D. Ah.	10 K
	42 K.	D. Ah.	37 K.	D. Ah.	32 K.	D. Ah.	27 K.	D. Ah.	22 K
	60 K.	D. Ah.	55 K.	D. Ah.	50 K.	D. Ah.	45 K.	D. Ah.	40 K
II. APPARENT WIND DIRECTION IS 4 POINTS (BROAD) OFF THE BOW	4 K.	11 pts.	4 K.	14 pts.	8 K.	15 pts.	12 K.	15 pts.	17 K
	8 K.	7 pts.	6 K.	11 pts.	7 K.	13 pts.	11 K.	14 pts.	15 K
	12 K.	6 pts.	9 K.	9 pts.	9 K.	11 pts.	11 K.	13 pts.	14 K
	16 K.	5 pts.	13 K.	7 pts.	11 K.	10 pts.	12 K.	11 pts.	14 K
	22 K.	5 pts.	19 K.	6 pts.	16 K.	8 pts.	15 K.	9 pts.	16 K
	30 K.	5 pts.	27 K.	6 pts.	24 K.	7 pts.	22 K.	8 pts.	21 K
	42 K.	4 pts.	39 K.	5 pts.	36 K.	6 pts.	33 K.	6 pts.	31 K
	60 K.	4 pts.	57 K.	5 pts.	53 K.	5 pts.	51 K.	6 pts.	48 K
III. APPARENT WIND DIRECTION IS 8 POINTS OFF THE BOW (ABEAM)	4 K.	13 pts.	6 K.	14 pts.	11 K.	15 pts.	16 K.	15 pts.	20 K
	8 K.	11 pts.	9 K.	13 pts.	13 K.	14 pts.	17 K.	14 pts.	22 K
	12 K.	10 pts.	13 K.	12 pts.	16 K.	13 pts.	19 K.	13 pts.	23 K
	16 K.	10 pts.	17 K.	11 pts.	19 K.	12 pts.	22 K.	13 pts.	26 K
	22 K.	9 pts.	23 K.	10 pts.	24 K.	11 pts.	27 K.	12 pts.	30 K
	30 K.	9 pts.	30 K.	10 pts.	32 K.	10 pts.	34 K.	11 pts.	36 K
	42 K.	9 pts.	42 K.	9 pts.	43 K.	10 pts.	45 K.	10 pts.	47 K
	60 K.	8 pts.	60 K.	9 pts.	61 K.	9 pts.	62 K.	10 pts.	63 K
IV. APPARENT WIND DIRECTION IS 12 POINTS OFF THE BOW (BROAD ON THE QUARTER)	4 K.	14 pts.	8 K.	15 pts.	13 K.	15 pts.	18 K.	15 pts.	23 K
	8 K.	14 pts.	12 K.	14 pts.	17 K.	15 pts.	21 K.	15 pts.	26 K
	12 K.	13 pts.	16 K.	14 pts.	20 K.	14 pts.	25 K.	15 pts.	30 K
	16 K.	13 pts.	20 K.	14 pts.	24 K.	14 pts.	29 K.	14 pts.	33 K
	22 K.	13 pts.	26 K.	13 pts.	30 K.	14 pts.	34 K.	14 pts.	39 K
	30 K.	13 pts.	34 K.	13 pts.	38 K.	13 pts.	42 K.	14 pts.	46 K
	42 K.	12 pts.	46 K.	13 pts.	50 K.	13 pts.	54 K.	13 pts.	58 K
	60 K.	12 pts.	64 K.	13 pts.	67 K.	13 pts.	71 K.	13 pts.	75 K

CONVERSION OF POINTS OFF BOW TO TRUE DIRECTION OF WIND

	POINTS OFF BOW	BOAT'S HEADING—TRUE							
		000°	045°	090°	135°	180°	225°	270°	315°
I. WHEN WIND DIRECTION OBTAINED FROM TABLE ABOVE IS OFF STARBOARD BOW	Dead Ahead	N	NE	E	SE	S	SW	W	NW
	4 points	NE	E	SE	S	SW	W	NW	N
	8 points	E	SE	S	SW	W	NW	N	N
	12 points	SE	S	SW	W	NW	N	NE	S
	Dead Astern	S	SW	W	NW	N	NE	E	S
II. WHEN WIND DIRECTION OBTAINED FROM TABLE ABOVE IS OFF PORT BOW	Dead Ahead	N	NE	E	SE	S	SW	W	NW
	4 points	NW	N	NE	E	SE	S	SW	W
	8 points	W	NW	N	NE	E	SE	S	SW
	12 points	SW	W	NW	N	NE	E	SE	S
	Dead Astern	S	SW	W	NW	N	NE	E	S

TO USE THIS TABLE

Abreviations: D. As. = Dead Astern. D. Ah. = Dead Ahead. K. = Knots. pts. = Points off bow.

1. **With Wind Direction Indicator:** Determine Apparent Wind Direction off the Bow.

2. **With Anemometer:** Determine Apparent Wind Velocity, in Knots.

3. **Enter Upper Part of Table:** Use portion for nearest Apparent Wind Direction Opposite Apparent Wind Velocity and under nearest Speed of Boat, read Wind Direction in Points off Bow and True Wind Velocity in Knots. Note whether True Wind Direction is Starboard or Port Bow.

4. **Enter Lower Part of Table:** Use portion for proper Bow: Starboard or Port. Opposite Points off Bow and under nearest Boat's True Heading, read True Wind Direction.

5. **Log:** Record True Wind Direction as obtained from Lower Part of Table and True Wind Velocity as obtained from Upper Part of Table in Boat's Weather Log.

above the standard FM band, special receivers are necessary. These are available from manufacturers of marine radio electronic equipment, in a variety of models.

Each station is in continuous 24 hour operation, with a taped weather message which recycles when completed. Tapes are updated regularly to include the latest forecasts or observations. Routine reports are interrupted when necessary for severe weather warnings.

A typical broadcast contains the following information:

1. The overall weather picture.
2. A radar weather summary.
3. Marine forecasts.
4. Observations of wind, weather, visibility, and sea conditions from U.S. Coast Guard stations.
5. A local area forecast.
6. A regional forecast.
7. Degree-day information during winter months.
8. The extended outlook.
9. Occasional Notices to Mariners.
10. All pertinent weather warnings.
11. Selected weather reports from National Weather Service stations.

National Weather Service VHF-FM Stations as of March, 1975:

162.55 MHz

Portland, Me.—KDO-95
New York, N.Y.—KWO-35
Washington, D.C.—
   KHB-36
Norfolk, Va.—KHB-37
Charleston, S.C.—KHB-29
Jacksonville, Fla.—KHB-39

Miami, Fla.—KHB-34
Tampa, Fla.—KHB-32
New Orleans, La.—
   KHB-43
Lake Charles, La.—
   KHB-42

WEATHER

162.40 MHz

Boston, Mass.—KHB-35   New London, Conn.—
Atlantic City, N.J.—   KHB-47
  KHB-38   Cleveland, Ohio—KHB-59

163.275 MHz

Galveston, Tex.—KHB-40   Chicago, Ill.—KWO-39
Corpus Christi, Tex.—   St. Louis, Mo.—KDO-89
  KHB-41   Kansas City, Mo.—KID-77
Los Angeles, Calif.—   Honolulu, Ha.—KB4-99
  KWO-37   Canton-Akron, Ohio—
San Francisco, Calif.—   KDO-94
  KHB-49   Sandusky, Ohio—KHB-97

169.075 MHz

Maui, Ha.

Marine Weather Services Charts

Coast Guard vessels now display storm warning signals. Headquarters of the Coast Guard are supplied with weather information by the National Weather Service and Coast Guard vessels receive instructions to fly the proper signals when bad weather is approaching.

The shore stations where storm warning signals are displayed are prominently marked on the *Marine Weather Services Charts,* a series which is published annually by the Weather Service. These charts also contain detailed information concerning the times of weather broadcasts from commercial stations, the radio frequencies of marine broadcast stations, the specific type of storm warnings issued, and the visual display signals which are used in connection with the warnings. This series consists of fourteen charts, twelve of which cover the coastal waters of the United States and the Great Lakes. The remaining two charts are for (a) the Hawaiian Islands, and (b) Puerto Rico and the Virgin Islands. They can be purchased from the Superintendent of Documents, Government Printing Office, Washington, D. C. 20402.

FOG

Fog is merely a cloud whose base rests upon the earth, be the latter land or water. It consists of water droplets, suspended in the air, each droplet so small that it cannot be distinguished individually, yet present in such tremendous numbers that objects close at hand are obscured.

If we are to have innumerable water droplets suspended in the air, there must be plenty of water vapor originally in that air. If droplets are to form from this vapor, the air must be cooled

WEATHER

Table 5-3

WIND AND BAROMETER INDICATIONS

Wind direction	Barometer reduced to sea level	Character of weather indicated
SW. to NW.	30.10 to 30.20 and steady	Fair, with slight temperature changes, for 1 to 2 days.
SW. to NW.	30.10 to 30.20 and rising rapidly	Fair, followed within 2 days by rain.
SW. to NW.	30.20 and above and stationary	Continued fair, with no decided temperature change.
SW. to NW.	30.20 and above and falling slowly	Slowly rising temperature and fair for 2 days.
S. to SE.	30.10 to 30.20 and falling slowly	Rain within 24 hours.
S. to SE.	30.10 to 30.20 and falling rapidly	Wind increasing in force, with rain within 12 to 24 hours.
SE. to NE.	30.10 to 30.20 and falling slowly	Rain in 12 to 18 hours.
SE. to NE.	30.10 to 30.20 and falling rapidly	Increasing wind, and rain within 12 hours.
E. to NE.	30.10 and above and falling slowly	In summer, with light winds, rain may not fall for several days. In winter, rain within 24 hours.
E. to NE.	30.10 and above and falling rapidly	In summer, rain probable within 12 to 24 hours. In winter, rain or snow, with increasing winds, will often set in when the barometer begins to fall and the winds sets in from the NE.
SE. to NE.	30.00 or below and falling slowly	Rain will continue 1 to 2 days.
SE. to NE.	30.00 or below and falling rapidly	Rain, with high wind, followed, within 36 hours, by clearing, and in winter by colder.
S. to SW.	30.00 or below and rising slowly	Clearing within a few hours, and fair for several days.
S. to E.	29.80 or below and falling rapidly	Severe storm imminent, followed, within 24 hours, by clearing, and in winter by colder.
E. to N.	29.80 or below and falling rapidly	Severe northeast gale and heavy precipitation; in winter, heavy snow, followed by a cold wave.
Going to W.	29.80 or below and rising rapidly	Clearing and colder.

by some means so that the vapor will condense. If the droplets
are to condense in the air next to the earth, the cooling must take
place at the surface of the earth. If the fog is to have any depth,
successively higher layers of air must be cooled sufficiently to
cause condensation in them. Fog forms from the ground up. Thus,
the land or water must be colder than the air next to it; the lower
layers of air progressively must be colder than the layers above
them.

If water vapor is to condense out of the air, then the temperature of the air must be lowered to or below the *dew-point temperature,* that is, the temperature at which the air is saturated
with water vapor and below which condensation of water vapor
will occur.

Air is said to be *saturated* with water vapor when its water-
vapor content would remain unchanged if it were placed above
a level surface of pure water at its own temperature. The amount
of water vapor which is required to saturate a given volume of
air depends on the temperature of the air, and increases as the
temperature increases. The higher the temperatures the more
water vapor can the air hold before it becomes saturated, and
the lower the temperature the less water vapor can the air hold
before it becomes saturated.

If a mass of air is originally in an unsaturated state, it can be
saturated by cooling it down to a temperature at which its content of water vapor is the maximum containable amount, that is
to say, to the dew-point temperature. Or we can saturate it by
causing more water to evaporate into it, thereby raising the dew-
point temperature to a value equal to the air temperature. In regard to the latter process, unsaturated air, as it passes over rivers
and lakes, over the oceans or over wet ground, picks up water
vapor and has its dew point raised. Also, rain falling from higher
clouds will increase the amount of water vapor in unsaturated air
near the earth.

WEATHER INSTRUMENTS

Sling Psychrometer

How do we determine the dew point? By means of a simple-to-operate, inexpensive little gadget known as a *sling psychrometer*. A sling psychrometer is merely two thermometers, mounted in a single holder with a handle that permits it to be whirled overhead. One thermometer, known as the *dry bulb,* has its bulb of mercury exposed directly to the air. This thermometer shows the actual temperature of the air. The other thermometer, known as the *wet bulb,* has its bulb covered with a piece of gauze. We

WEATHER

Table 5-4   **CLOUD FORMATIONS**

Type and description	Approx. height (feet)	Weather portent
Cirrus—Very high white strands of cloud; commonly known as "Mare's Tails."	25,000-35,000	Probable approach of a depression with wind and rain
Cirro-Stratus—Spreading white film or veil through which the sun can still be seen, probably with a halo effect.	Ditto.	More definite forecast of rain
Cirro-Cumulus—Compressed bunches of cloud forming a more clearly defined pattern; commonly known as a "Mackerel sky."	Ditto.	Changeable
Alto-Stratus—Watery grey layer or heavy veil of cloud; sun usually just visible.	10,000-20,000	Almost certain rain
Alto-Cumulus—An even layer of fairly dense cloud, often resembling the pattern of sand on the sea bed. Also sometimes called a "Mackerel sky."	Ditto.	Usually more settled weather; perhaps a chance of thunder
Strato-Cumulus—A lower version of Alto-Cumulus, with perhaps a more distinct definition.	5,000-10,000	Fairly settled conditions
Cumulus—Clearly defined fleecy clouds with a firm, dark base, often increasing in size and number during the day.	2,000-5,000	Fair conditions
Cumulo-Nimbus—Larger, more menacing development of Cumulus, with towering grey and white masses, often rising to an anvil-shaped plateau.	Rising from a fairly low base up to perhaps 25,000	Big air disturbances with possibility of thunder, heavy showers or hail
Nimbo-Stratus—Heavy, dark, amorphous cloud, driving hard with the wind.	Mostly below 7,000	Prolonged rain likely; fresh or strong wind certain
Stratus—Blanket of fog or mist-like cloud suspended low in the sky.	500-20,000	Generally humid with prospect of rain or mist

Table 5-5   **WAVE HEIGHTS**

Maximum values for wave heights at various wind velocities

Wind Velocity (mph)	Wave Height (ft.)	Wave Length (ft.)	Wave Period (sec.)	Sea-room "Fetch" (Naut. mi.)	Wind Duration (hours)
12	3.2	180	5.9	230	44
25	13	590	10.8	790	80
37	30	1,443	16.8	2,000	125
50	56	2,625	22.5	3,600	167

Sea-room and wind duration indicate the minimum values required for the wind velocities given in order to produce waves of the height stated. The greatest wave height ever definitely confirmed—82'—has been measured in the South Pacific.

soak this gauze in water so that the bulb is moistened. If the air is not saturated with water vapor, evaporation then takes place from the wet-bulb thermometer, and the wet bulb is cooled, since the process of evaporation requires the expenditure of heat. The reduced temperature shown by the wet-bulb thermometer, the so-called "wet-bulb temperature," represents the lowest temperature to which the air can be cooled by evaporating water into it.

When we whirl the psychrometer we create a draft around the instrument. The ventilation so produced increases the efficiency of the evaporation process and makes the wet-bulb reading more reliable than it would be if there were little or no air movement past the wet bulb. This is the reason why the psychrometer is designed for whirling.

From the wet-bulb temperature and dry-bulb temperature, the dew point may be determined by referring to a suitable table. As we are far more interested, however, in knowing the *spread, or difference, between the air temperature and dew point,* we will save ourselves some work by using another table (Table 5-6), its use being explained in the next two paragraphs.

If the air is already actually saturated with water vapor, then no water can evaporate from the gauze and both thermometers must show the same value. The dew point then has this same numerical value and so the spread between air temperature and dew point must be zero. But, as explained above, if the air is not already saturated with water vapor, the wet-bulb thermometer will give a lower reading than the dry-bulb thermometer. We subtract the wet-bulb temperature from the dry-bulb temperature. With this difference and the dry-bulb (the air) temperature, we consult Table 5–6 and find directly the corresponding spread between the air temperature and the dew-point temperature. This is the figure we want.

If, in the late afternoon or early evening, the spread between the air temperature and dew point is less than approximately 6°F, and the air temperature is falling, fog or greatly restricted visibility will probably be experienced in a few hours. These critical

Table 5-6

AIR TEMPERATURE—DEWPOINT SPREAD

(All figures are in degrees Fahrenheit at 30″ pressure)

Difference Dry-Bulb Minus Wet-Bulb	Air Temperature Shown By Dry-Bulb Thermometer												
	35	40	45	50	55	60	65	70	75	80	85	90	95
1	2	2	2	2	2	2	2	1	1	1	1	1	1
2	5	5	4	4	4	3	3	3	3	3	3	3	2
3	7	7	7	6	5	5	5	4	4	4	4	4	4
4	10	10	9	8	7	7	6	6	6	6	5	5	5
5	14	12	11	10	10	9	8	8	7	7	7	7	6
6	18	15	14	13	12	11	10	9	9	8	8	8	8
7	22	19	17	16	14	13	12	11	11	10	10	9	9
8	28	22	20	18	17	15	14	13	12	12	11	11	10
9	35	27	23	21	19	17	16	15	14	13	13	12	12
10	—	33	27	24	22	20	18	17	16	15	14	14	13
11	—	40	32	28	25	22	20	19	18	17	16	15	15
12	—	—	38	32	28	25	23	21	20	18	17	17	16
13	—	—	45	37	31	28	25	23	21	20	19	18	17
14	—	—	—	42	35	31	28	26	24	22	21	20	19
15	—	—	—	50	40	35	31	28	26	24	23	21	21

Opposite—Difference Dry-Bulb Minus Wet-Bulb and
Under   —Air Temperature Shown By Dry-Bulb Thermometer
Read   —Value of Spread: Air Temperature minus Dewpoint Temperature
Based on U.S. Weather Bureau Psychrometric Tables

WEATHER

values are emphasized by the heavy line above which they lie in Table 5–6. Incidentally, should we ever want to know the dewpoint temperature itself, all we need do is to subtract the spread

Table 5-7

BOAT WEATHER LOG

Yacht_____At/Passage_____ to _____
Day_____ Date_____ Time Zone_____Skipper_____

1. Latest Weather Map: Date_____Time_____Summary of forecast and of
   principal regional weather features: _____
   _____
   _____
   _____
   _____

2. Radio Weather Reports Received (state source and time): _____
   _____
   _____
   _____
   _____

3. Local Weather Observations

4. Remarks and Local Forecast for Next_____Hours (state time forecast
   effective):_____
   _____
   _____
   _____
   _____
   _____
   _____
   _____

figure given in the table from the temperature shown by the dry-bulb thermometer. Thus, when the dry-bulb thermometer indicates an air temperature of 70°F and the difference between

Table 5-8

LOCAL WEATHER OBSERVATIONS

Time

Latitude—degrees, minutes

Longitude—degrees, minutes

Course—degrees mag.

———degrees true

Speed—Knots

Barometer—in. or mb.

———tendency

Clouds—form

———moving from

———amount

———changing to

Sea—condition

———swells

———moving from

Temperatures—air, dry bulb

———dewpoint

———water

Visibility

Wind—direction, true

———shifting to

———velocity, true

———force (Beaufort)

Weather—present

ELECTRONICS

the dry-bulb and wet-bulb temperatures is 11°F, the spread is 19°F and the dew point is 51°F.

The Barometer

Another weather instrument is the *aneroid barometer*. A good instrument will have *pressure scales*. Barometric pressure is often expressed in terms of *inches of mercury*, so the outer scale is graduated in these units. Weather maps are now printed with the pressures shown in *millibars* and many radio weather reports specify this value. Consequently, the inner scale is graduated in millibars. Also, it has the usual reference hand, so you can keep track of changes in pressure.

The words "Fair—Change—Rain," in themselves, when they appear on the face of an aneroid barometer, are meaningless. It is not the actual barometric pressure that is so important in forecasting; it is the *direction* and *rate of change of pressure*.

The Anemometer

For measuring *wind velocity* we need something else. This is an *anemometer*. The anemometer is essentially a speedometer. It consists of a rotor with conical cups attached to the ends of spokes and is designed for mounting at the masthead, where the wind is caught by the cups, causing them to turn at a speed proportional to the speed of the wind. Indications of the rotor's speed are transmitted to an indicator which may be mounted in the cabin.

DESTRUCTIVE WAVES

Unusual sudden changes in water level can be caused by tsunamis or violent storms. These two types of destructive waves have become commonly known as tidal waves, a name which is technically incorrect as they are not the result of tide-producing forces.

Tsunamis (seismic sea waves) are setup by submarine earthquakes. Many such seismic disturbances do not produce sea waves and often those produced are small, but the occasional large waves can be very damaging to shore installations and dangerous to ships in harbors.

These waves travel great distances and can cause tremendous damage on coasts far from their source. The wave of April 1, 1946, which originated in the Aleutian Trench, demolished nearby Scotch Cap Lighthouse and caused damages of $25 million in the Hawaiian Islands 2,000 miles away. The wave of May 22–23, 1960, which originated off southern Chile, caused widespread death and destruction in islands and countries throughout the Pacific.

The speed of tsunamis varies with the depth of the water, reaching 300 to 500 knots in the deep water of the open ocean. In the open sea they cannot be detected from a ship or from the air because their length is so great, sometimes a hundred miles, as compared to their height, which is usually only a few feet. Only on certain types of shelving coasts do they build up into waves of disastrous proportions.

There is usually a series of waves with crests 10 to 40 minutes apart, and the highest may occur several hours after the first wave. Sometimes the first noticeable part of the wave is the trough which causes a recession of the water from the shore, and people who have gone out to investigate this unusual exposure of the beach have been engulfed by the oncoming crest. Such an unexplained withdrawal of the sea should be considered as nature's warning of an approaching wave.

Improvements have been made in the quick determination and reporting of earthquake epicenters, but no method has yet been perfected for determining whether a sea wave will result from a given earthquake. The Honolulu Observatory of the National Ocean Survey is headquarters of a warning system which has field reporting stations (seismic and tidal) in most countries around the Pacific. When a warning is broadcast, waterfront

WEATHER

areas should be vacated for higher ground, and ships in the vicinity of land should head for the deep water of the open sea.

Storm waves.—A considerable rise or fall in the level of the sea along a particular coast may result from strong winds and sharp change in barometric pressure. In cases where the water level is raised, higher waves can form with greater depth and the combination can be destructive to low regions, particularly at high stages of tide. Extreme low levels can result in depths which are considerably less than those shown on nautical charts. This type of wave occurs especially in coastal regions bordering on shallow waters which are subject to tropical storms.

Seiche is a stationary vertical wave oscillation with a period varying from a few minutes to an hour or more, but somewhat less than the tidal periods. It is usually attributed to external forces such as strong winds, changes in barometric pressure, swells, or seismic sea waves disturbing the equilibrium of the water surface. Seiche is found both in enclosed bodies of water and superimposed upon the tides of the open ocean. When the external forces cause a short-period horizontal oscillation of the water, it is called *surge.*

The combined effect of seiche and surge sometimes makes it difficult to maintain a ship in its position alongside a pier even though the water may appear to be completely undisturbed, and heavy mooring lines have been parted repeatedly under such conditions. Pilots advise taut lines to reduce the effect of the surge.

WIND CHILL TABLE
Prepared by the National Center for Atmospheric Research
Boulder, Colorado

Little Danger   Increasing Danger   Great Danger That Exposed Flesh will Freeze

Wind Velocity (MPH)

Temp. °F	0	5	10	15	20	25	30	35	40	45	50
—10	—10	—15	—31	—45	—52	—58	—63	—67	—69	—70	70
—5	—5	—11	—27	—40	—46	—52	—56	—60	—62	—63	—63
0	0	—6	—22	—33	—40	—45	—49	—52	—54	—54	—56
5	5	1	—15	—25	—32	—37	—41	—43	—45	—46	—47
10	10	7	—9	—18	—24	—29	—33	—35	—36	—38	—38
15	15	12	—2	—11	—17	—22	—26	—27	—29	—31	—31
20	20	16	2	—6	—9	—15	—18	—20	—22	—24	—24
25	25	21	9	1	—4	—7	—11	—13	—15	—17	—17
30	30	27	16	11	3	0	—2	—4	—4	—6	—7
35	35	33	21	16	12	7	5	3	1	1	0
40	40	37	28	22	18	16	13	11	10	9	8

6.
ELECTRONICS

ELECTRICAL UNITS

Volts, ohms, amperes, and watts are the terms used to describe electromotive force, electrical resistance, current strength, and electric power, respectively. One volt is the force that will produce a current of one ampere in a conductor with a resistance of one ohm. One watt is the power developed by one ampere of current at one volt.

RADIO TERMINOLOGY

Amplitude: The height of a radio wave.

Frequency: The number of times per second that a radio wave goes through its cycle. All radio waves travel at the speed of light. The shorter the wave-length, the more times per second it will go through its cycle, or the higher the frequency.

Carrier Wave: A radio wave of constant amplitude and constant frequency that is emitted by the transmitter when you press the button but do not speak into the microphone.

Modulation: The manner in which the carrier wave is changed or varied when you speak into the microphone.

AM stands for Amplitude Modulation. A process by which speech waves are impressed on the carrier wave by varying the amplitude of the carrier wave.

Side Bands are produced when speech frequencies are added to the carrier frequency. In conventional amplitude modulation (AM) two sidebands are produced, an upper sideband containing the carrier wave frequency *plus* all the speech frequencies present, and a lower sideband containing the carrier wave frequency *minus* all the speech frequencies present.

DSB stands for Double Side Band, the conventional AM radiotelephony in use today, in which a carrier wave and two side bands are transmitted. If the radiated power is 30 watts, ⅔ of the power, or 20 watts would be consumed by the carrier wave, leaving only ⅓ of the power, or 10 watts, to be divided between the two sidebands. Each sideband would then contain 5 watts of power. The distant receiver picking up this signal discards the carrier wave and one sideband and uses only the one remaining sideband. Thus, 5/6 of the radiated power is wasted, only 1/6 of the power doing any useful work.

SSB stands for Single Side Band, a newer method of radiotelephony. In SSB transmission, the carrier wave and one sideband are suppressed, only one sideband being transmitted. All the power can then be put into this one sideband, increasing the "speech power" six times. Thus, a 30-watt SSB radiotelephone would be equivalent to a 180-watt DSB radiotelephone.

FM stands for Frequency Modulation, a process by which speech waves are impressed on the carrier wave by varying its frequency.

MF stands for Medium Frequency, a radiotelephone frequency band extending roughly from 2000 Khz to 3500 Khz. (Kilohertz and Megahertz are now used in place of the familiar Kilocycles and Megacycles).

RADIOTELEPHONES

Three types of radio systems are used aboard boats; two of these are designed and licensed specifically for marine use. The third is the Citizens Band radio system.

VHF-FM marine radios are considered to be the prime system for marine communications over distances of up to about 30 miles. There are 55 channels in the VHF band for marine use; some of these are special-purpose bands for commercial use only; others are for linkup with shoreside telephone systems. Two channels are mandatory for all boats: channel 6 (156.300 MHz), for intership safety communications; and channel 16 (156.800 MHz), the distress, safety and calling frequency. There also are channels for linkup with shoreside facilities such as marinas and yacht clubs.

For long-distance communications, a Single Sideband (SSB) marine radio is required, but it can be installed only if the boat is equipped with a VHF-FM set, and the owner can demonstrate a need for the long-range set. On this equipment, the international distress and calling frequency is 2182 kHz. Pleasure boats can operate with sets having about 80 to 100 watts output power, giving a range of more than 100 miles.

Citizens Band radios are often used as an adjunct to the normal marine radios, for informal, short-distance communication. There is no CB channel monitored by the U. S. Coast Guard, and there is no linkup with the telephone system ashore. CB range is about 10 to 15 miles, but the distance may be greater to a base station ashore, with a high antenna. Since a CB license permits operation of up to 5 sets, an owner may set up such a base station at home, or carry walkie-talkie type sets for use in communicating with part of the crew ashore. While true marine radios must be used only for "ship's business," there is no such restriction on the CB sets.

In areas where the Coast Guard is not operating, CB radios provide the only means for calling for help in an emergency.

ELECTRONICS

PRIORITY LIST OF VHF-FM CHANNELS
FOR RECREATIONAL BOATS

Channel	Frequency (MHz)		Communications Purpose
Number	Transmit	Receive	
16	156.800	156.800	DISTRESS SAFETY and CALLING (mandatory)
06	156.300	156.300	Intership safety communications (mandatory)
22	157.100	157.100	Primary liaison with USCG vessels and USCG shore stations, and for Coast Guard marine information broadcasts
68	156.425	156.425	Non-commercial intership and ship to coast (marinas, yacht clubs, etc.)
09	156.450	156.450	Commercial and non-commercial intership and ship to coast (commercial docks, marinas, & some clubs)
26	157.300	161.900	Public telephone, first priority
28	157.400	162.000	Public telephone, first priority
25	157.250	161.850	Public telephone
27	157.350	161.950	Public telephone
13	156.650	156.650	Navigational—Bridge to Bridge (1 watt only). Mandatory for ocean vessels, dredges in channels, and large tugs while towing. Army installing for communications with boats in their locks. Will be found, also, on Army operated bridges
14	156.700	156.700	Port Operations channel for communications with bridge and lock tenders. Some Coast Guard shore stations have this channel for working
70	156.525	156.525	Non-commercial only, intership
12	156.600	156.600	Port Operations—traffic advisory—still being used as channel to work USCG shore stations.
72	156.625	156.625	Non-commercial intership (2nd priority)
WX-1		162.550	Weather broadcasts
WX-2		162.400	Weather broadcasts
WX-3		162.475	Weather broadcasts
69	156.475	156.475	Non-commercial intership and ship to coast
71	156.575	156.575	Non-commercial intership and ship to coast
78	156.925	156.925	Non-commercial intership and ship to coast

Installation and Maintenance

Radio equipment may be physically installed and electrically connected by the boat owner or any person. Before it is put on the air, however, the set must be checked out by a person holding a first or second class license who will make certain tests required by the FCC rules. Radio installations on gasoline-powered boats will generally require some form of ignition noise suppression or shielding; this is a job for a technician. With regard to maintenance, an unlicensed person is limited to matters which will not affect the quality of the signal on the air. For example, he can replace bad fuses, tubes, etc., but cannot change crystals or adjust antenna loading.

RADIO LICENSES

To control the use of radio stations, hold down interference and make possible emergency and essential communcations, a system of licenses is used. Recognizing that harmful interference could result from either malfunctioning equipment or from misuse of a properly operating set, licenses are required for both the station and the person operating it. Although it is termed a station license, the FCC authorization is essentially concerned with the transmitting component only. The set owner need not concern himself with the many technical requirements for equipment provided that he has a set that is "type accepted."

The Station License

A station license may be issued to a U.S. Citizen or an alien individual, but not a foreign government or its representative (if a corporation, see section 82.23 of the FCC Rules.) Application is made on Form 502 which is either mailed to the FCC, Gettysburg, Penna. 17325, or taken to one of the more than 30 FCC field offices. The fee for a station license is $4 for the five-year term. The actual issuance of the license will take perhaps as long as 30 days, but if the applications is personally taken to an FCC office, you will be given an interim license which will permit immediate use of your set; the fee for station license plus interim permit is $10.

Radio station licenses are issued in the name of the *owner* and the *vessel*. A station license is not automatically transferred to another person upon sale of the boat, nor may a license be moved

ELECTRONICS

with the radio set to a new craft owned by the same person. A simple change in the name of the boat or licensee (but not a change in ownership), or his address does *not* require license modification. Just send a letter to the FCC advising them of the change; a copy of this letter must be posted with the license. Neither modification of license nor letter is required for a change in type-approved equipment operating in the same frequency band. If VHF is to be added to a 2–3 MHz station, a modification is needed.

The regulations require that a station license be conspicuously posted aboard the vessel. At the end of its five-year term, it must be renewed if continued operation of the station is desired. Form 405-B is used for renewal; it should be sent to Gettysburg with a $20 renewal fee before the expiration of the license. If, but only if, timely application for renewal has been made, operation may continue even should the renewed license not be received before the expiration date. If the use of the radio station is permanently discontinued at any time, the license must be returned to the FCC in Washington for cancellation.

The Operator's Permit

A personal license is required for the operation of any marine band radio station. The average boatman will obtain either a *Restricted Radiotelephone Operator Permit* or a *Third Class Radiotelephone Operator Permit*. Higher class licenses are available for persons with technical training and experience, but they are needed only for making tuning adjustments and repairs. An unlicensed person may talk into the microphone of a radio, but a licensed operator must be present and responsible for the use of the station.

An applicant for any grade of license may be either a U.S. citizen or an alien. A Restricted Permit is obtained by submitting an application on FCC Form 753. This form contains all necessary instructions, including where to mail it; there is no need to appear in person at any FCC office. The permit is issued, without test or examination, by "declaration." The applicant must be at least 14 years old and "certify" that he (1) can receive and transmit spoken messages in the English language; (2) can keep a rough log in English, or in a foreign language translatable into English; (3) is familiar with the applicable laws, treaty provisions, rules, and regulations; and (4) understands his responsibility to keep currently informed of the regulations, etc. The Restricted Permit fee, $4, is valid for the lifetime of the person to whom issued, unless, of course, it is suspended or revoked.

For the Third Class Operator Permit, there is no age limit, but an examination is required. This test is non-technical, covering only operating rules and procedures; questions are all of the multiple-choice type. You will find the examination not at all difficult if you prepare yourself for it properly. A free Study Guide is available from FCC offices. For skippers of recreational boats the privileges of this higher class license are no greater than those of a Restricted Permit, but it is a matter of pride for many to qualify and post it on their craft. Boats that carry more than six passengers for hire, however, are "compulsorily equipped" and must have a crewman with at least a Third Class Permit. The fee for a Third Class Permit is $4, and it is issued for a five-year term; the fee for renewal for another five years is $2.

If your radio operator permit is lost, or becomes so mutilated that it is illegible, you should immediately apply for a duplicate. The fee is $2 and the same form as for an original is used. State the circumstances fully, and, if the license has been lost, you must certify that a reasonable search has been made. Continued operation is authorized if a signed copy of the application for a duplicate is posted. Should a lost license be found later, either it or the duplicate must be sent at once to the FCC for cancellation.

The Radio Log

Log keeping for a radio station on a voluntarily equipped boat has been made much easier than it used to be, but don't let this

ELECTRONICS

MARINE TELEPHONE LOG   YACHT_____CALL LETTERS_____

DATE	TIME	YACHT OR STATION CALLED	CALL LETTERS OR TELEPHONE NUMBER	LOCATION OF CALLED NUMBER	NAME OF OPERATOR

Fig. 601   Sample radio log.

simplification stop you from meeting the present minimum requirements of the FCC. Each page of the log must show the name of the vessel and the radio call sign; each entry must be signed by the person making it. Entries are required for all distress calls heard or transmitted, for all urgent and safety communications transmitted, and any information related to maritime safety. The log must also show the time of starting and ending a listening watch on 2182 kHz or 156.8 MHz, *but remember that the keeping of such a watch is not mandatory on recreational boats.*

All installation, service, and maintenance work performed on the radio equipment must be logged. It is *not* necessary to make entries for ordinary communications to other boats, the Coast Guard, or shore stations. Logs must be retained for one year following the last entry, except for unusual circumstances described in the Rules. Logs must be made available for inspection upon request from any authorized FCC representative. Inspection of the station by such an official must be permitted at any reasonable hour, and at such frequent intervals as may be determined necessary in the discretion of the FCC.

How to Make a Call

Listen carefully to make sure that the channel you want to use is not busy. If it is busy, you will hear voices, or from most public shore stations, an intermittent busy tone. Except in a safety emergency, don't interrupt.

ELECTRONICS

Standard Phonetic Spelling Alphabet

A	ALFA	**N**	NOVEMBER
B	BRAVO	**O**	OSCAR
C	CHARLIE	**P**	PAPA
D	DELTA	**Q**	QUEBEC
E	ECHO	**R**	ROMEO
F	FOXTROT	**S**	SIERRA
G	GOLF	**T**	TANGO
H	HOTEL	**U**	UNIFORM
I	INDIA	**V**	VICTOR
J	JULIETT	**W**	WHISKEY
K	KILO	**X**	X-RAY
L	LIMA	**Y**	YANKEE
M	MIKE	**Z**	ZULU

When the conversation is to take place on a ship-to-ship frequency—unless you have reached an agreement in advance as to the time and frequency, establish contact on 2182 kHz (or 156.8 MHz) and then shift to the agreed-upon intership channel.

When the conversation is to take place through a commercial shore station—make your initial contact on a working frequency of that station; this will speed your call.

Both of these practices are designed to relieve the load on 2182 kHz and 156.8 MHz and keep them clear for safety purposes.

Steps to Follow in Making a Call
(other than a Distress, Urgency, or Safety Call)

Boat-to-boat calls—Make sure 2182 kHz (or 156.8 MHz) is not busy. If it is free, put your transmitter on the air and say—

"(Name of boat called) This is (Name of your boat and call sign), Over." To avoid confusion, always observe the proper sequence of call signs—state the name or call sign of the *other station first*, then give your own identification after saying 'This is.'

(If necessary, the identification of the station called, and your boat's name and call sign may each be given two or three times, but not more; the entire calling transmission must not take longer than 30 seconds.)

Listen for a reply. If no contact is made, repeat the above after an interval of at least two minutes. After establishing contact switch to the agreed upon intership working channel. One exchange of communications shall not exceed three minutes after establishing contact on the working frequency. After conversation is completed, say—

"This is (name of your boat and call sign), Out."

You shall not establish contact thereafter with the same boat until 10 minutes has elapsed.

Ship-to-Shore Service

Listen to make sure that the working channel you wish to use is not busy. If it is clear, put your transmitter on the air and say—

"(Location) Marine Operator This is (Name of your boat and call sign), Over."

Listen for a reply. If no contact is made, repeat after an interval of at least two minutes.

When the Marine Operator answers, say—

"This is (Name of your boat and call sign) calling (telephone number desired), Over."

After the telephone conversation is completed say—

"This is (Name and call sign of your boat), Out."

How to Receive a Call

Your boat can be reached only when your receiver is turned on and tuned to the frequency over which you expect.

The receiver you use to maintain watch on 2182 kHz (or 156.8 MHz) will assure that you get calls addressed to you by other boats. For calls from public shore stations, you will generally need to keep a receiver tuned to a working frequency of the station for that area. It is urged that you have one receiver for watch-keeping and a second one to ensure that you can be reached by a public shore station over a working channel. This will help to keep 2182 kMz and 156.8 MHz free for their primary purpose.

Steps in Receiving a Call

Boat-to-boat calls—When you hear your boat called, put your transmitter on the air and say—

"(Name of boat that called) This is (Name of your boat and call sign), Over."

Switch to the agreed upon intership channel. After the conversation is completed, say—

"This is (Name of your boat and call sign), Out."

Shore-to-ship calls—When you hear the name of your boat called, put your transmitter on the air and say—

"(Name of station that called) This is (Name of your boat and call sign), Over."

After the conversation is completed, say—

"This is (Name of your boat and call sign), Out."

ELECTRONICS

DEPTH SOUNDERS

Depth sounders are a modern replacement for the hand-held lead line used for uncounted centuries to determine the depth of water beneath a ship. This electronic device furnishes a vastly greater amount of information, and does it with much greater ease, especially in nasty weather. It provides safety as well as convenience in boating, and so is doubly advantageous to have on board.

How Depth is Measured

Depth is determined by measuring the round-trip time for a pulse of ultrasonic energy to travel from the boat to the bottom of the water and be reflected back to the point of origin. See fig. 601. The frequency of the audio pulses generally lies between 50,000 and 200,000 cycles per second, too high to be heard by human ears. Their average velocity through the water is approximately 4800 feet per second; slight variations in speed will occur between salt and fresh water and with different temperatures. The resulting small errors, however, can be safely ignored for the relatively shallow depths of interest to the operators of recreational boats.

Probably the greatest advantage of the electronic device over the hand-held line is the essentially continuous nature of the information furnished. Depth sounders vary widely in the rate at which readings are taken, but in all cases many more soundings are taken than could be accomplished by hand. Current equipment takes readings at rates between 1 and 30 *each second.*

Components of a Depth Sounder

The major components of a depth sounder are a source of energy (transmitter), a means of sending out the pulses and picking up the echoes (transducer), a receiver to amplify the weak echoes, and a visual presentation of the information. The transducer usually takes the form of a round block of hard ceramic

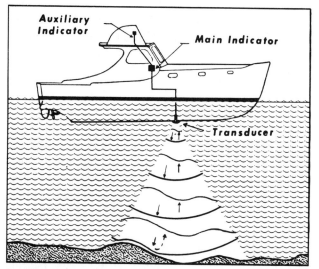

Fig. 602   An electronic depth sounder measures depth by sending pulses of high frequency sound waves, reflected back from bottom. Distance is measured by time taken by pulses for the round trip.

ELECTRONICS

material several inches in diameter and an inch or so thick. In many cases, it is given an oblong, streamline shape to reduce drag.

The visual presentation of information on the depth of the water is accomplished by either an "indicator" or a "recorder." The indicator provides a non-permanent indication of the depth, in some cases by the use of a flashing light; in many units an ordinary electric meter is used with a suitably calibrated dial. Some new units provide a direct readout in digital number. The flashing light is mounted on the end of an arm which rotates around a scale much like the second hand of a clock, only much faster. The zero of the scale is usually at the top of the dial and a flash of light occurs there when the outgoing pulse leaves the transducer on the boat's bottom. A second flash occurs when the pulse is received back at the transducer, having been reflected back from the bottom of the water. The deeper the water, the longer it will take for the echo to return to the boat; the longer this takes, the farther the arm will have rotated around the dial. Thus the scale of depths increases clockwise around the face of the indicator.

RADIO DIRECTION FINDERS

On the seacoasts of the United States, and on the Great Lakes and other large inland bodies of water, a *radio direction finder* (RDF) is an important piece of electronic equipment. Primarily installed as a safety item, it can also be a great convenience to the boat operator. It is the primary radio aid to navigation for small craft.

A complete radio direction finding system consists of four components:

1. One or more radio transmitters at known locations.
2. An RDF set on the boat.
3. Charts covering both the location of the transmitters and the area of operation of the boat.
4. A person who knows the operation of the system.

To be fully effective, the RDF system must be used with competence and confidence—an incorrect radio bearing can lead to disaster; a correct bearing that is ignored because of mistrust can be equally disastrous.

Special RDF Features

Basically, an RDF is a radio receiver with two additional features. First and vitally important is the directional antenna. Usually, this antenna is rotatable so that the set may be secured firmly in a convenient location. The directional antenna employed with an RDF set is an improved version of the simple loop used on portable receivers, the directional characteristics of which are familiar to most boatmen. This antenna may take the form of a loop a foot or so in diameter or it may appear as a plastic bar measuring about an inch square by some six inches in length.

Both types will be mounted on top of the set; either will do the job.

As the antenna it rotated through 360°, these directional antennas show two positions of maximum signal strength and two positions of minimum sensitivity called "nulls." With properly balanced construction and no local interfering objects, the two maximum signal positions will be separated by 180°, as will be the nulls which are found 90° in either direction from the maximums. It is characteristic of these antennas that the maximum signal points are broad and poorly defined, while the nulls are marked and precise. For this reason, the nulls are used for direction finding.

The second feature of RDFs is a visual null indicator. While the operator can judge by ear the position of the antenna at minimum signal with fair accuracy, a more precise bearing can be obtained by observing a visual indicator. This is normally a small electric meter, read for either a maximum or minimum deflection of its needle in accordance with the instructions for the particular set being used.

How to Take a Radio Bearing

To take a radio bearing, follow these steps:

1. Set the scale built into the set, usually around the base of the antenna, so that 000° is dead ahead.

2. Rotate the directional antenna until a null point is precisely located, read the angle from the scale; this is the uncorrected relative radio bearing. Caution: the boat must be directly on course at the moment that the bearing is taken as any error in heading will be reflected in the resultant radio bearing.

3. If there is any doubt as to whether the reading just taken is the direct or reciprocal bearing, use the sense antenna to identify it. If the reading is the reciprocal, do *not* add or subtract 180°, take a new bearing.

4. Having determined the direct bearing angle, apply the

ELECTRONICS

proper deviation correction; the sum is the corrected relative radio bearing.

5. Add the boat's *true* heading, subtracting 360° if the sum exceeds that amount; this is now the true radio bearing from the boat, plot in the same manner as a visual bearing.

The above steps outline in basic terms the correct procedures to be followed in taking a radio bearing. In the use of any particular RDF set, however, the manufacturer's manual should be studied and the instructions followed closely.

Automatic Radio Direction Finders

An automatic radio direction finder (ADF) indicates on a dial the direction to a transmitter once it has been tuned in—no swinging of a loop, no 180° ambiguity.

ADFs cover the same frequency bands as manual RDFs and use the same types of transmitting stations. They are, of course, more complex in circuitry and thus more expensive. The antenna is continuously rotated, either mechanically or electronically, whenever the set is turned on. Often such equipment is a fixed installation with a remote antenna, but portable models are available.

The advantages of ADFs lie in their ease and speed of operation. They are, however, subject to the same radio deviation as manual RDFs and a correction table must be prepared.

RADAR

Radar is an excellent means of marine navigation and is used on vessels of all sizes down to boats about 30 feet in length. Although size, power requirements, and cost limit its use on recreational boats, its capabilities and limitations should be known to all boatmen for their own safety when cruising on waters navigated by radar-equipped vessels.

Radar Principles

A radar set sends out brief pulses of super-high frequency radio waves that are reflected by objects at a distance. The time that it takes for the pulse to go out and the echo to return is a measure of the distance to the reflecting object. In broad principles, this is the same technique as previously described for depth sounders, except that transmission is through air rather than water, and radio waves have been substituted for ultrasonic pulses. A refinement has been made in that the radar pulses are sent out in a very narrow beam which can be pointed in any direction around the horizon and used to determine direction as well as distance.

Components of a Radar Set

The major components of a radar set are:

1. The *transmitter* which generates the radio waves; it includes the *modulator* which causes the energy to be sent out in brief pulses.

2. The *antenna* which radiates the pulses and collects the returning echoes. The antenna is highly directional in its horizontal characteristics, but 8 to 10 times wider vertically. The beam pattern can be thought of as being like a fan turned up on edge. The beam's narrow horizontal directivity gives it a fairly good angle-measuring capability, while its broadness in the vertical plane helps keep the beam on an object despite any rolling or pitching of the vessel.

3. The *receiver* which detects the returned reflections and amplifies them to a usable strength.

4. The *indicator* which provides a visual display of objects sending back reflections.

Radars operate at frequencies far above the usual radio communications bands. At such super-high frequencies, radar pulses act much like light waves in that they travel in essentially straight lines. They travel at the speed of light, 186,000 miles per second. For each nautical mile of distance to the target, only a fraction more than 12 microseconds are required for the round-trip of the outgoing pulse and the returned echo. Pulses, each of which lasts for only a fraction of a microsecond (one millionth of a second), are sent out at a rate of from 600 to 4000 each second depending upon the design of the equipment. The directional antenna rotates at a rate of one revolution in about 4 seconds. The round-trip time for a pulse is so short that the antenna has not appreciably moved before the reflection is returned.

The Plan Position Indicator (PPI)

Marine navigational radars use a Plan Position Indicator (PPI) type of display. A circular cathode ray tube of a special type from 5 to 20 inches in diameter is used. The center of the face represents the position of the radar-equipped vessel and the presentation is roughly like that of a navigational chart.

A bright radial line on the face of the tube represents the radar beam; it rotates in synchronism with the antenna. Reflections show up as points or patches of light depending upon the size of the echo-producing object. The persistence of the screen is such that the points and patches of light do not completely fade out before the antenna has made another rotation and they are restored to brilliance. Thus the picture on the radarscope is repainted every few seconds.

Radar Range Scales

The relative bearing of an object is indicated directly on the screen; a position corresponding to the "12" on a clock face is directly ahead. The distance to the object is proportional to the distance from the center of the screen to the point of light which is the echo. On most radars, concentric circles of light are used as range markers to make the estimation of distances both easier and more accurate. All radar sets have multiple range scales which may be selected to suit the purpose for which the radar is being used. Longer range scales provide coverage of greater areas, but at a cost of less detail and poorer definition.

Radar sets have both a maximum and a minimum range, each of which is of importance in the operation of the equipment. The maximum range is determined by the transmitter power and the receiver sensitivity, provided, of course, that the antenna is at a sufficient height above water that the range is not limited by the distance to the horizon. (The radar pulses normally travel with just a slight amount of bending; thus the radar horizon is about 15% farther away than the visual horizon.)

Because a radar pulse has a definite duration, and therefore occupies a definite length in space as it moves outward from the antenna, there is a minimum range within which objects cannot be detected. This minimum range, usually between 20 and 50 yards, is important when maneuvering in close quarters, as when passing buoys at the side of a narrow channel.

Units for Small Craft

Radar sets for small craft usually consist of two units. Modern design of the components makes it possible to combine the antenna, transmitter, and a portion of the receiver into a single unit installed on a mast or on the pilothouse. This unit, usually weighing between 60 and 120 pounds, should be located as high as possible in order to avoid limiting the range of the set. The antenna should have an unobstructed "look" in all directions. The remainder of the receiver and the indicator are located near the helmsman's position. Improved design techniques have resulted in indicator units so small that they may be fitted into a pilothouse in any number of positions.

Because radar sets radiate radio frequency energy, they must be licensed by the FCC, but this is not difficult to do for commercially produced equipment. No license is required to operate a radar, but for its installation and maintenance, the technician must have a second- or first-class radio operator's license with a special "ship radar" endorsement. The owner and station licensee of a marine radar installation is responsible that only a properly licensed individual does all of the technical work on the equipment.

Principal Applications

Radars have two principal applications aboard ships and small craft. They are often thought of primarily as anti-collision devices, but are even more often used to assist in the piloting of the vessel.

Radar was originally conceived for the detection and tracking of ships and aircraft. It offers an excellent means of extending the coverage of a visual lookout, especially at night and under conditions of reduced visibility. This greater range of detection affords more time for a ship to maneuver to avoid another craft or an obstacle.

Radar serves another valuable function in the piloting of a vessel approaching a coastline or traveling in confined waters. It has real advantages even in the daytime, and, of course, becomes particularly helpful at night or in fog.

Passive Radar Reflectors

The motorboat owner who does not have a radar can still do something to increase his safety in relation to this item of electronic equipment. He can equip his craft with a *passive radar reflector*. This simple and inexpensive item consists of thin lightweight metal sheets, or areas of fine-mesh metal screening, arranged in mutually perpendicular planes. These may fold for storage, but must remain rigid with respect to each other when opened for use. A relatively small reflector with each metal surface only about two feet square will provide a radar reflection as strong as that from a medium-sized steel ship. The echo from the wooden hull of a small craft is so weak as to be easily overlooked in the echoes from the waves if a reflector is not used. With a passive reflector hoisted as high as possible, the operator of a small craft can be sure that his boat will be detected on the radar screens of passing ships. Often Coast Guard or other rescue craft searching for a boat in distress are radar-equipped; the use of a passive radar reflector greatly increases the chances of being quickly spotted.

ELECTRONIC NAVIGATION SYSTEMS

There are a number of electronic navigation systems that are available to skippers of offshore cruising and fishing boats as well as to navigators of larger ships. These vary in degree of complexity and cost of receiving equipment. Many boatmen will probably never use any of them personally, but it is desirable to have a general familiarity with their method of operation, and their advantages and disadvantages.

The most widely used electronic navigation system is *Loran* which is currently operational in two versions, Loran-A and Loran-C. (A third form, Loran-D, is for military applications only.) Another system is *Omega* which is now operational with only eight transmitting stations needed to provide coverage on all navigable ocean waters of the world.

Decca is a short-range, high-accuracy electronic navigation system that is available only in limited areas; it is more widely used in Europe than North America. Decca is unique in that in the United States it is commercially operated rather than by a governmental agency.

The aeronautical VHF navigations system called *VOR*, or *Omnirange*, is sometimes used by boats, but its short range is a severe limitation. (Aircraft can use this system out to hundreds of miles by reason of their high altitudes; Omni-equipped boats are limited to about 10-20 miles by the line-of-sight characteristics of the signals.)

There is also an electronic navigation system based on the use of satellites, but the complexity and cost of equipment eliminates it from consideration by boatmen.

ELECTRONICS

LORAN

Loran (LOng RAnge Navigation) now exists in two forms: Loran-A, also called Standard Loran, and Loran-C. These are both basic navigation systems for ocean-going ships and offshore fishing vessels; they can also be used to advantage by boats on open-water passages. Loran has the disadvantage of being dependent upon the reliable operation of electronic equipment both on shore and on the vessel.

Loran is a passive system; there is no transmitter on board the vessel, but a relatively complex and expensive receiver is required. Loran is a valuable supplement to celestial navigation, particularly when weather conditions prevent the taking of sights.

Loran-A

Frequencies between 1750 and 1930 kHz are employed by Loran-A. A pair of transmitters send out pulses of radio waves which are received on board the vessel. The difference in time of arrival of the pulses from each station is measured electronically, and this information is used to determine a line of position. The pulses are not sent out simultaneously, but are synchronized in a predetermined manner. A second pair of pulses is used to determine another LOP and the result is a Loran fix. Normally, one station is common to each of the two pairs; it is called the "master" and the others are "slaves."

A line of position can usually be determined in about two minutes; training in the use of a Loran receiver is required, but skill is soon acquired with practice. Loran stations must be accurately identified and the controls of the receiver manipulated properly to measure the time difference in arrival of the pulses. Thereafter, the position may be obtained from tables or plotted directly on readily available charts. As with other navigational techniques, three LOPs will give a better fix than two; coverage is such as to make this possible in many areas.

Loran-A has different day and night ranges because of the radio frequencies involved. Daytime reception using "ground waves" is the most accurate and average ranges are about 500 miles. This can be extended by the use of "sky waves" to as much as 1200 miles as determined by the power of the transmitter. Reception at night, also using sky waves, may extend out to 1400 miles, but with lessened accuracy. Range is reduced when the pulses must cross land areas, but accuracy is not degraded.

Accuracy of a Loran-A line of position varies over the coverage area of the stations used; it is greatest near the base line (line *between* the two stations). Ground wave LOPs should give a fix within 1½ miles accuracy over 80% of the normal coverage area. The accuracy when using sky waves wil be degraded to a position uncertainty of 5 to 7 miles.

Loran-C

The transmitters of Loran-C operate on 100 kHz in groups of one master and several slave stations. This system uses pulse matching (as in Loran-A) and cycle matching techniques for rough and fine positioning respectively.

As a result of the lower frequency, Loran-C has a ground wave (most reliable) range of up to 1200 miles, with sky wave reception extending out to more than 3000 miles. Accuracy of position depends upon the method of reception. Automatic equipment gives more precise locations than manually operated receivers. Automatic tracking and cycle matching will provide positions within ¼-mile or less to a nominal distance of 1000 miles from the master station. Manual reception, with cycle matching will give locations accurate to 1 to 3 miles out to 700 miles. Without cycle matching, this reduces to 3 to 10 miles at the same distances from the master station.

Loran-C is scheduled to eventually replace Loran-A but the changeover will be gradual and dependent upon expansion of the Loran-C network. Overlap of the two systems will be provided and Loran-A will not be finally phased out until 1979 in some areas and 1980 in other areas.

ELECTRONICS

Loran receivers

Receivers for Loran are widely available in many models. The simpler, less expensive units require manual tuning and human-operator matching of the signals. More sophisticated models feature automatic tracking, and some even provide for automatic signal acquisition.

Basic models of receivers are for Loran-A only, but units are also made that will receive both "A" and "C" signals. Dual receivers are available which will track and display two Loran readings simultaneously, enabling the navigator to plot a fix more quickly and easily than by having to take sequential readings. Loran receivers are not inexpensive, the price is several times that of a radiotelephone, but they do provide full-time, all-weather navigational assistance.

OMEGA

The *Omega* electronic navigation system uses very low frequency (VLF) radio waves; three different frequencies from 10.2 to 13.6 kHz are used. Such VLF signals have considerable range and stability over day and night paths. An advantage of the system is that complete global coverage can be obtained by the use of only six transmitters properly situated. Ideally, stations would be located at the North and South Poles and 90° apart on the Equator; such a requirement must, of course, be modified to meet practical considerations. In actual practice, the Omega network will have eight transmitting sites to allow for possible equipment failures and off-air time for routine maintenance. The transmitters are located approximately 6,000 miles apart and at any point signals from at least four stations will be usable. As the global network of stations is established, transmitters will be operated by the U.S. (by USCG personnel) and by foreign nations.

The Omega system

The Omega system was originally developed by the U.S. Navy for its submarines, surfaced or submerged (VLF signals can be received while under water), as well as for surface vessels and aircraft. Receiving equipment is now available, however, for civilian ships and aircraft, including fishing and recreational boats. Omega equipment is now quite expensive, but advancing technology and increased production can be expected to bring price reductions.

Omega fixes

Omega stations transmit continuous-wave signals, rather than pulses, for approximately one second out of every ten seconds on each frequency used. Signals from a single pair of stations on a single frequency can furnish a hyperbolic line of position, but rough position knowledge is required to within about eight miles to identify the set of lines, called a "lane," within which the receiver is located. Use of a second frequency reduces the need for position knowledge to 24 miles, and use of a third frequency extends this to 72 miles.

Two or more lines of position are combined in the normal manner to obtain an Omega fix. Station pairs should be selected so as to get lines crossing at large angles, as near 90° as possible for two lines, or 60° for three lines. As with Loran, special charts are used with over-printed Omega lines of position. Receivers have "lane counters" to keep a record of the number of lanes crossed since the counter was re-set after a fix was established, and so lessen the problem of lane identification.

Omega signals are affected by sky-wave propagation conditions and it is necessary to refer to published correction tables in the use of this system. The nominal all-weather accuracy is one mile in the daytime and two miles at night. Special techniques are available within local areas for increased degree of precision in position fixing, this is known as *differential omega,* and is useful for high-accuracy work such as surveys.

DECCA

Decca electronic navigation system depends on radio signals sent out by four transmitters: a master station and three "slaves." The three slaves are located at the corners of an approximately equal-sided triangle, and the master station is in the center. Distance from master to each slave is about 60 miles. For convenience in identification, the slaves are known as red, green, and purple, and the Decca charts show lines in these colors.

In operation, the Decca receiver compares the wave arriving from each slave with that arriving from the master. This comparison is made possible by a natural phenomenon known as "standing waves." When two waves of slightly different frequencies are imposed together, the confluence is marked by many points at which one either amplifies or neutralizes the other. At these points there will be a peak or valley which does not move with the waves. The Decca receiver takes the intervals developed by these "standing waves," and translates them into a pulse which rotates a scale pointer to give a line of position reading.

The pulses arrive in a definite order: master, red, green, and purple, with a 2½ second gap between each.

A "Minidec" unit is available for recreational craft installation that can operate off the boat's battery. A whip antenna and a good ground are required. The crystal for the desired chain is inserted, and the selection knob is set to the "sync" position. The first pulse should set the pointer at zero; if not, the "hold" button is pushed while a manual reset knob is turned to make the correction.

Turn the selector knob to "Coarse," and the readings will appear at their 2½ second intervals. Find the corresponding Decca lines on the special chart, and you have a fix. If necessary, the selector knob can be turned to the "Fine" position to provide the last two significant digits in the coordinates.

7.
RACING

Speed always has been a challenge for many boatmen, whether to see how fast a given boat could go, or in competition with other boats. Here are some of the outstanding records for speed on the water—power and sail, commercial and recreational vessels, in solo runs or passages, and in races.

Here, too, is information on the major power and sail races, and the organizations that conduct them.

AMERICAN POWER BOAT ASSOCIATION

All major power racing in this country is sanctioned by the American Power Boat Association, and the races are run under the rules established by APBA. Racing classifications include Unlimited Hydroplanes, Cruiser (predicted log racing), Drag, Inboard, Offshore, Outboard, Stock Outboard, and Outboard Performance Craft.

Listed here are the national officers of APBA, including the vice presidents for each of the racing divisions, plus the region chairman. See fig. 701. These are the individuals who can give

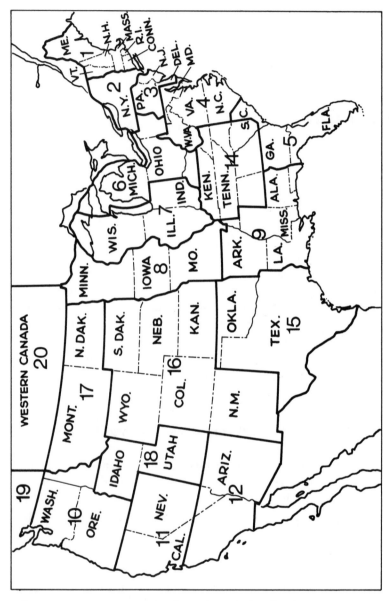

Fig. 701 American Power Boat Association Regions.

you any information you may need in the field of power boat racing.

APBA COUNCIL MEMBERS

President—Richard W. Sandstrom, 20918 46th St. S.E., Bothell, WA 98011

Senior Vice President—Wil Pergande, 16630 Martha Dr., Brookfield, WS 53005

Treasurer—Mike Jones, P.O. Box 1025, Kent, WA 98031

Secretary—Don Allen, 22166 Hall Rd., Woodhaven, MI 48183

Vice President, Cruiser—R. Kenney Baker, P.O. Box 147, Augusta, ME 04330

Vice President, Drag—Dione T. Williams, 501 Fernwood Dr., Moraga, CA 94556

Vice President, Inboard—Raymond T. Beber, 1177 Cadieus Rd., Grosse Pointe Park, MI 48230

Vice President, Inboard Endurance—Art Field (*Pro-Tem*), P.O. Box 2073, Gardena, CA 90247

Vice President, Modified Outboard—Jo Anne Ellis, 105 Willow Dr., Springboro, OH 45066

Vice President, Offshore—S. Sandy Satullo, 3861 W. Valley Dr., Fairview Park, OH 44126

Vice President, Outboard Performance Craft—Robert E. De-Grenier, 2172 Plainfield Dr., Des Plaines, IL 60018

Vice President, Professional Racing Outboard—Ralph Donald, 1073 Terrell Mill Rd., Marietta, GA 30060

Vice President, Stock Outboard—Jon Stone, 47 Thorncliff Rd., Spencerport, NY 14559

Vice President, Unlimited—George W. Byers, Jr., 3115 E. Broad St., Columbus, OH 43209

RACING

COUNCIL MEMBERS AT LARGE

Terms Expire 1977

Gerald L. Bangs, 1700 Westlake N., Suite 420, Seattle, WA 98109

Mani Costa, 617 Nottingham Dr., Virginia Beach, VA 23452

Kay Hallet, Box 2415, Oakland, CA 94614

Leonard Spangenberg, Harbor Towers, 85 India St., Apt. 11B, Boston, MA 02110

James Wilson (Past President), 3811 N.E. 27th Ave., Pompano Beach, FL 33064

Mel Zikes, 4309 Garden Hwy, Sacramento, CA 95837

Term Expires 1978

Bill Giles, 409 Cohannet St., Tuanton, MA 02780

Charles F. Hornickle, 444 Stanfield Rd., Springfield, PA 19064

James H. Jost, 11707 W. Locust St., Wauwautosa, WS 53222

Paul Kalb, Outboard Marine Belgium N.V., Pathkoekeweg 72, 8000 Bruge, Belgium

Bill Muncey, 10364 Russell Rd., La Mesa, CA 92041

Term Expires 1979

Molly Ballou, 41035 Park Ave., Hemet, CA 92343

Fred J. Miller, 1879 Boxford, Trenton, MI 48183

Bob Nordskog (Past President), 16000 Strathearn St., Van Nuys, CA 91406

Edgar Rose, 741 Sycamore La., Glencoe, IL 60022

Charles D. Strang, 1576 Tara La., Lake Forest, IL 60045

Eugene M. Whipp, 2520 Par Hills Ave., Dayton, OH 45419

Chief Counsel

William A. Smith, 30 Bay St., Staten Island, NY 10301

Fig. 702 Profiles of some APBA classes. There are 11 "stock" classes of outboard hydros and runabouts. Note that some inboard classes feature both rear-engine and forward-engine designs.

PROFILES OF SOME APBA CLASSES

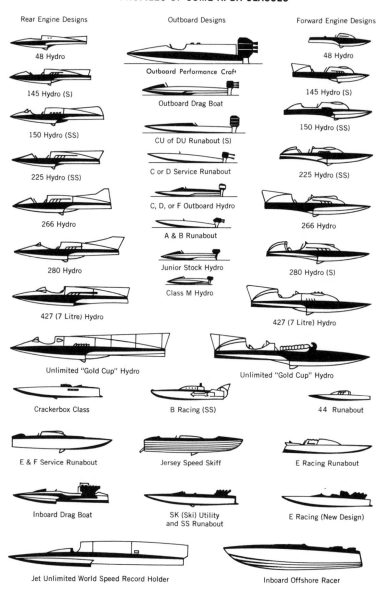

Rear Engine Designs

48 Hydro

145 Hydro (S)

150 Hydro (SS)

225 Hydro (SS)

266 Hydro

280 Hydro

427 (7 Litre) Hydro

Unlimited "Gold Cup" Hydro

Crackerbox Class

E & F Service Runabout

Inboard Drag Boat

Jet Unlimited World Speed Record Holder

Outboard Designs

Outboard Performance Craft

Outboard Drag Boat

CU of DU Runabout (S)

C or D Service Runabout

C, D, or F Outboard Hydro

A & B Runabout

Junior Stock Hydro

Class M Hydro

Unlimited "Gold Cup" Hydro

B Racing (SS)

Jersey Speed Skiff

SK (Ski) Utility
and SS Runabout

Inboard Offshore Racer

Forward Engine Designs

48 Hydro

145 Hydro (S)

150 Hydro (SS)

225 Hydro (SS)

266 Hydro

280 Hydro (S)

427 (7 Litre) Hydro

44 Runabout

E Racing Runabout

E Racing (New Design)

RACING

MAJOR POWER BOAT RACES

Unlimited Events

Gold Cup Challenge Trophy. The Gold Cup is the American Power Boat Association's perpetual challenge trophy for unlimited hydroplanes. The race is meant to be the world's fastest water competition and is the most popular of the high-powered speedboat races.

The Gold Cup Race sponsor and location each year are decided mainly on the basis of bids received by the Unlimited Racing Commissioner of the APBA during its annual meeting, usually held in November.

Offshore Events

Benihana Grand Prix. Run annually in early summer by the New York Offshore Power Boat Racing Association, this race had its origin in 1959 as the Around Long Island Marathon. Since 1970 it has been run in the open ocean off the New Jersey coast, and from 1965 through 1974 it was one of the Hennessy Cognac-sponsored offshore races. It is sanctioned by both APBA and the UIM (Union Internationale Motonautique), so it counts toward both the national and international championships. Race distance is about 180 statute miles, with a short course of about 90 miles for Production Class boats.

Marina City Classic. APBA-UIM sanctioned offshore race dates back to 1965, and is produced by the Pacific Offshore Power Boat Racing Association. Offshore race courses tend to be changed from year to year; this one has been run out of Long Beach, and recently out of Marina Del Rey, with courses that include the circling of Catalina. A short course for Production Class boats is provided.

Barcardi Trophy Race. An APBA-UIM event operated by the Offshore Power Boat Racing Association, a Florida club that is

Table 7-1

Unrestricted Class World Water Speed Records Since 1928

1928 Gar Wood, "Miss America VII" at Detroit.. 92.862
1930 Sir Henry Segrave, "Miss England II" at Windermere (died immediately after)............... 98.7
1931 Kaye Don, "Miss England II" in Argentina...103.48
1931 Kaye Don, "Miss England II", Lake Garda..110.24
1932 Gar Wood, "Miss America IX", Miami, Florida..111.65
1932 Kaye Don, "Miss England III", Loch Lomond (first man to reach 100 knots)...................119.75
1932 Gar Wood, "Miss America X", at Detroit...124.86
1937 Sir Malcolm Campbell, "Blue Bird", Lake Maggiore..129.5
1938 Sir Malcolm Campbell, "Blue Bird", Lake Hallwil, Switzerland..................................130.94
1939 Sir Malcolm Campbell, "Blue Bird", Lake Coniston..141.74
1950 Stanley Sayres, "Slo-mo-shun IV", Lake Washington..160.323
1952 Stanley Sayres, "Slo-mo-shun IV", Lake Washington..178.497
1955 (July 23)   Donald Campbell, "Bluebird", Ullswater...202.32
1955 (Nov. 16)   Donald Campbell, "Bluebird", Lake Mead, Nevada....................................216.25
1956 (Sept. 19) Donald Campbell, "Bluebird", Coniston Water..225.63
1957 (Nov. 7)   Donald Campbell, "Bluebird", Coniston Water..239.07
1958 (Nov. 10)   Donald Campbell, "Bluebird", Coniston Water..248.62
1959 (May 14)   Donald Campbell, "Bluebird", Coniston Water..260.35
1964 (Dec. 31)   Donald Campbell, "Bluebird" Lake Dumbleyung, Australia.............................276.33
1968 (June 30)   Lee Taylor, Jr., "Hustler", Guntersvilla, Ala......................................285.21

the oldest organization in the APBA offshore division. The race course cuts across the Gulf Stream and includes Miami and Bimini.

RACING

Table 7-2

RECORD OCEAN PASSAGES

DATE	SHIP	FROM	TO	NAUT. MILE DISTANCE	TIME
SAILING VESSELS					
1854	"James Blaine"	Boston Light	Light Rock	—	12d 6h
1854	"Flying Cloud"	New York	San Francisco	15,091	89d
1860	"And. Jackson"	New York	San Francisco	13,700	89d 20h
1868-69	"Thermopylae"	Liverpool	Melbourne	—	63d 18h
1853	"Northern Light"	San Francisco	Boston	—	76d 6h
—	"Red Jacket"	New York	Liverpool	3,150	13d 1h
1846	"Yorkshire"	Liverpool	New York	3,150	16d
1905	"Atlantic"	Sandy Hook	England	3,013	12d 4h
POWER VESSELS					
1819	"Savannah"	Savannah	Liverpool	—	16d
1838	"Great Western"	Bristol	New York	—	15d
1910	"Mauretania"	Queenstown	New York	2,780	4d 10h 42m
1933	"Rex"	Gibraltar	Ambrose Lt.	3,181	4d 13h 58m
1934	"Bremen"	Cherbourg	Ambrose Lt.	3,092	4d 14h 27m
1937	"Normandie"	New York	Southampton	2,936	3d 22h 07m
1938	"Queen Mary"	Ambrose Lt.	Bishop's Rock	3,120	3d 20h 42m
1952	"United States"	Ambrose Lt.	Bishop's Rock	2,942	3d 10h 40m

San Francsico Offshore Power Boat Race. Another APBA-UIM race that counts toward the national and world championships, this event has its start and finish just inside the Golden Gate Bridge. Offshore legs include a run out to the Farallon Islands.

Key West Race. Final race of the year on the UIM offshore calendar and first for the following year's APBA circuit, this November event covers 162 nautical miles from Key West to the Dry Tortugas and back. It is organized and operated by the Key West Boat Race Association.

Stroh's Grand National. Run on the waters of Lake Erie by the Great Lakes Offshore Power Boat Racing Association, this can be one of the most punishing events on the U. S. Circuit. It carries both APBA and UIM sanctions.

MAJOR SAIL BOAT RACES*

America's Cup. International yachting's most coveted award, the America's Cup, was inaugurated by the Royal Yacht Squadron of England during the London Exhibition of 1851. The prize got its name when it was won for the first time by the United States entry, *America*, a schooner which had been built and sent over by the New York Yacht Club. The sole U.S. entry defeated a fleet of 17 sailing craft from the Royal Yacht Squadron in a 58-mile race around the Isle of Wight.

Although the original value of the "Ould Mug" was only $500, millions of dollars have been spent by U.S. defenders and would-be defenders, as well as by a long series of valiant but unsuccessful challengers. Until 1970, all challenges were by English-speaking people (English, Irish, Scottish, Canadian and Australian). In 1970, the French and Australians issued challenges.

Because yacht construction costs have made investments in

* *Source: National Association of Engine & Boat Manufacturers.*

huge racing machines impractical, America's Cup racing has been conducted with sleek 12-Meter boats since 1958.

Recent Cup races have been held in Rhode Island Sound off Newport, R.I., during September. Conditions of the race, including time and place, are dependent on the applicable rules set by the current defender of the Cup, the New York Yacht Club. At present challenges must be spaced three years apart. Summaries of all the races are given in this section.

Newport-Bermuda Race. Sailed biennially in June (alternating with the Annapolis to Newport Race), the 635-mile race starts at Brenton Reef Tower off Newport, R.I., and finishes at Mount Hill Light on St. David's Head, Bermuda. The event, open to sailing yachts and under rules of the Cruising Club of America, is sponsored by the CCA and the Royal Bermuda Y.C. Yachts are handicapped according to rating of the International Offshore Yacht Racing Rules.

Annapolis to Newport Yacht Race. Sailed in June every other year, alternating with the Newport-Bermuda Race, the Annapolis (Md.) to Newport (R.I.) ocean race is 473 miles long and is sponsored by the New York Yacht Club, the Annapolis Yacht Club and the U.S. Naval Academy Sailing Squadron.

Transpacific Race. This sailing race is held every odd numbered year in July, going from Los Angeles to Honolulu. It is sponsored by the Transpacific Yacht Racing Association.

Transpacific Catamaran Race. Alternating with the Transpacific Race, this event is for multihulls every July in even numbered years. It is sponsored by the Seal Beach (Cal.) Y.C., and the Ocean Racing Catamaran Association.

Chicago to Mackinac. This 333-mile fresh-water sailboat race is sponsored annually by the Chicago Y.C., in July.

Southern Ocean Racing Conference. This series of races generally consists of six events, five of which count toward a high point championship. The races are: St. Petersburg to Venice (Fla.); St. Petersburg to Ft. Lauderdale; Miami to Lucaya; Sir Thomas Lipton Cup (day race off Miami); Miami to Nassau, and

AMERICA'S CUP SUMMARIES

Year	Winner (U.S.)	Challenger
1851	*America*	U.S. schooner *America* defeated Royal Yacht Squadron fleet in race around the Isle of Wight, England.
1870	*Magic*	*Cambria*, England
1871	*Columbia, Sappho*	*Livonia*, England
1876	*Madeline*	*Countess of Dufferin*, Canada
1881	*Mischief*	*Atalanta*, Canada
1885	*Puritan*	*Genesta*, England
1886	*Mayflower*	*Galatea*, Scotland
1887	*Volunteer*	*Thistle*, Scotland
1893	*Vigilant*	*Valkyrie II*, England
1895	*Defender*	*Valkyrie III*, England
1899	*Columbia*	*Shamrock*, Ireland
1901	*Columbia*	*Shamrock II*, Ireland
1903	*Reliance*	*Shamrock III*, Ireland
1920	*Resolute*	*Shamrock IV*, Ireland
1929	*Enterprise*	*Shamrock V*, Ireland
1934	*Rainbow*	*Endeavor*, England
1937	*Ranger*	*Endeavor II*, England
1958	*Columbia*	*Sceptre*, England
1962	*Weatherly*	*Gretel*, Australia
1964	*Constellation*	*Sovereign*, England
1967	*Intrepid*	*Dame Pattie*, Australia
1970	*Intrepid*	*Gretel II*, Australia
1974	*Courageous*	*Southern Cross*, Australia

the Nassau Cup Race, off Nassau, Bahamas. Racing is conducted under International Offshore Rules, during the first two or three months of the year.

Acapulco Race. Sponsor of this 1,430-mile sail is the San Diego Y. C., which runs it every even numbered year in February.

Ensenada Race. A highly popular (over 500 yachts) sailing event going from Newport Beach, Cal., to Ensenada, Mexico, a distance of about 130 miles, the Ensenada Race is sponsored by the Newport Ocean Sailing Association, on the weekend closest to May 5, each year.

Congressional Cup. Round Robin match racing among the nation's top sailors is sponsored each year by the Long Beach (Cal.) Y.C. The trophy for this invitational series was created by the United States Congress.

World Ocean Racing Championship. This three-year competition, initiated in 1969 by Jack Powell and the St. Petersburg (Fla.) Y.C., was won by Ted Turner in American Eagle in 1971. A championship, of the same duration, the Salty Tiger Trophy, sponsored by Yachting Magazine, was initiated in 1972 with the St. Petersburg-Ft. Lauderdale Race. Seven out of 19 races around the world must be started, and the boat and skipper must be the same for all races to be eligible.

ONE-DESIGN
CLASS ASSOCIATION SECRETARIES

Reprinted from Sail Magazine's '75 Sailboat & Equipment Directory, with permission.

A

ALBACORE: John Ranken
   3717 Camelot Dr., Annandale VA 22003
ALBERG TYPHOON: Charles Waaser
   c/o Cape Dory Co. Inc., 373 Crescent St.,
   W Bridgewater MA 02379
ALDEN OCEAN SHELL: Ernestine Bayer
   385 Washington Rd., Rye NH 03870
AMPHIBI-CON: Francis G. Shaw
   272 Woodland Rd., Chestnut Hi.l MA
   02167
AQUARIUS 21 & 23: Gary L. Russell
   417 Vista Suerte, Newport Beach CA
   92660
ARIEL COMMANDER: Milton F. Thrasher
   80 Fairway Ave., Rye NY 10580
ARROW: Rosalind B. Schmitt
   120 Woodbine, Wilmette IL 60091

B

BALBOA 20 & 26: Gary L. Russell
   417 Vista Suerte, Newport Beach CA
   92660
BANSHEE: Barry Bruch
   12186 Winton Way, Los Altos Hills CA
   94022
BEETLE CAT: Charles E. Clapp II
   One Hospital Trust Plaza, Povidence RI
   02903
BOBBIN: R. F. Collins
   2 Crown Rd., New Malden, Surrey
   ENGLAND
BONITO: G. Ashley Boden
   Maythorne House, Maythorne, South-
   well, Nottinghamshire ENGLAND
BUCCANEER (US): Woody Swope
   459 Bentleyville Rd., Chagrin Falls OH
   44022

BUCCANEER (CANADA): Patrick J. Mc-
Grath 2 Thorncliffe Park Dr. Un. 47,
Toronto, Ont. CANADA
BULL'S EYE: George S. Burr
166 Edmunds Rd., Wellesley MA 02181
BUTTERFLY: Terry Bischoff
PO Box 184, Hartland WI 53029

C

CAL-20: Stan Scott
2249 Ocana Ave., Long Beach CA
90805
CAL-25: N. C. Walton
2314 Murray Ridge, San Diego CA
92123
CAPE DORY 10: Charles Waaser
c/o Cape Dory Co. Inc., 373 Crescent St.,
W. Bridgewater MA 02379
CAPE DORY 14: Charles Waaser
c/o Cape Dory Co. Inc., 373 Crescent
St., W. Bridgewater MA 02379
CATALINA 27: W. F. Featherstone
PO Box 5354, San Mateo CA 94402
CATASTREAK: Alexis Smith
4 Soule St., Warwick RI 02886
CELEBRITY: Peter & Neil Oakes
8 Bay First St., Islip NY 11751
CHALLENGER 15: Terry Kaines
3656 Percy King, Waterford MI 48095
CHEETAH-CAT: Laurent C. Deschamps
20 S. Cherry Grove Ave., Annapolis
MD 21401
C-LARK 14: Dana H. Collins
1725 Grand Ave., Medford OR 97501
COLUMBIA 26: Kent Ross
50 Corte Real, Apt. 3, Greenbrae CA
94904
COLUMBIA CHALLENGER: Stan Cook
1028 Ave., A, Redondo Beach CA 90277
CONTENDER: Raoul Guertin
2015 Eunice, Berkeley CA 94709
CORONADO 15: Carol Winn
4058 Third Ave., San Diego CA 92103
CS 22: Trevor Kingsley-Jones
76 Ramona Blvd., Markham, Ont.
CANADA
CYGNUS: Mrs. H. Brunner
PO Box 94, Maitland, Ont. CANADA

D

DAY SAILER: Dolores Bayer
2801 Raleigh La., Cincinnati OH 45215
DC-14 CATAMARAN: Duncan D. Sutphen,
Jr., PO Box 83, Old Lyme CT 06371

DEMON: Carol Kuse
PO Box 4544, Overland Pk KS 66212
DINGO CATAMARAN: Marjorie A. Penoyer
55 Fourth Ave., Union City PA 16438
DN 60 ICEBOAT: Douglas J. Harvey
11850 Clinton River Rd., Sterling Hts.
MI 48078
DRAGON: V. H. Craig
PO Box 189, Santa Paula CA 93060

E

ENSENADA 20: Gary L. Russell
417 Vista Suerte, Newport Beach CA
92660
ENSIGN: Harry J. Perlberg, Jr.
43 Greenhaven Rd., Rye NY 10580
ENTERPRISE (U.S.): Kenneth Goetz
557 Davidson Rd., Piscataway NJ 08854
ENTERPRISE (CANADA): Frank Bristol
731 Temperance St., Saskatoon, Sask.
CANADA
ETCHELLS 22: Karl K. Gleeson
11 Pleasant View Pl., Old Greenwich
CT 06870

F

FINN: David C. Leach, Jr.
524A Poplar, Wilmette IL 60091
FIREBALL: Gail DuVal
330 Eight Ave., Indialantic FL 32903
505: Bill Salvo
c/o John G. Alden Inc.
89 Commercial Wharf, Boston MA
02110
FLYING FIFTEEN (U.S.): Irving Rubin
1609 Channing Way, Berkeley CA
94703
FLYING FISH: D. Bruce Connolly
PO Box 1345, Waterbury CT 06720
FLYING SCOT: Harold E. Marcus, Jr.
2155 Hallmark Dr., Pensacola FL 32503
FOLKBOAT: Lennart Buch
74 Landlystvej, DK 2650 Hvidovre
DENMARK
FORCE 5: Warren W. Bowes, AMF Alcort
PO Box 1345, Waterbury CT 06720
4.45: G. R. Northrup
2218 Ramsey Rd., Monroeville PA 15146
420: International 420 Class Assoc.
9 Rockefeller Plaza, New York NY 10020
470: Brownie Lewis
PO Box 169, Pewaukee WI 53072

G

GIG: Natalie Brandon
2905 SW Second Ave., Ft. Lauderdale
FL 33315
GREAT PELICAN: Muriel S. Short
203 Hawthorne Ave., Larkspur CA
94939
GRENADIER: G. R. Northrup
2218 Ramsey Rd., Monroeville PA 15146
GULF COAST 14: J. Gordon
2525 Winrock #143, Houston TX 77027
GULF COAST 15: Jim Uroda
113 Talisman, Lake Jackson TX 77566
GULF COAST 20: Louis J. Martin, Jr.
7602 Highmeadow, Houston TX 77042

H

HANDY CAT: Charles Wasser
c/o Cape Dory Co. Inc., 373 Crescent
St., W. Bridgewater MA 02379
HOBIE CAT 14, 16, MONO-CAT: Pat
Larabee 2026 McGraw Ave., Irvine CA
92625
HORNET: Roger J. Robertson
37 Fleet La. London ENGLAND

I

INDIAN: William Halliwell
895 Hope St., Bristol RI 02809
INTERCLUB: James H. Hunt,
O'Day, 1848 Airport Rd., Fall River MA
02720
INTERLAKE: F. K. Holtzman
2534 Boxford Rd., Trenton MI 48183
INTERNATIONAL ONE-DESIGN: Christian
Becker, One Marshall St., Irvington NJ
07111
INTERNATIONAL 110: Albert P. Peloquin
505 S. Birney, Bay City MI 48706
INTERNATIONAL TEMPEST: David McComb
15 Mountain Ridge Terrace, Apt. 87,
New Haven CT 06513

J

JET 14: Mary C. Ungemach
26 Pontiac Dr., Wayne NJ 07470
JOLLY BOAT: Natalie A. Brandon
2905 SW Second Ave., Ft. Lauderdale
FL 33315

K

KESTREL: G. H. Williams

High Beeches, The Old Carriageway
Chipstead Sevenoaks, Kent ENGLAND
KITTIWAKE 24: Charles Brand
801 Berquist, Manchester MO 63011
KNARR (U.S.): Knud Wibroe
57 Post St., San Francisco CA 94104
KNICKERBOCKER: Milton S. Taffet
31 Elliot Rd., Great Neck NY 11021

L

L-16: William C. Fundenberg, Jr.
230 E. 17th St., Costa Mesa CA 92627
LA PAZ 25: Gary L. Russell
417 Vista Suerte, Newport Beach CA
92660
LASER: Arthur E. Warrener
91 Hymus Blvd., Pointe Claire, Que.
CANADA
LIGHTNING: Helen Limbaugh
808 High St., Worthington OH 43085
LISTANG: Adrian Jardine,
c/o BEBS (Marine) Ltd., Quay Works,
Burnham on Crouch, Essex ENGLAND

M

MARBLEHEAD TRAINER: W. T. Butler
PO Box 123, Marblehead MA 01945
MARINER: William Finkle
1548 Holiday Park Dr., Wantagh NY
11793
MATILDA: Linda Masterman
52 Decarie Cir., Islington, Ont. CANADA
MERCURY: Albert L. Runge
901 Main St., Hingham MA 02043
MINIFISH: D. Bruce Connolly, AMF Alcort
PO Box 1345, Waterbury CT 06720
MOBJACK: J. David Arnold
501 Harton Cir., Virginia Beach VA
23452
MONTGOMERY 12: Nancy Kilpatrick
13½ Beacon Bay, Newport Beach CA
92662
MOTH: Benjamin Krothe III
317 Ocean Ave., Ocean City, NJ 08226

N

NADIR: Lee M. Brown
3914 Gibsonia Rd., PO Box 35, Gibsonia
PA 15044
NEWPORT 20: Tannie Bussell
23012 Kent Ave., Torrance CA 90505
NEWPORT 27: Albert Castillon
626 N. Irena Ave., Redondo Beach CA
90277

RACING

NEWPORT 41-S: Richard Meine
3270 Via Campesina, Palos Verdes CA
90274

O

OD-11: G. L. Pierce
1770 Arrowhead Dr., Oakland CA
94610
OK DINGHY: Mrs. Henry Huston
McKitrick Rd., R.R. #3, Plain City OH
43064
OPTIMIST PRAM: Dave Gulkis
PO Box 1031, Clearwater FL 33517

P

P-CAT: Larry Owen
302-30th Pl., Hermosa Beach CA 90254
PEARSON 30: Joseph W. Halliday
23 Revere Rd., Scarsdale NY 10583
PETREL: R. Argue
c/o Aluminum Goods, 158 Sterling Rd.
Toronto, Ont. CANADA
PINTAIL: Claude Horton
115 Washington Ave., Cuyahoga Falls
OH 44221
POINT JUDE 15: P. L. Greene
PO Box 129A, Saunderstown RI 02874
PUFFER: James C. Bonner
AMF Alcort, PO Box 1345, Waterbury
CT 06720

R

RAINBOW: Robert Marder
710 Howard Rd., Pikesville MD 21208
RANGER 20: Richard E. Hanson
32736 35th Ave., SW, Federal Way
WA 98002
RASCAL: David Hyder
3747 Elm Lawn, Toledo OH 43610
RAVEN: Wilfred L. Hand
10555 Bergtold Rd., Clarence NY 14031
REBEL: Lee Helphinstine
209 E. Goodwin Pl., Mundelein IL 60060
REDSTART VOYAGER: Adrian Jardine,
c/o BEBS (Marine) Ltd.
Quay Works, Burnham on Crouch,
Essex ENGLAND
RENEGADE ICEBOAT: Cora Lee Millenbach
8068 Lamphere, Detroit MI 48239
RHODES BANTAM: Paul Valigosky
4256 Ann Rose Ct., Toledo OH 43611
ROBBER: Adrian Jardine
c/o BEBS (Marine) Ltd., Quay Works,
Burnham on Crouch, Essex ENGLAND

ROBIN: Richard H. Lemmon
136 Canaveral Dr., Pittsburgh PA 15235
ROOSTER: Michael P. Smith
Hawthorne Rd., Jamestown RI 02835

S

SABOT (NAPLES): Peggy Brown
5552 Chelsea Ave., La Jolla CA 92037
SABOT (WIN'ARD): Gene Levinthal
4581 Deseret Dr., Woodland Hills CA
91364
SAILAWAY: R. F. Collins
2 Crown Rd., New Malden, Surrey
ENGLAND
SAILFISH: Jack Evans
PO Box 1345, Waterbury CT 06720
SAN FRANCISCO PELICAN: Robert A.
Wooll, 62 Blossom Dr., San Rafael CA
94901
SAN JUAN 21: Cindy Mattson
11504 23rd St. SW. Seattle WA 98146
A, C, E, & M SCOWS: Terry Bischoff
PO Box 117, Nashotah WI 53058
MC SCOW: J. B. Crum
PO Box 1435, Barton FL 33830
M-20 SCOW: William Hanson
524 E. Cecil St., Neenah WI 54956
SEA SPRAY 15 (U.S.): Barry Moore
2547 Nipomo Ave., Long Beach CA
90815
SEA SPRAY 15 (CANADA): Fred J. van
Zuiden, 301 Cumberland House, Rideau
Towers, Calgary, Alb CANADA
SEA SPRITE: Everett Hall
45 Pleasant St., N. Kingstown RI 02852
SHARK (U.S.): Jim Hagwood
3745 Arbor Rd., Suffolk VA 23435
SHARK (CANADA): J. A. Johnson
46 Sherbourne St., Toronto, Ont.
CANADA
SIDEWINDER: Malvene M. Hill
811 Winston Dr., Monroe MI 48161
SKIMMER 45: David Gebow
14545 Robson, Detroit MI 48227
SKIPJACK: Chuck Atkinson
Rt. 5, PO Box 279-S, Ft. Worth TX
76126
SKYLARK: Quentin Patterson
110 E. King, Hillsborough NC 27278
SNIPE: Lowry Lamb
Privateer Rd., Hixson TN 37343
SOL CATAMARAN: Diego A. Kahr
1932 E. Pomona St., Santa Ana CA
92705
SOLING: Terry Bischoff
PO Box 185, Hartland WI 53029

SOLO: D. W. Butler
15 Cherrywood Ct., Cambridge Rd.,
Teddington, Middlesex ENGLAND
SOUTH COAST 21: T. Eugene Caldwell
PO Box 1704, Jackson MS 39205
SPINDRIFT: Mrs. Sieb Vandestadt
PO Box 7, Owen Sound, Ont. CANADA
SR-2: N. W. Gooderham
467 Chartwell Rd., Oakville, Ont.
CANADA
STAR: John W. Allen
1301 Waukegan Rd., Glenview IL 60025
SUNBIRD: W. W. Bowes
PO Box 1345, Waterbury CT 06720
SUNFISH: Jack R. Evans, AMF Alcort
PO Box 1345, Waterbury CT 06720
SUNSPOT: K. V. Loimand
743 Kennedy Rd., Scarborough, Ont.
CANADA
SWEET 16: Lona Jewell
6301 N. Wabash Dr., Gladstone MO
64118

T

TANZER 16 (U.S.): Emmett Y Stafford
PO Box 26003, Raleigh NC 27611
TANZER 16 (CANADA): Gord Forth
PO Box 67, Dorion, Que. CANADA
TANZER 22: John G. Charters
54 Lakeview Rd., Baie D'Urfe, P. Q.
CANADA
TARTAN: Gina Hamister
24212 Lake Rd., Bay Village OH 44140
TELSTAR: Larry R. Baker
1110 NW 43rd Ave., Lauderhill FL
33313
THISTLE: Honey Abramson
1303 Ridgewood Dr., Highland Pk. IL
60035
TIGERCAT: Arthur Gronkowski
Rte. 1, PO Box 135, Roscommon MI
48653
TORNADO CAT: Pete Jung
1560 Catalina Blvd., San Diego CA
92107
TRIAD: J. C. Dobler
801 Eighth St., Manhattan Beach CA
90266
TRIKINI TRIMARAN: Len Susman
1010 SE 12th Ct., Cape Coral FL 33904
22 SQ. METER: Don Glasell
331 Kedzie, Evanston IL 60202

U

UDELL ONE-DESIGN: Don Glasell
331 Kedzie, Evanston IL 60202
US 1 (SINGLEHANDER): Richard D. Starks
7906 NW Potomac, Parkville MD 64152

V

VICTORY: R. D. Walker
2039 Cordoba Pl. Carlsbad CA 92008
VITA: J. C. Dobler
801 Eighth St., Manhattan Beach CA
90266

W

WAYFARER: Jo Jones
23161 Cromwell, Dearborn MI 48128
WHISTLER: Tom Schroth
15904 Longmeadow Dr., Dearborn MI
48120
WIANNO SENIOR: Stanley W. Moore
Stanley Pl., Hyannis MA 02601
WIDGEON: James H. Hunt
O'Day, 848 Airport Rd., Fall River MA
02720
WINDFLITE: Tom Sportsman
Sobstad Sailmakers
PO Box 385, Old Saybrook CT 06475
WINDMILL: Terry Bischeff
PO Box 183, Hartland WI 53029
WINDSURFER: Diane Schweitzer
1038 Princeton Dr., Marina Del Rey CA
90291

Y

YACHTCRAFT 26: Bob Alcumbae
618 N. Baker, Santa Ana CA 92703
YARE: Natalie A. Brandon
2905 SW Second Ave., Ft. Lauderdale
FL 33315
YARE JR: Natalie A. Brandon
2905 SW Second Ave., Ft. Lauderdale
FL 33315
Y-FLYER: Mrs. C. Brink
1299 Glenora Dr., London, Ont.
CANADA

RACING

8.
AMENITIES & DIVERSIONS

A lot of little things can add to the pleasure of boating. Making life aboard more comfortable is one of them; another is knowledge of common boating customs and etiquette. Here are a number of useful tips in the galley and housekeeping departments, suggestions for the boatman's library ashore and afloat, information on pets and boats, and even a short course on photography for the boatman. In short, here are boating's amenities and diversions.

HOUSEKEEPING HINTS*

Those Wire Clothes Hangers Can Be Rust Proofed

A good coat of colorless nail polish prevents the hanger from rusting. This type of rust-free hanger takes up much less room than plastic or wooden ones. And bear in mind that where the hanging hook is attached to the plastic and wooden hangers is where the neck of the terry cloth robe or cotton sweatshirt always touches, making a most identifiable rust mark.

* From Ruth Lundgren Williamson's column, "The Companionway," in *Motor Boating & Sailing* magazine.

Table 8-1   TABLE OF EQUIVALENTS

Beans, dried	1 cup	1/2 lb.
Butter	2 cups	1 lb.
	1 stick	1/2 cup
	1 stick	8 tablespoons
Chocolate	1 square	1 oz.
Cheese	5 cups grated	1 lb.
Dates	2 cups pitted	1 lb.
Eggs	5 whole	About 1 cup
Egg whites	8	About 1 cup
Egg yolks	16	About 1 cup
Meat	2 cups diced	1 lb.
Nut meats	4 cups chopped	1 lb.
Raisins	3 cups seedless	1 lb.
Rice	1 cup raw	3 to 4 cups cooked

SUBSTITUTIONS

Baking powder	1 teaspoon	=	1/4 teaspoon baking soda plus 1/2 teaspoon cream of tartar
Butter	1 cup	=	7/8 cup cottonseed, corn, nut oil or lard
Chocolate	1 square	=	3 tablespoons cocoa plus 1½ teaspoons fat
Cornstarch	1 tablespoon	=	2 tablespoons flour when used for thickening purposes
Cracker crumbs	3/4 cup	=	1 cup bread crumbs
Cream, sour, heavy	1 cup	=	1/3 cup butter and 2/3 cup milk in any sour-milk recipe
Flour, cake, sifted	1 cup	=	7/8 cup sifted all-purpose flour (1 cup less two tablespoons)
Milk	1 cup	=	1/2 cup evaporated milk and 1/2 cup water

Table 8-2   ROASTING TIME

ROAST	Weight	Oven Temp. Constant	Temp. Inside Meat	Minutes Per Pound
BEEF				
... standing ribs	6-8	300°F.	140°F.	18-20
			160°F.	25-27
			170°F.	27-30
... standing ribs (1 rib)	1-8	350°F.	140°F.	33
			160°F.	45
			170°F.	50
... rolled ribs	6-8	300°F.	140°F.	30-32
			160°F.	45-48
chuck ribs	5-8	300°F.	150-170°F.	25-30
... rump	5-7	300°F.	150-170°F.	25-30
PORK—FRESH				
... loin—center	3-4	350°F.	185°F.	35-45
whole	12-15	350°F.	185°F.	15-20
ends	3-4	350°F.	185°F.	45-50
... shoulder—whole	12-14	350°F.	185°F.	30-35
boned and rolled	4-6	350°F.	185°F.	40-45
cushion	4-6	350°F.	185°F.	35-40
pork butt	4-6	350°F.	185°F.	45-50
fresh ham	10-12	350°F.	185°F.	30-35
LAMB				
leg	6½-7½	300°F.	165-180°F.	30-35
shoulder-rolled	3-4	300°F.	165-180°F.	40-45
shoulder	4½-5½	300°F.	165-180°F.	30-35
VEAL				
leg roast	7-8	300°F.	165-170°F.	25
loin	4½-5	300°F.	165-170°F.	30-35
rack—4 to 6 ribs	2½-3	300°F.	165-170°F.	30-35
shoulder	7	300°F.	165-170°F.	25
shoulder—rolled	5	300°F.	165-170°F.	40-45

This chart can be used for both the searing and constant temperature methods.

AMENITIES

When It Comes to Pots and Pans

It is generally felt that rust-resistant stainless steel or enameled cookware is best for the boat. We have always been for high, fairly narrow cookware. It saves space in a galley and prevents liquids from sloshing over when the going gets rough. Shop for the widest two pots that will fit on a two-burner. Water boils faster in a wide pot (the same amount, of course) and, with the pot covered, one-dish meals simmer in absolutely no time. Both time and alcohol are conserved.

About Ice Chests

They leak and sweat. They also rot. Which isn't so much their fault as the ice that's in them. Ice melts and chests have to be drained. On some boats they drain through the hull, but on many boats the drain goes into the bilge. Of course, what makes the ice chests rot is that this is fresh water. Some people carry this rotten idea further. Like down the bilge. A famous boating lady from Puerto Rico mentions cow licks. She suggests you get a cow lick and put it directly under the drain. Every drop from the ice chest is converted into salt water before it settles into those dark recesses in the bilge beyond the reach of the probing penknife. They can be ordered from a farm supply house. If you don't know a farm supply house call up your local Department of Agriculture Extension Service office. If you don't have room for a cow lick, simple rock salt of the sort you sprinkle on winter sidewalks, generously distributed, will work pretty well.

How to Prevent and Remove Mildew

A useful little pamphlet on this subject is available from the Office of Information, U. S. Dept. of Agriculture in Washington, D.C. Mildew is caused by molds that grow on anything from which they can get enough food. Boatwives do not need to be told that as the molds grow they cause damage and have a musty odor. Obviously, it's pretty hard to get rid of the dampness that encourages the mildew but there are some things you can do to protect your interests. Providing ventilation is the first rule. Give some articles special care. Plastic bags are a joy here. Boat sheets, pillow cases, towels and extra blankets should always be stored in plastic bags when they're on the boat and if anybody lives on the waterfront it's a good idea to keep all home and boat linens in plastic. It reduces the dampness—never known or had a piece of cloth mildew in a plastic bag. In season, these bags also keep leather and canvas shoes dry and mildew-free. And plastic covers are a must for cotton mattresses. Nice on foam, too, but essential on cotton. There are now mildew-resistant finishes that can be put on some surfaces to protect them. The little pamphlet suggests the following to remove mildew already present on fabrics: use lemon juice and salt solution, perborate bleach or chlorine bleach. And use talcum powder in books.

Reusable-Disposable Bed Sheets

These bed sheets and pillow cases can be slept on for seven nights before throwing them away. Soft and cozy the whole week-long, with nary a rip or tear, and they're attractive to boating wives for another reason. They store in about a quarter of the space of ordinary bed linen.

A Boat Bucket With a Lid

Rubbermaid puts out such a bucket. It's rectangular, has a 14-quart capacity, and is handy for a dozen things aboard. It can be used to hold bait one day, for icing beverages the next, and for mopping the deck after that—it's that easy to keep clean. The lid is what gives it added value.

Pressure Cookers

Some boatwives seem to feel that for cooking in a hurry, they're great. They reduce cooking time for just about everything by two-thirds or more. Sometimes this is important. Sometimes it's not, especially if you're looking forward to a long, beautiful cruising day and have plenty of time to spare. At any rate, you can use a pressure cooker as long as there's a steady source of heat and cold water. Some recipes for quick-cooking foods like fresh vegetables require the cold water for reducing pressure immediately after the recommended cooking time to prevent overcooking. Otherwise you let the pressure drop of its own accord. It doesn't take much cold water, though. Running the cooker under the water faucet or pouring cold water over it is enough. Or even just placing it in a pan of cold water. National Presto Industries, Eau Claire, Wisconsin, makes one of the most popular cookers; you can get them electric or non-electric, with or without Teflon.

Galley Stoves

Galley stoves are never far removed from a mate. But we wouldn't want to forget them if we could. They are one of the facts of life. The point is they should never be taken lightly.

AMENITIES

Table 8-3   **PURCHASING GUIDE FOR FRESH VEGETABLES**

Item	Market Unit	Approx. Measure as Purchased	Approx. No. of Servings per Unit
Asparagus	1 lb.	16-20 stalks	6
Beans, lima shelled	1 lb.	2 cups	6
Beans, snap	1 lb.	3 cups	5
Beets	1 lb.	2 cups diced	4
Broccoli	1 lb.	—	3
Brussels sprouts	1 lb.	1 quart or less	5
Cabbage—Served raw	1 lb.	1/2 small head	7
Served cooked	1 lb.	—	4
Carrots	1 lb.	4 cups diced or shredded	5
Cauliflower	1 lb.	1½ cups	2
Celery	1 lb.	2 med. bunches 4 cups diced	4 (cooked)
Corn, ears	12 medium	3 cups cut	6
Greens	1 lb.	—	4
Mushrooms	1 lb.	35-45	6
Onions	1 lb.	3 large	4
Peas, in pod	1 lb.	1 cup shelled	2
Potato, sweet	1 lb.	3 medium	3
Potato, white	1 lb.	3 medium	3
		2½ cups diced	
Rutabaga	1 lb.	2⅔ cups sliced	4
Squash, summer	1 lb.	—	3
Tomato	1 lb.	4 small	3 (cooked)
Turnip	1 lb.	3 medium	4

Table 8-4   COOKING MEASURES

3 teaspoons	1 tablespoon
4 tablespoons	1/4 cup
5⅓ tablespoons	1/3 cup
16 tablespoons	1 cup
7/8 cup	3/4 cup plus 2 tablespoons
2 cups	1 pint
2 pints	1 quart
4 quarts	1 gallon
8 quarts	1 peck
16 ounces	1 pound
4 pecks	1 bushel

COOKING TEMPERATURES

Simmering (water)	180° F.
Boiling (water)	212° F.
Soft Ball stage (candies and sauces)	234°-240° F.
Jellying stage	220°-222° F.
Very slow oven	250°F.
Slow oven	300° F.
Moderately slow oven	325° F.
Moderate oven	350° F.
Moderately hot oven	375° F.
Very hot oven	450°-500° F.
Hot oven	400° F.

Something you're going to be fooling with every day deserves some thought even if it does not contribute greatly to your comfort and pleasure. Most boat women will agree, and many ask for the final answer as to type, fuel, size, etc. Many stoves have many good qualities, depending somewhat on the space available, your own temperament, your budget for stoves etc. However, the more burners the better. Some cooks can do all right with one burner, but darn few. And of those few, all could do better with more burners. It may be pointed out (because boating people are such literal people) that when camping one fire can be made to make do. But a camp fire is many fires, and properly made, can serve many purposes. With one burner you have one source, one heat—and that's it. Sometimes we have little choice because of space, but most of the time things can be rearranged, oh so little, to accommodate two burners rather than one. You can give up on almost anything else and if by doing so, you could get the kind of galley stove to suit you, it would be worth the effort.

Use Your Laundry Marker

To label the tops of all cans aboard. It is to be pointed out that moisture can cause labels to fall off and "pot luck" ceases to be fun after a day or two. Any kind of paper packaging is not for boats. Transfer things like flour and sugar to air-tight plastic containers (Tupperware is a fine choice). Or else put the paper package into a tightly-tied plastic bag. If you've got some good heavy plastic bags, incidentally, you can stuff them with canned foods, seal them and drop them into the bilge. In that way, you'll never be without variety for your menus. And it's in the best tradition of the sea.

Top-of-Stove Grilling

Handy O'Reily. This is a flat oblong piece of cast aluminum with a one-inch lip and high ridges and deep grooves covering its surface. The grooves catch the fat as meat is grilled on top of the stove and the high ridges brown the meat. It's got a handle, just like a frying pan, but that's where the resemblance ends. The meat tastes broiled. It is inexpensive and obtained in department stores such as Gimbels or some store in your own area. You'll find it very handy on the boat.

AMENITIES

Coffee and Tea Canisters

You have discovered Tupperware somewhere along the line but you'll be happy to learn about new canisters they have added to their line. They're brown and big and labelled. One for coffee holds a whole pound and the matching tea canister stores from 75 to 100 tea bags. The unique Tupperware seal can be counted on, as most boating women know, not only to keep things fresh but to keep things in, in case of a heavy sea.

SKIPPER'S HOME AND ON-BOARD LIBRARIES

by Tony Gibbs

The only thing more impossible than picking someone else's neckwear is choosing his reading matter. People who love books are very touchy (and rightfully so, I think) about others telling them what they ought to be reading. So this list is offered very tentatively as one man's opinion, in the hope that it will inspire readers to seek out their own favorites.

One other point: the titles listed here are for the most part older books which are either still in print or generally available at good public libraries. If you're interested in buying any of the volumes listed, one of the major mail order nautical book specialists will probably be able to help you. Three of the best are *Sailing Book Service*, 34 Oak Ave., Tuckahoe, NY 10707; *International Marine Publishing Co.*, 21 Elm St., Camden, ME 04843; and *Nautical Book Service*, 2825 Newport Blvd., Newport Beach, CA 92660.

On Board

The number of books you can (and want) to carry abroad your boat will depend a lot on how much room you have to stow them (for suggestions, see the end of this article). Assuming you've got a bare minimum of dry lockerage, you'll want to keep your library down to basic, operational books.

Engine book: It may be that your particular engine's service manual covers this heading—some of them, like the excellent book on the Universal Atomic-4, are all the engine literature you need. But if your owner's manual is inadequate or missing, you may want to carry a substitute. Outboard skippers cannot do better, I think, than the appropriate volume of *Glenn's Outboard Motor Repair and Tune-Up Guide.* These complete, hardcover books now cover all the major U.S. outboards—Chrysler, Evinrude, Johnson, McCulloch, Mercury and Sears, one book to a manufacturer, and they are about $7 apiece.

The owner of an inboard has nothing so specific. Very small engines are covered by Boyd Daugherty's *Servicing Small Gasoline Engines,* a good, clear introduction. More elaborate installations are a problem. At this writing, the best book in the field is the text of the U.S. Power Squadrons' *Engine Maintenance Course*—so if you're already a Squadron member, it would certainly help you to take the course and have the book aboard for reference.

Log Book: Basically, the boating world seems to be divided between log-keepers and non-log-keepers—with the latter in the great majority. Even if you're not the systematic type, it can pay you to keep some records of your boat's operation, and some of her vital statistics—major equipment serial numbers, sail plans, stowage plan, etc. The standard *Yacht Log and Guest Register* published by *Motor Boating & Sailing Books* is very good for the power cruising man. Besides the standard trip-notation pages, it has space for a radiotelephone and guest log, and heavy-paper envelopes attached inside the front and back covers for miscellaneous papers (the spare parts list for the galley stove, for instance).

For the cruising sailor, I can think of no better log than the loose-leaf version, in large and small sizes, published by West Products (161 Prescott St., E. Boston, MA 02128). Its removable pages include many of the same headings as the MB&S volume, but it also has sections peculiar to sailing skippers, for recording sail inventory or racing records.

If your vessel has a radiotelephone, you'll need a radio log, and it must be permanently bound to be legal. There are probably enough pages in the MB&S log referred to above to handle most skippers' loggable messages, but you may also want to invest in a small, informative booklet called *Marine Radio Telephony*, available from Radio Technical Commission for Marine Services, c/o FCC, Washington, D.C. 20554. While having this book aboard will not relieve you of the obligation to carry the relevant FCC Rules, those rules are incomprehensible to just about everyone except the people who wrote them. *Marine Radio Telephony*, which costs less than a dollar, tells you how to operate your R/T legally and effectively.

Medical Emergencies: Most good marine first aid kits come with a pamphlet-sized manual enclosed. If you feel yours isn't good enough—and it probably isn't—there are several books you can get to supplement it. Two titles are put out by the American Red Cross—*First Aid* and *Life Saving and Water Safety.* Another very fine book, of special pertinence to the yachtsman, is *First Aid Afloat,* by Paul Sheldon, M.D. Whichever first aid book you decide on, check the ingredients of your first aid kit against those noted in the book, to make sure you'll have what you need to follow the doctor's orders.

Forecasting: The complete pleasure boatman's weather book is yet to be published. In the meantime, however, there are three worthy volumes to consider. For on-board use, one of the most helpful publications I've ever encountered is the *Sager Weathercaster.* It has a set of cardboard dials on the front cover, which can be set to correspond to the present weather conditions and trend, and the resultant coded read-out will provide the skipper with a local forecast for the next 12–24 hours. All you need besides the book is a reliable barometer.

Thorn Bacon's *Weather for Sportsmen,* published by Motor Boating & Sailing Books, presents basic forecasting information, but the emphasis throughout is on how to use nature's signs for better, and safer boating, fishing, hunting, camping, etc.

One-volume reference: If your shoreside nautical library were restricted to a single book, you could do far worse than make it a copy of the revised *Piloting, Seamanship and Small Boat Handling,* by Charles F. Chapman. Virtually everything you need to know is in *Chapman's,* and a recent overhaul, now complete, makes the book both thoroughly up to date and far easier to use than ever before.

Beyond the basics, there are literally hundreds of worthy volumes the skipper can consider for home or boat. There's only room to list the most outstanding ones here—ones known personally to the compiler or by reliable recommendation.

Learning to Sail

Basic Sailing, by M.B. George. A self-teaching text for beginners.

Sailing, by Peter Heaton. Also for the beginner, but with a pronounced British flavor.

Glenans Sailing Manual, by Philippe Harlé. The textbook of France's Glenans sailing school, in translation. Practical and thorough.

Practical Sailing, by Tony Gibbs. How to sail and why, plus some information on boats and equipment currently available.

Hand, Reef and Steer, by Richard Henderson. Perhaps the best young person's introduction to sailing.

More Advanced Sailing and Racing

Yachtsman's Omnibus, H.A. Calahan. The famous writer's *Learning to Sail, Race* and *Cruise* in one volume. Old fashioned but charming.

Yacht Racing, by Manfred Curry. First of the great yachting theorists, and still controversial and thought-provoking.

Sailing to Win, by Robert N. Bavier, Jr. An excellent introduction to competitive sailing.

AMENITIES

Race Your Boat Right, by Arthur Knapp. A classic for those learning to race.

Sailing Theory and Practice, by C.A. Marchaj. Double-dome in the extreme, but fascinating if you have the advanced math to follow the author's arguments.

Cornelius Shields on Sailing. Another racing classic: like golf books, there never seem to be enough.

Wind and Sailing Boats, by Alan Watts. A theoretical approach, but not too technical for the intelligent reader.

Offshore Boats and Sailing

Cruising, by Peter Heaton. A charming paperback introduction to the sport. Very old fashioned and British.

Heavy Weather Sailing, by Adlard Coles. There are few hard and fast rules when the going gets tough. Most of them are here.

Cruising Under Sail and *Voyaging Under Sail,* by Eric Hiscock. How it's done, by a man who has made most of the significant voyages there are.

Practical Boating, by W.S. Kals. Not specifically for sailors alone, this is a compendium of useful information for far voyagers.

The Racing-Cruiser, by Richard Henderson. A new and very good introduction to the sport of distance racing, by an American author.

Further Offshore, by John Illingworth. Successor to the classic *Offshore,* this is a revision of the earlier volume. American readers will find it still useful, but incomplete.

Ocean Racing and Offshore Yachts, by Peter Johnson. The author is a large figure in the JOG, Britain's version of the Midget Ocean Racing Club. His book concentrates on smaller offshore boats. It is up to date and very good.

The Compleat Cruiser, by L. Francis Herreshoff. The author is a man of many strong opinions—but who is more entitled to hold them? Lots of useful hints and tips.

The Proper Yacht, by Arthur Beiser. An experienced cruising man's informed ideas on what goes into a live-aboard sailing boat.

Boatbuilding and Design

Boatbuilding, by Howard I. Chapelle. A classic, if somewhat dated.

Boatbuilding Manual, by Robert Steward. An excellent and up-to-date volume that goes from A to Z. Mostly about wooden craft.

Ferro-Cement Boat Construction, by Jack R. Whitener. Covers every detail of concrete boatbuilding, from the trowel up.

Boatkeeper's Project Book, by Tom Bottomley. Ideas and specifications for modifications, improvements, and installations on all types of boats.

Modern Marine Materials, by Ernest Zadig. Everything you need to know about every material used in your boat.

Modern Marine Maintenance, by John Duffett. The most comprehensive and up-to-date volume on boat care now available.

Your Boat's Electrical System, by Conrad Miller. The layman's book that deals at a practical level with everything electrical aboard a boat, power or sail.

Skene's Elements of Yacht Design, by Francis Kinney. The great classic in the field.

Understanding Boat Design, by Brewer and Betts. A very good introduction to elementary factors of design.

Sailor's Skills

Ashley Book of Knots. Perhaps the most complete knot book ever compiled, though most of it is of use only to antiquarians.

Knight's Modern Seamanship. Another of the non-fiction classics of the sea, this one is not of great pertinence to the pleasure boatman.

Arts of the Sailor, by Hervey Garrett Smith. Fancy ropework— a small gem of a book.

Celestial Navigation for Yachtsmen, by Mary Blewitt. A method of approaching deep-water navigation that may appeal to amateurs because of its simplicity.

AMENITIES

Primer of Navigation, by G.W. Mixter. A navigation text designed for class use.

Art of Knotting and Splicing, by Cyrus Dey. A good, complete book—if not so complete as Ashley.

Dutton's Navigation and Piloting, by Dunlap and Shufeldt. The latest revision of an old classic.

Knots & Lines Illustrated, by Paul and Arthur Snyder. How to handle most rope-and-line situations on a modern sailboat. Highly practical.

Reference

Safety Standards for Small Craft, issued periodically by the American Boat & Yacht Council. Recommended construction, design and installation practices for pleasure boats. Technical but sound.

International Maritime Dictionary, by René de Kerchove. Heavily weighted toward commercial shipping terms, it is still the only game in town.

Modern Powerboats, by Jack West. The boats themselves, the equipment for them, and how to install and care for it.

Sailboat & Sailboat Equipment Directory, by Institute for Advancement of Sailing. Annual paperback directory.

Sails, by Jeremy Howard-Williams. With a British bias, this is still the best general book on the design and construction of sails.

Mariner's Notebook, by William Crawford. A self-teaching course in piloting and boat handling.

American Practical Navigator, better known as *Bowditch.* Not really very useful to the pleasure boatman, but fun to have just the same.

Power Boat Annual. Not as good as the Sailboat Directory, but adequate.

Boat Owner's Buyer's Guide, by the Editors of *Yachting.* Annual compendium of where-to-get-it information. A lot easier than trying to keep track of individual catalogs.

Yachtsman's Eight Language Dictionary. Most pleasure boating terms rendered into French, German, Dutch, Danish, Italian, Spanish, Portuguese, and—you guessed it—English.

PETS AND BOATS

Some dog breeds such as retrievers and spaniels take to boating readily. Poodles, beagles, and dachshunds seem to be natural sailors. Short-haired breeds seem to do better than those with long hair, and most puppies can usually accomodate themselves to the water. Old dogs who have a violent dislike of the water should not be forced to go along on boats.

If your dog swims in salt water as part of his boating experience, wash him off with fresh water at least once a day, dry him well, and keep him away from drafts. Salt water, if left on the dog, can cause skin problems.

Some pets will drink excessive amounts of salt water, causing them to become nauseous. Give a small amount of Pepto-Bismol, and do not feed the animal for awhile. Fresh water should be available at all times; renew it four or five times a day, if necessary, to make sure it is fresh and pure. Avoid excessive ice water, however, as this can lead to diarrhea.

Canned dog foods are ideal for the boat; dry foods tend to pick up the dampness and become soggy. Most table scraps are all right, but avoid all bones, and double-check condition of leftovers from the ice box or refrigerator. Don't overfeed your pet.

Dogs need plenty of exercise, and should have it, ashore, three or four times a day. Make sure there's a total of at least an hour a day for exercise. Dogs find it necessary to relieve themselves with some degree of regularity, and scheduled times should be provided. Most of them prefer to have this opportunity after they have eaten, so a good walk following the evening meal is recommended.

Don't allow your pet on deck when coming in alongside a pier or another boat. Most dogs regard the boat as family property,

AMENITIES

to be guarded, and may try to bite anyone who reaches aboard to take a line, or steps aboard for any reason. A dog or cat moving about on deck also could be a tripping hazard.

Don't go off from the boat at night and leave a noisy dog in the cabin, and don't allow your dog to run loose in a marina.

It should be noted that cats make excellent cruising companions. They do not need trips ashore for exercise, and an on-board "Kitty Litter" pan serves them very well. They can swim, too, in case one falls overboard.

DESIGN YOUR PERSONAL FLAG

There's no rule governing the shape of flags, or assigning a particular significance to a shape, but there is a general practice, as follows: rectangular flags—national or regional associations (like the United States Power Squadrons or the Coast Guard Auxiliary, or groups of yacht clubs associated for racing); triangular pennants—yacht club burgees, Coast Guard Auxiliary officers; swallow-tail (or burgeed) flags—private signals, certain appointed officers of the Coast Guard Auxiliary and Power Squadrons.

In the matter of swallow-tailed flags, it's interesting to note that, according to one flag maker, about 50% of private signals are tapered swallow-tails, about 25% untapered burgeed flags, and the rest of a variety of shapes. The man designing his own may pretty well make up his own mind what shape to use, while yacht clubs—judging by the entries in Lloyd's Register of American Yachts—stick almost entirely to the triangular pennant.

In order to increase legibility of your flag, it's good practice to follow the dictates of the "science" of heraldry: tinctures (the colors red, blue, green, purple, and black) must alternate with metals (silver, white, gold, and yellow). Never place a tincture alongside a tincture, because the line of demarcation is hard to see at a reasonable distance, and the two tints will blend, with both of them losing authority. This color rule makes a lot of

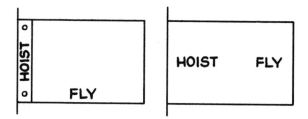

Fig. 801 Hoist and fly are two words that can confuse. They refer to the height and length of a flag, and they also refer to the parts nearest and farthest from the staff.

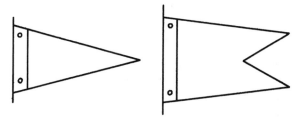

Fig. 802 Common shapes for flags, other than the rectangle, are the triangle used for yacht club burgees, and the swallowtail.

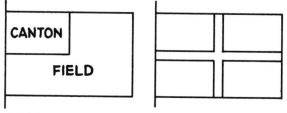

Fig. 803 Canton is another term that has two meanings. It can refer to the upper left hand portion of a flag, or it can refer to any of the quarters when the flag is so divided.

sense, especially when one considers two very necessary qualifications to it.

The first concerns cantons (fig. 803), which may be either the four quarters of a rectangular flag, equal in size, or, when referred to as *the* canton, a square or rectangle somewhat less than a quarter of the flag's area in the upper, left-hand corner of the flag. (Flags, by the way, are always drawn with the staff or halyard edge—the hoist—at the viewer's left.) An example of the canton is the 50-starred segment of the U.S. flag. Cantons are presumed to be separate from the rest of the flag's design, and the color rules don't pertain to them: in a quartered flag, like that of Panama or the State of Maryland, each quarter (or canton) stands by itself, and the color rules apply only within the canton.

If, for good and sufficient reasons, your main design and background are both tinctures (or metals), it's still possible to achieve a striking, visually effective flag: simply edge the design with a contrasting metal (or tincture, as the case may demand) in a narrow band. This process is technically called *fimbriating,* and the best-known example of it appears on the Confederate battle flag. That basic design is, of course, a blue saltire with 13 white stars on a red field; to make the layout legible at a distance, the designers fimbriated the St. Andrew's cross, edged it in white, and came up with a banner whose popularity far outstripped the national flag of the Confederacy.

Both the colors and design of a flag may have symbolic meanings, but color symbolism varies widely from place to place—white, for instance, means purity in some areas and death in others. The essential meaning of a flag is usually expressed by the devices that appear on it. Illustrations of things, technically called *charges,* can be animal, vegetable, or mineral; anything from the mind of man or the material world is legitimate, so long as it can be drawn. Or one may use geometrical forms, related to the shape of the flag or not, as the main design. Many yachtsmen employ their initials as part of their private signal, twisting or altering them if necessary to fit the flag. It is, by the way, considered rather bad taste to write out words on a flag, but the prohibition is a lot less strong than it once was.

The first step for a flag designer is picking a theme, a general illustrative subject; at this point, a lot of people go off the rails, and a good maxim to bear in mind is, *If in doubt, leave it out.*

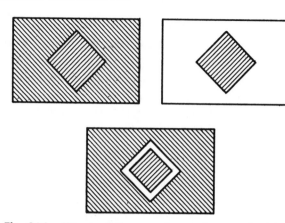

Fig. 804 "Tinctures" are the colors red, blue, orange, green, purple, and black. "Metals" are yellow (gold) and white (silver). Never use two tinctures or two metals next to each other (left). Use a tincture with a metal, or vice versa (right). If you must use two tinctures, separate them with a metal.

Often, in trying to design a flag, you won't even have a wisp of an idea for a theme. There are a number of natural categories for flag themes that provide good source material for a designer to work from. Here are a few:

First is history, where your emblem harks back to a famous person, place, or event connected to your subject. For private signals, family emblems, crests, or coats of arms make good starting points, but it's important to stick to just one element—the major design on the shield, *or* the crest above it, *or* a badge derived from it, but not all of them at once. If you want to see why, take a look at the state flag of New York or Connecticut; neither of them is legible at any distance, even in the large sizes flown from official flagstaffs; there's just too much detail.

In most parts of the country there are genealogical and historical societies that can offer assistance. The library is also a good place to begin looking, starting with the section on your area's history.

AMENITIES

Or consider occupational symbols, ones that refer to your business or profession, as the basis for your flag design. Everyone's familiar with the traditional devices—the doctor's caduceus, the teacher's lamp of learning, for instance—and the tools of modern trades, if they can be simplified for illustration, are just as good. You don't even have to use a gadget that's actually employed in your business: an advertising man might well choose a trumpet for the device on his flag.

Which brings us more or less deviously to rebuses, or visual puns. In earlier times, plays on words and names were taken as a matter of course, and every educated man prided himself on being able to rip off an appropriate pun on occasion. If you twist them a bit, most personal names today can be made to yield a meaningful word or phrase, though it may not be an English one, or suitable for reproduction. One small caution: the funniest, most apropos joke ever embodied in an owner's flag can swiftly become a weary drag when you have to explain it over and over.

A little earlier, I mentioned that many boat owners draw on the alphabet as a source for flag themes. Because of the problems attendant on double-thick flags, you're probably well advised to steer clear of initials on flags unless your name begins with one of the following, which read correctly on obverse and reverse: A, H, I, M, O, T, U, V, W, X, and Y.

As it must to all institutions, progress has come to flag making. No longer is the only material for outdoor flags heavy cotton bunting—thick, but subject to wear and fading. In addition, the range of available colors has increased, and the shades are brighter than ever. Cotton, of course, is still widely used where cost is an important factor and for flags that are only occasionally exposed to severe weather.

Wool, renowned for bright colors, isn't suitable alone for outdoor flags, but the flagmaking firm of Annin has created a trademarked blend named Nylanin, which is one part wool and three parts nylon, for a good compromise of strength, brightness, and cost.

Flags of 100% nylon are certainly the most common ones in use today. They're bright, durable, and lightweight, and while they cost more than those made from other fabrics, nylon flags make up the difference in durability.

The cost of any flag is directly proportional to four considerations: fabric, size, quantity ordered, and simplicity of design. In the cases of private signals and club burgees, where quantity is usually small, the fourth factor noted above is even more important: a complex flag design and/or one that requires a double-thick flag, can cost twice as much as a simple layout that reads correctly on one side and backward on the reverse.

The appropriate size of flag or pennant depends, of course, on the size of the boat flying it. A generally agreed-upon rule of thumb says that the ensign—U.S., yacht, or U.S.P.S.—when flown at the stern, should be one inch on the fly for each foot of the boat's length. All other flags (club, owner's, Coast Guard Auxiliary, officer's, U.S.P.S.), when flown at the yardarm, should be ⅝″ on the fly for each foot of a powerboat's overall length and ½″ on the fly for each foot of a sailboat's vertical clearance afloat.

Since flags are made in standard sizes, the ratio between banner and boat will often be approximate; price aside, it is usually more satisfactory from a visual standard to hoist flags slightly larger than the ordinary, and I think only the smallest boat would want a pennant less than 12″x18″.

The stern staff from which the national ensign or yacht ensign is flown should be of adequate length. While there is no regulation covering this, the recommended length is three times that of the ensign's hoist. When there's no breeze, the flag will not dangle below the bottom of the staff.

PHOTOGRAPHY AFLOAT

It's easy to take good pictures of boats and boating—*good* pictures, not the blurred, improperly-exposed and composed snapshots or slides that are seen so often. Here are a few tips that will put you on the right track. The photography magazines and your camera dealer can help fill in the details.

Camera

An inexpensive Instamatic type camera cannot produce pictures that are as sharp as those shot with expensive equipment. But the expensive camera *can* produce results that are worse than those from the Instamatic.

Basic to the inexpensive cameras are fixed-focus lenses and slow, single-speed shutters. If the scene is too bright for the film being used, the picture will be over-exposed; if there's not enough light, it will be underexposed. Background detail will be just as sharp as foreground detail.

An increase in camera price generally indicates an increase in the quality of the lens, in addition to other details. The better the lens, the sharper the detail in the finished print or slide. Also, the better lenses can be focused to provide maximum sharpness at a distance from the camera ranging from a few feet to infinity. With the proper lens aperture and shutter adjustments, a picture will have a foreground subject clear and sharp, with a softly blurred background, or sharp detail in the distance framed by a blurred foreground. This is actually the way your eyes operate. It's also possible to have *everything* sharp under normal conditions.

Other advantages of more expensive cameras are the ability to adjust lens apertures to compensate for the amount of existing light, and a range of shutter speeds that permits "stopping" fast action or taking pictures in fairly dim light without a flash attachment.

Another bonus of the more expensive cameras is the availability of interchangeable or add-on lenses for wide-angle and telephoto pictures. The latter is particularly useful in getting close-up detail in subject matter that would be lost with an ordinary lens.

With inexpensive cameras, you don't have to worry about any adjustments; with expensive equipment, you'll get better pictures —if your adjustments are correct.

Film

There are three basic film choices: black and white, color for slides, and color for prints. Most Instamatic type cameras use a medium-speed black and white film, such as Kodak's Verichrome Pan. Outdoors, it provides good results in the hours of maximum daylight. Faster films are available for the more expensive roll film cameras to permit taking pictures at speeds up to 1/1000th of a second in normal light, or at slow shutter speeds in dim light.

Choice of color film depends on whether color prints or slides are wanted. For color prints, a film such as Kodacolor should be used; for slides, use Kodachrome or Ektachrome, or their equivalent. Some provide richer colors, others a better grain structure. It's worth experimenting to see which meets your needs. It's also possible to make black and white prints from Kodacolor negatives, or black and white conversions from color slides. These do not have the quality of prints made from regular black and white film negatives.

Filters

A medium yellow filter is recommended for best results when using black and white film outdoors. It brings out detail in clouds, darkens the water, and adds sparkle to highlights. Orange and red filters also can be used for more dramatic effects; a deep red filter can transform a bright afternoon into a moonlight scene in the final print.

For color film, an almost clear "skylight" filter can be used, or a polaroid filter, to cut haze and to emphasize cloud detail.

When using a filter, it will be necessary to increase exposure by the applicable "filter factor." As the filter reduces the amount of light hitting the film, you must use a slower shutter speed, or a larger aperture to compensate. A skylight filter has no filter factor, and normal exposures are used.

Composition

A basic premise of the professional photographer is that film is cheap. Take a lot of pictures, and the law of averages will turn

AMENITIES

up some that are good, some that are fair, and some that are poor. Still, try to plan your pictures. Decide what is to be the point of interest. See what elements of foreground or background best emphasize it. Try to avoid conflicts of subject and background such as a mast that appears to grow out of the First Mate's head.

Scenic shots are plentiful, but make sure you can identify them later. Including an element of crew activity will personalize these. When taking pictures of people or activities on the water, try to move around your subject as much as possible, shooting from various angles and distances. Don't worry about the direction from which the light is coming; except for early morning or late evening, there's no problem. Do try to keep faces in an even light.

Shooting

If you are on a boat, you are in motion unless the boat is hard aground in a flat calm. If you are ashore, and taking a picture of a boat in action, it is in motion. With an inexpensive fixed-focus single-speed shutter camera, motion means blurs. Always brace the camera against your face or body with both hands, and hold it as steady as possible while you apply even pressure to the shutter release. Don't trip the shutter with a hard snap; you'll jar the camera.

When taking a picture of a boat that's moving at a good clip, "pan" with the action: move the camera to keep the boat centered. It will come out sharp and clear in the picture, and the background will be slightly blurred. Or get in a position so the boat is coming directly toward you or heading directly away. This minimizes apparent motion.

With cameras that have adjustable shutter speeds and lens apertures, you may use a speed that freezes action—whether your motion or that of your subject. Or you can use a slow speed and pan as above to give the feeling of motion to the finished picture. Use of a light meter is recommended. Be sure it is set for the speed of the film you are using, and that you read the light on your subject, not its background.

Processing

You can take your exposed black and white film to your drug-store, and have it sent to a central mass-production laboratory that will grind it out quickly and cheaply. That's the best that can be said about this method. No attempt is made to compensate for differences in type of film or exposure. Even the best exposures, the best compositions, lose a lot.

If possible, send your film to one of the custom processors listed in the yellow pages of your phone book. Each roll of film gets individual attention, and you can order contact sheets. A whole roll of film can be printed on one 8"x10" contact sheet. Check the contact sheets to indicate which negatives you want printed, and order the prints in any of the standard sizes available—up to 11" x 14" or larger. The larger the print, the higher its cost, but you'll find that you won't want prints of everything you shoot. With the drugstore, you don't have a choice. Every negative that has an image is printed.

CUSTOMS AND ETIQUETTE

YACHTING ETIQUETTE

Etiquette in yachting takes many forms, but all are essentially the act of showing consideration and courtesy to others. The range of correct etiquette extends from simple everyday actions to formal daily routines and official ceremonies.

Daily Color Ceremonies

If a boatman is at a yacht club, or a military or naval base, where formal morning and evening color ceremonies are held, he should follow the actions of local personnel who are not in formation. If he is outdoors when the flag is raised or lowered, and he is wearing a uniform or visored cap, he should face the flag and give a hand salute, holding it until the ceremony is completed. If he is wearing a civilian hat, this should be removed and held over the left breast. If no headgear is worn, the right hand should be placed over the left breast. This is the "breast salute." Women not in uniform stand at attention and give the breast salute. Automobiles are stopped and personnel remain inside.

The above rules do not, of course, apply if the boatman is engaged in hoisting or lowering his own colors. He should complete his actions and then, if the official ceremonies have not ended, he should stand at attention, and salute if appropriate.

On official occasions, the same salutes as above are given for the playing of the Star Spangled Banner or national anthem of another country.

Boarding another Boat

The etiquette to be observed when coming on board another person's boat is derived from that for boarding a naval vessel. Salutes are seldom exchanged, but a simple request for permission to come aboard is always in good taste. An occasion for saluting might be if the individual boarding were wearing a uniform cap and the craft were that of the commodore of the yacht club or the commander of a Power Squadron.

When leaving another's boat, the naval form of requesting permission is not used. A simple statement of thanks for the hospitality or best wishes for a pleasant cruise is sufficient.

SALUTES BETWEEN VESSELS

In formal ceremonies such as a rendezvous of a yacht club or Power Squadron, the fleet of boats present may pass in review before the flagship of the commodore or USPS commander. In such cases, each craft will salute as it passes. In other isolated instances, joining a club cruise or passing a ship with a high public official embarked, salutes may be exchanged between vessels.

Dipping the Ensign in Salute

Federal law prohibits dipping the Flag of the United States (the 50-star flag) to any person or thing, and only government vessels are permitted to dip the national ensign in reply to a dip.

The law does, however, permit organizational or institutional flags to be dipped. Thus the U.S. Power Squadrons Ensign, when flown from stern or gaff, may be dipped to salute another craft, or dipped in reply to a dip.

The status of the Yacht Ensign (13 stars in a circle around an anchor on a blue field) is not spelled out clearly, but since the law specifically covers only the Flag of the United States, the assumption has been made that the Yacht Ensign may be dipped.

In a fleet review of a unit of the Power Squadrons, the USPS Ensign should be flown from the stern staff or gaff if a suitable size flag is available. In this way, the flag dipped would be that of the organization holding the review.

All vessels in any review, flying either the USPS or Yacht Ensign at the stern or gaff, should dip that flag when their bow comes abreast of the stern of the flagship and return it to full height when their stern clears the bow of the flagship.

On this occasion, the Flag of the United States should *not* be flown, but if it is, *do not dip it* and use only the hand salute described below. Do not dip any flag other than the flag being flown at the stern staff or the gaff (including the equivalent position on a Marconi sail).

Hand Saluting

When a vessel is officially reviewing a parade of other vessels, the senior officer present stands on the deck of the reviewing ship with his staff in formation behind him. Only he gives the hand salute in return to salutes rendered him.

On a boat passing in review, if the skipper has his crew and

AMENITIES

guests in formation behind him, only he gives the hand salute. If the crew and guests are in uniform and standing at attention at the rail facing the reviewing boat as they pass, they all give the hand salute. The criterion is whether or not the other persons aboard are in formation. If in formation, only the skipper salutes; but if not in formation, all salute.

For both situations, the hand salute is given as the flag is dipped and is held until it is raised again.

Gun Salutes

Guns should not be used in salutes between yachts unless ordered by a national authority or by the senior officer present.

YACHT ROUTINES

The following regulations, particularly applicable to a consideration of yachting etiquette, are taken from that portion of the New York Yacht Club code entitled *Yacht Routine*. These deal with salutes, boats (meaning tenders and dinghies), and general courtesies. Other sections, not given here, relate primarily to the display of flags, signaling, and lights.

The routines of other yacht clubs may be considerably less formal and detailed than that which follows, but whatever routines are used they are likely to have been derived from the procedures of the New York Yacht Club.

Salutes

All salutes shall be made by dipping the ensign once, lowering the ensign to the dip and hoisting it when the salute is returned. All salutes shall be returned.

Whistles shall never be used in saluting.

Guns may be used to call attention to signals, but their use otherwise shall be avoided as much as possible.

Vessels of the United States and foreign navies shall be saluted.

When a flag officer of the Club comes to anchor, he shall be saluted by all yachts present, except where there is a senior flag officer present.

When a yacht comes to anchor where a flag officer is present, such officer shall be saluted. A junior flag officer anchoring in the presence of a senior shall salute.

Yachts passing shall salute, the junior saluting first.

All salutes shall be answered in kind.

A yacht acting as Race Committee boat should neither salute nor be saluted while displaying the Committee flag.

Boats

Upon entering and leaving boats, deference is shown seniors by juniors entering first and leaving last.

When in boats, flag officers display their flags, captains (owners) their private signals, and members (non-owners) the club burgee. When on duty, the fleet captain and race committee display their distinctive flags. The flag of the senior officer embarked takes precedence. A flag officer embarked in a boat not displaying his distinctive flag should be considered as present in an unofficial capacity.

When two boats are approaching the same gangway or landing stage, flag officers shall have the right of way in order of seniority.

Whenever possible, boat booms shall be rigged in at night. Otherwise, a white light shall be shown at the end. All boats made fast to the stern of a yacht at anchor shall show a white light at night.

Courtesies

When a flag officer makes an official visit, his flag, if senior to that of the yacht visited, shall be displayed in place of the burgee while he is on board.

A yacht may display the personal flag of a national, state, or local official when such individual is on board, or the national ensign of a distinguished foreign visitor. This flag should be dis-

AMENITIES

played in place of the private signal or officer's flag for the President of the United States, and in place of the burgee for all other officials and visitors.

On Independence Day, and when ordered on other occasions, a yacht shall, when at anchor and the weather permits, *dress ship* from morning to evening colors.

After joining the Squadron during the Annual Cruise, a yacht shall request permission before leaving.

CRUISING

When cruising away from home waters, the wise skipper keeps a sharp eye out for local customs. It is a mark of courtesy to conform to local procedures and practices.

While visiting at a yacht club of which you are not a member, observe the actions and routines of the local owner-members, and particularly the club officers. This is especially important with respect to evening colors. Not all clubs strictly calculate the daily time of sunset, and some may be earlier than you would normally expect.

If you will be off your boat at the time of evening colors—in the clubhouse for dinner, for example—be sure to take down your flags before you leave your craft.

Be a Good Neighbor

Consideration of the other skipper is an important element of yachting etiquette. Don't anchor too close to another boat so as to give cause for concern for the safety of both craft; consider the state of the tide and the effect of its range on the radius about which you will swing. Use a guest mooring only with permission; tie up to a fuel pier only briefly.

Fig. 805 "Dressing ship" is done only on special occasions, and the proper procedures must be followed to be correct. Although the pattern is in effect random, flags should be in sequence shown.

In the evening hours at an anchorage, don't disturb your neighbors on other boats. Sound travels exceptionally well across water and many cruising boatmen turn in early for dawn departures. Keep voices down and play radios only at low levels. If you should be one of the early departees, leave with an absolute minimum of noise.

Be a good neighbor in other ways, too. Don't throw trash and garbage overboard. Secure flapping halyards; they can be a most annoying source of noise for some distance. When coming into or leaving an anchorage area, do so at a dead slow speed to keep your wake and wash at an absolute minimum.

Passing other Boats

A faster boat overtaking and passing a slower one in a narrow channel should slow down *sufficiently* to cause no damage or discomfort. Often overlooked is the fact that it may be necessary for the *slower* boat itself to reduce speed. If that boat is making, say, 8 knots, the faster boat can only slow down to about 10 knots in order to have enough speed differential left to get past. At this speed, the passing boat may unavoidably make a wake that is uncomfortable to the other craft. In such cases, the overtaken boat should slow to 4 or 5 knots to allow herself to be passed at 6 or 7 knots with little wake.

If adequate depths of water extend outward on one or both sides of the course, it is the courteous thing for the passing boat to swing well out to a safe side to minimize the discomfort of the overtaken boat.

Proper etiquette calls for power boats to pass sailing craft astern or well to leeward.

GUESTS ABOARD

If you are invited to go cruising for a day, a weekend, or a more extended period, there are many things to be considered— clothes, promptness, gifts, aids, noise, smoking, privacy, and time.

Take a minimum of *clothes,* packed in collapsible containers, or at least in suitcases that will nest inside each other when empty—storage space is severely limited aboard boats. Bring one outfit of "city clothes" for use at those places ashore requiring such dress. Bring two bathing suits if you plan to do much swimming—at times, things dry slowly around a boat.

For the *stowage of clothing* you bring aboard, the skipper may assign a special locker which he has cleared for your convenience. Don't scatter gear and clothing all over the boat. Use the locker provided, keep it orderly, and thus help the skipper keep things shipshape.

When a *sailing time* is given, be there ahead of time. The skipper generally chooses a time with a purpose in mind—the tides and currents, normal weather patterns, the length of the planned run, etc.

Meal times are set for the convenience of the galley hand. It is inconsiderate for a tardy guest to delay meals. In any event, it is bad manners to be late for a meal.

Rising and *bedtimes* are a matter of convenience to everyone aboard because of the generally limited washing and toilet facilities. Get up promptly when the skipper or paid hands are heard moving about. Use the head as expeditiously as possible, make up your bunk, stow any loose gear about the cabin, and appear on deck. When the skipper suggests that it is time to retire for the evening, take the hint and bed down.

Noise on a boat seems to amplify, so walk and speak softly and your shipmates will be glad you're aboard.

Smoking is stopped, of course, when gasoline is to be taken aboard, but care is the order of the day even when smoking is permissible. A carelessly flicked cigarette ash or butt has started many a fire in a chair, awning, or compartment. Cigars leave a particularly unpleasant after-odor and should be enjoyed only in the open air.

Many small particles—pipe tobacco and ashes, peanut shells, bits of potato chips, crumbs, etc.—have a way of getting into

cracks, crevices and corners, and there defying the ordinary cleaning facilities found on a boat. Use care with all of these things.

Privacy becomes valuable on a protracted cruise. Part of every
day should be set aside for getting away from everyone else
aboard. Your cruisemates will be more glad of your company if
it is not constant.

Should occasions arise where you board the boat from a *dinghy,*
or have an opportunity to use the skipper's dinghy (with his permission, of course) use care in coming alongside. Unship oarlocks which could scar the boat's planking, and stow oars in the
boat; never leave them in the oarlocks.

Gifts are certainly not expected, but are always acceptable. Be
sure, however, that they are appropriate for boating—if in doubt,
make it liquid and consumable. When invited on board for a day
or a week, ask what you can bring. If the owner wants to provide
all of the food and drink, the guest might take the cruising party
ashore for a good dinner at the first port of call. Buying part of
the fuel is looked upon as a partial charter by some government
agencies, but bringing food or liquid refreshment is not so regarded.

Assistance on board a boat can be useful, or it can do more
harm than good. If you don't know what to do, sit down out of
the way and be quiet. Always keep out of the line of vision of the
helmsman and be particularly quiet and unobtrusive when the
craft is being docked or undocked.

If being on board is not a new experience, or you wish to learn
to be more useful, you may ask what you can do to help. Ask,
however, when things are calm and uneventful; don't ask in the
midst of getting under way or coming alongside a pier.

Above all, if you are assigned to do something, do exactly that.
If you think that the instructions were wrong, say so, but don't
go off on your own when the skipper thinks that you are doing
what he asked.

9.
INFORMATION SOURCES

ORGANIZATIONS

One way to get more pleasure from your boating is to join with others with similar boating interests. And if you need special information, or want your voice as a boatman heard in legislative councils, there are organizations that can provide the help you need.

Listed here are major national organizations, and a brief statement of purpose of each. For complete details, write to the group's headquarters.

General Organizations

United States Coast Guard Auxiliary, Washington, D.C. 20591. This civilian arm of the Coast Guard provides free boating classes, and courtesy safety examinations of pleasure boats. It also assists in Search & Rescue operations under Coast Guard orders.

United States Power Squadrons, P.O. Box 30423, Raleigh, NC 27612. This is a fraternal organization of boatmen that provides free basic boating classes to the public, as well as advanced courses in seamanship and navigation practices to its members,

INFORMATION

along with courses covering such topics as weather, engine maintenance, and marine electronics.

American National Red Cross, 17th and D Streets, N.W., Washington, DC 20006. Safe boating classes offered at local Red Cross chapters are: Basic Rowing, Basic Canoeing, Basic Sailing, and Basic Outboard Boating. Swimming and water safety courses are also offered, ranging from Beginner to Advanced, as well as a variety of first aid courses.

Boat Owners Association of the United States (BOAT/U.S.), 5261 Port Royal Rd., Springfield, VA 22151. Richard Schwartz, Executive Director. A full-service representational membership organization of recreational boatmen, offering group-rate marine insurance, a boating equipment savings program, charts, books, cruise planning, consumer complaint bureau, theft protection, correspondence courses, and other services for members, and is active in legislative and conservation programs related to boating and waterways.

Boat Owners Council of America, 534 N. Broadway, Milwaukee, WS 53202. Provides members with cruising information, *Water-Sport* magazine, special boat owners insurance rates, and other services, and—through its affiliation with the Boating Industry Association,—represents boating needs before legislative bodies.

Boy Scouts of America, U.S. Highway No. 1, N. Brunswick, NJ 08902, Wm. J. Lidderdale, director, Health and Safety Service. This organization provides boating safety training for boys through its more than 600 camps and the National Sea Exploring Program.

National Boating Federation, 275 Madison Ave., New York, NY 10016, Barry Golumb, Secretary. A federation of state and regional boating organizations (of yacht clubs) keeps members informed of news on boating legislation, etc., and provides a responsible voice of the boating public nationally.

Outboard Boating Club of America, 401 N. Michigan Ave., Chicago, Ill. 60601. This branch of the Boating Industry Association keeps local boat clubs informed of boating legislative developments at local, state, and national levels.

Special Interest Organizations

American Canoe Association, 32 Avenue of the Americas, Rm. 860, New York, N.Y. 10013. Contact L. M. Schindel.

American Water Ski Association, Seventh St. & Avenue G., S.W., Winter Haven, Fla. 33880. William D. Clifford, Executive manager. Sponsors and sanctions water ski shows and competitions, promotes safe ski practices, and publishes magazine for its members.

Antique Boat & Yacht Club, % Rose York Assoc., 1040 Avenue of the Americas, New York, N.Y. 10018. Alan S. York, Commodore. An association of owners of old boats.

Houseboat Association of America, P.O. Box 7285, Asheville, N.C. 28807. Organization of houseboat owners and enthusiasts furnishes chart service, houseboat plans, newsletter, special buying service, and special subscription rate to *Family Houseboating* magazine.

Turtles. Box 66, New York Yacht Club, 37 W. 44th St., New York, N.Y. 10036. Informal international fraternal organization for the recreational boating trade and public.

Racing Organizations, Power

American Power Boat Association, 22811 Greater Mack Ave., Detroit, MI 48080. This organization sanctions all major power boat races in the United States.

Union Internationale Motonautique, Centre International Rogier, Passage International, 29, Residence "HERA" 8me etage, B-1000, Brussels, Belgium. The Union of International Motorboating sanc-

tions all major international power boat races. It is represented
in the U.S.A. by the American Power Boat Association.

Racing Organizations, Sail

The Corinthians, P.O. Box 3224, Grand Central Station, New
York, NY 10017. Alexander H. Danzberger, Secretary. An organization of amateur yachtsmen which helps to provide crews.

Cruising Club of America, % Pratt, Read & Co., Ivoryton, CT
06442. Peter H. Comstock, secretary. This club sponsors selected
races.

International Yacht Racing Union, 60 Knightsbridge, Westminster,
London, S.W. 1X 7JX England. Responsible for international sail
racing, including technical arrangemets for Olympics. Committee
formed to work in legislative areas affecting boating.

Midget Ocean Racing Club, Box 44, City Island, NY 10464 Fred
Hamburg, Secretary. This group establishes racing rules and
sponsors races for small cruising/racing sailboats under 30′ overall
length.

U.S. Yacht Racing Union, 1133 Avenue of the Americas, New
York, NY 10036. Henry H. Anderson, Jr., executive director. An
association of individual members and yacht clubs which encourages and promotes the racing of sailing yachts, and the unifi-
cation of rules, in an advisory capacity. Thirteen major championship races are sailed under its auspices each year.

Slocum Society, Box 1774, Hilo, HI 96720. Neal T. Walker, Secretary. An organization established in 1955 to record, encourage
and support long-distance passages in small boats. Publishes
quarterly journal, "The Spray." Dues $10 per year.

Storm Trysail Club, Inc., % Ivy Hill Litho, 18 E. 48th St., New
York, N.Y. 10017. Victor A. Romagna, Secretary. A racing association which sponsors major cruising sailboat races on the east coast
all throughout the boating season.

United States International Sailing Association, 1133 Avenue of the Americas, New York, NY 10036. Henry H. Anderson, Jr., executive secretary. Membership fees help to provide boats, training for participants, for Olympic and other international sailing events.

United States Olympic Yachting Committee, 527 Lexington Ave., New York, N.Y. 10017. Paul H. Smart, chairman. This organization helps to raise funds to facilitate U.S. participation in Olympic yachting competition.

Government Agencies

National Oceanic and Atmospheric Administration (NOAA), Rockville, Md. 20852. This branch of the Department of Commerce includes the National Weather Service and the National Ocean Survey, among other services. It publishes nautical charts, and a wealth of other material useful in piloting and seamanship. See the listings of available publications and chart sources in this section.

Corps of Engineers, Department of the Army, Washington, D.C. 20314. This branch of the U.S. Army is charged with the maintenance of all Federal navigation projects within the United States.

National Association of State Boating Law Administrators, Embassy Square, 2000 N Street N.W., Washington, DC 20036. Morris Rosenbloom, executive secretary. Organization is instrumental in development of uniform boating legislation at the state level.

United States Coast Guard, Coast Guard Headquarters, 400 7th St., N.W., Washington, D.C. 20591. This is the government organization charged with responsibility for pleasure boating safety and regulation on a national level.

Industry Associations

American Boat and Yacht Council, Inc., 15 East 26th St., New York, NY 10010. G. James Lippmann, executive director. Technical society develops safety standards and recommended practices for

INFORMATION

design, construction, equipment, and maintenance of all types of recreational boats.

American Sailing Council, % National Association of Engine & Boat Manufacturers, P.O. Box 5555 Grand Central Station, New York, NY 10017. This committee of NAEBM is devoted to the promotion of sailing, and provides free movies, a guide to the organization of sailing clubs, general sailing information, and an illustrated catalog of class sailboats.

Boating Industry Association, 401 N. Michigan Ave., Chicago, IL 60611. Organization is active in all phases of the industry, including safety certification of small craft, legislative reporting, market research and sponsorship of national clubs for boat owners (see Outboard Boating Club listings).

Hiswa, Keizersgracht 412, Amsterdam, Holland. Hiswa is the name of the federation of Dutch Marine Industry, the organization that sponsors the Amsterdam Boat Show, and maintains an information service that provides prospective boat owners all over the world with details about the boats and other products of the marine industry produced in the Netherlands.

International Council of Marine Industries Associations, 31 Great Queen St., London, W.C. 2, England. Telephone: 01-405-7481. Thomas Webb, secretary general. Purpose of this group is to promote recreational boating on an international basis.

National Association of Engine and Boat Manufacturers, P.O. Box 5555 Grand Central Station, New York, NY 10017. Frank Scalpone, administrative vice president. Trade association has programs covering marinas, industry service, government relations, boating statistics, domestic and international marketing information, legislation and the distribution of general safety and boat ownership information. It sponsors the National Boat Show in New York as well as an annual Conference related to the boating industry. It provides scholarships, a trophy program for boat races, and maintains a boating films service.

National Safe Boating Association, % National Waterways Conference, Washington, DC. Group includes the NAEBM, American Waterways Operators, Inc., and various other commercial and recreational organizations. Purpose is to foster cooperation between pleasure boatmen and commercial boat operators using the nation's waterways.

National Safe Boating Committee, Office of Boating Safety, U.S. Coast Guard, Washington, D.C. 20590. Mr. Robert F. Burnside, chairman. Committee is made up of representatives of organizations who coordinate the presidentially-proclaimed National Safe Boating Week promotion.

Society of Small Craft Designers, William R. Mehaffey, 1174 S. Scoville Ave., Oak Park, Ill. 60304. Organization of naval architects exchanges technical information on materials and methods for boat construction.

Underwriters Laboratories, Marine Department, 2602 Tampa East Boulevard, Tampa, Fla. 33619. This UL department was formerly the Yacht Safety Bureau. The facility evaluates products or systems intended for marine use with respect to safety. For products found to comply with the Laboratories' requirements, manufacturers are authorized to use an appropriate listing mark on or in conjunction with such products.

PUBLICATIONS

Government Publications

Notice to Mariners. Prepared jointly by the Defense mapping Agency Hydrographic Center, National Ocean Survey, and U.S. Coast Guard, and published weekly by the Defense Mapping Agency Hydrographic Center, Washington, D.C. 20390, to advise mariners of important matters affecting navigational safety, including new hydrographic discoveries, changes in channels and navigation aids, etc. Besides keeping mariners informed generally, the *Notice to Mariners* also provides information specifically useful for updating the latest editions of nautical charts and publications produced by the Defense Mapping Agency Hydrographic Center, the National Ocean Survey and the U.S. Coast Guard. Marine information pertaining to the Intracoastal Waterway and other waterways and harbors within the United States that are not normally utilized by oceangoing vessels is not promulgated *in the weekly Notice to Mariners.*

Local Notice to Mariners. Issued as required, usually weekly, these contain marine information within the boundaries of the various Coast Guard Districts and may be obtained, free of charge, by making application to the appropriate District Commander (see listing of U.S. Coast Guard District offices in this section).

Coast Pilots. Books covering coastal waters and the Atlantic, Gulf, and Pacific coastal waters are published by the National Ocean Survey, Nationl Oceanic and Atmospheric Administration, Rockville, MD 20852. Book covering the Great Lakes is published as the *Great Lakes Pilot* by the National Ocean Survey, Lake Survey Center, 630 Federal Bldg., Detroit, MI 48226. These volumes supplement information carried on charts with detailed descriptions of routes, courses, distances, depths, harbors, sources of supplies, currents, weather, lists of yacht clubs and repair facilities.

Light Lists. Published by the U. S. Coast Guard, these are available from the Superintendent of Documents, Government Printing Office, Washington, D.C. 20402, or any of the Coast Guard Sales agencies listed semi-annually in the *Notice to Mariners* (see listing in this section). They describe lighted aids to navigation, radio beacons, fog signals, unlighted buoys, and daymarks. Vol. 1 covers Atlantic Coast from St. Croix Rover, Me., to Little River, S.C.; Vol. 2, Atlantic and Gulf Coasts from Little River, S.C., to Rio Grande River, Tex.; Vol. 3, Pacific Coast and Islands; Vol. 4, Great Lakes; Vol. 5, Mississippi River.

Tide Tables, Current Tables, Tidal Current Charts, and Tidal Current Diagrams. Available from the National Ocean Survey, National Oceanic and Atmospheric Administration, Rockville, MD 20852, from their distribution offices, and any of their sales agents listed semi-annually in the *Notice to Mariners.*

Rules of the Road. CG-169 is for "certain inland waters of the Atlantic and Pacific coasts and of the coast of the Gulf of Mexico; CG-172 is for the Great Lakes and their connecting and tributary waters and the St. Mary's River; and CG-184 is the Western Rivers and the Red River of the North. Published by the U.S. Coast Guard, they are available from Marine Inspection Offices in principal ports, or from the Commandant, U.S. Coast Guard, Washington, D.C. 20591.

Recreational Boating Guide. CG-340. Information on boat numbering, legal minimum requirements for equipment, recommended equipment, responsibilities when afloat, emergency procedures, and U.S. Coast Guard Auxiliary services are all covered. Booklet also contains text of Federal Boating Act of 1958 and Motorboat Act of 1940, sample of application for number form, boating accident report, and radio distress information sheet. Available from Superintendent of Documents, Government Printing Office, Washington, D.C., 20402.

Federal Requirements for Recreational Boaters. CG-290. Digest of boating laws and regulations published by the U.S. Coast Guard. Covers numbering, boating accidents, sales to aliens, law enforcement, and documentation, plus equipment requirements, listing of Coast Guard approved equipment, and. safety suggestions. Available from local Coast Guard offices

Aids to Marine Navigation of the United States. CG-193. Illustrated booklet gives basic principles underlying marking of coasts with lighthouses, fog signals, radio beacons, loran, and buoys. It also shows how their physical characteristics serve the mariner. Available from the United States Coast Guard, Washington, D.C. 20591.

INFORMATION

Rules and Regulations for Uninspected Vessels. CG-258. Coast Guard pamphlet gives requirements for all vessels not subject to inspection, including those subject to the Motorboat Act of 1940. Available from U.S. Coast Guard District offices, listed in this section.

Rules and Regulations for Numbering Undocumented Vessels. CG-267. Available from the U.S. Coast Guard District offices, or from the Commandant (CHS), U.S. Coast Guard, Washington, DC 20591. It is included in the *Federal Register for Reporting Casualties and Accidents, Vol. 37, No. 196, Part 2.*

Intracoastal Waterway Booklets. Comprehensive descriptions of the Intracoastal Waterway, with data on navigation charts, distances, etc. In two sections: (1) Atlantic Section, Boston to Key West, and (2) Gulf Section, Key West to Brownsville, Tex. Prepared by the U.S. Army Corps of Engineers, and sold by the Superintendent of Documents, Government Printing Office, Washington, DC 20402.*

Intracoastal Waterway Bulletins. Frequent bulletins are published by the U.S. Army Corps of Engineers, and are available from District offices at: 803 Front St., Norfolk, Va. 23510; P.O. Box 1890, Wilmington, N.C. 28401; P.O. Box 919, Charleston, S.C. 29402; P.O. Box 889, Savannah, Ga. 31402; P.O. Box 4970, Jacksonville, Fla. 32201; P.O. Box 2288, Mobile, Ala. 36601; and P.O. Box 1229, Galveston, Tex. 77551.

Marine Weather Services Charts (formerly ESSA *Weather Bureau Coastal Warning Facility Charts*), Government Printing Office, Washington, D.C. 20402. Fifteen charts covering the coastal waters of the U. S. Mainland, the Great Lakes, Alaska, Hawaii, and Puerto Rico contain radio weather schedules, warning display station locations, Weather bureau information telephone numbers, etc. (15 cents each).*

Weather Forecasting. National Weather Service, National Oceanic and Atmospheric Administration, Rockville, Md. 20852. Illustrated booklet gives generally accepted facts and theories of meterology and some of the principles of weather forecasting. Available from Superintendent of Documents, Government Printing Office, Washington, DC 20402.*

The Hurricane. National Weather Service, National Oceanic and Atmospheric Administration. 22-page booklet details growth and controlling factors of tropical storms. Superintendent of Documents, Government Printing Office, Washington, DC 20402.*

The American Nautical Almanac. United States Naval Observatory. Compact publication contains information essential to solution of navigational position problems. Contains a star chart which shows position of stars used in navigation, along with instructions for its use. Star chart may be purchased separately. Superintendent of Documents, U.S. Government Printing Office, Washington, DC 20402. $6.20 each.

The Ship's Medicine Chest and First Aid at Sea. Miscellaneous Publication No. 9, United States Health Service. Illustrated, 498-page book has special sections on emergency treatment, and first aid by radio. Superintendent of Documents, Government Printing Office, Washington, DC 20402.*

Cruising Guides

Cruising charts, guides, and booklets. Some of the large oil companies provide free cruising services for boatmen, and will send you cruising charts from which an itinerary can be planned; some have guides for safe boating and boat maintenance. Write to: Gulf Tourguide Bureau, Box 8056, Philadelphia, Penna. 19101; Texaco Waterways Service, 135 E. 42nd St., New York, N.Y. 10017. Esso, Phillips, and other oil firms offer cruising guides.

Cruising Guide to the New England Coast. Book by Fessenden Blanchard describes harbors, anchorages, and waterways of New England, plus the Hudson River, Long Island Sound, and the New Brunswick coast. Price, $10. Sailing Book Service, 34 Oak Ave., Tuckahoe, N.Y. 10707.

*The Superintendent of Documents may be out of stock, or the publication may be out of print. Perhaps you can refer to a copy at your local library.

INFORMATION

A Cruising Guide to the Chesapeake, by William T. Stone. Guide covers the area from Long Island Sound to Cape Henry. New marinas, changes in channels and harbors, new boat facilities, what to see and do; illustrations and charts included. $12.50, Dodd, Meade & Co.

Waterway Guide. Publication details marinas, boatyards, anchorages, restaurants, etc., and gives piloting hints for the east coast and the Intracoastal Waterway. Northern edition—New York to Cape Cod, Maine, Canada, and into the Great Lakes. Mid-Atlantic Edition—Lower New York Bay to the Georgia/Florida line. Southern Edition—Florida and the Keys, Gulf Coast to Brownsville, Texas. Price, $4.95 each edition; $5.75 by mail. Waterway Guide, P.O. Box 1486, Annapolis, MD 21401.

Boating Handbook for Maryland Waters. 26-page pamphlet gives basic rules and regulations for boats in Maryland, including Rules of the Road, Buoys, Speed Limit areas. Free. Maryland Department of Natural Resources, Natural Resources Bldg., Annapolis, Md. 21401.

Guide for Cruising Maryland Waters. Twenty full color charts with more than 200 courses and distances plotted. Price, $5 plus 20¢ Maryland sales tax. Maryland Department of Natural Resources, Natural Resources Bldg., Annapolis, MD 21401.

Maryland Tidewater Sportfishing Guide, Department of Natural Resources, Natural Tawes State Office Bldg., B-3, Annapolis, MD 21401.

Boating Atlas of Tidewater Virginia. An atlas of 53 full color charts covers ocean front, lower Chesapeake Bay, the James, York, Rappahannock, and Potomac Rivers. Included are buoyage systems, rules of the road, location of marine facilities, state and Coast Guard regulations, notes from the Coast Pilot, Tide Tables, safety suggestions, and a course protractor. Distributed by Paxton Co., 1111 Ingleside Rd., Norfolk, Va. 23502.

Yachtsman's Guide to the Great Lakes. Harbors, services, supplies on the Great Lakes, St. Lawrence, and the New York State Barge Canal. Price, $3.00, plus 25¢ for postage and handling. Seaport Publishing Co., 843 Delray Ave., S.E., Grand Rapids, MI 49506.

Yachtsman's Guide to the Bahamas. Cruising areas, pilotage, facilities, light list, tides, weather and other useful information is presented in book published by Tropic Isle Publishers, Inc., as an official publication of the Bahamas Ministry of Tourism. Send order to P.O. Box 340866, Coral Gables, FL 33134. Price is $4.95 plus $1.00 postage.

Yachtsman's Guide to the Virgin Islands. Cruising areas, pilotage, facilities, charting information, tides and weather are set forth in this guide published by Tropic Isle Publishers, Inc. Send order to P.O. Box 340866, Coral Gables, FL 33134. Price is $4.95 plus $1.00 postage.

Yachtsman's Guide to the Caribbean. Complete guide for cruising to or in the Caribbean, through the Bahamas to Trinidad, off South America. Lists fueling spots, repair services, safe anchorages, things to see and do on each island. Price, $6. Seaport Publishing Co., 843 Delray Ave. S. E., Grand Rapids, MI 49506. Add 25¢ for postage and handling.

Quimby's Harbor Guide (to the Mississippi River, Arkansas and Illinois Waterways). Guide covers the Upper and Lower Mississippi, Minneapolis to New Orleans; Arkansas from mouth to Catoosa, Okla.; the Illinois, mouth to Lake Michigan at Chicago. Book provides information on harbors, locks, dams, cruising problems, cities and towns. Price, $3.00 by third class mail; $3.20 first class mail. Mildred Quimby, Box 85, Prairie du Chien, WI 53821.

Yachtsman's Guide to the Caribbean. Complete guide for cruising to or in the Caribbean, through the Bahamas to Trinidad, off

South America. Lists fueling spots, repair services, safe anchorages, things to see and do on each island. Price, $6. Seaport Publishing Co., 843 Delray Ave. S.E., Grand Rapids, Mich. 49506.

Books

There are literally hundreds of sailing and boating books available, covering technical, practical, historical, romantic, and fictional aspects of boating. See pages 163-167. Three books, however, deserve special mention here:

Piloting, Seamanship and Small Boat Handling, by Charles F. Chapman. This is the "Bible of Boating," now in its 55th year of publication. The revised 52nd Edition has more than 650 pages that cover everything the serious boatman should know about his vessel and its operation. "Chapman's" is the major text and reference book used in U.S. Power Squadrons and U.S. Coast Guard Auxiliary classes. Price, standard edition, $11.95; Deluxe edition, $14.95. Motor Boating & Sailing Books, P.O. Box 2316, New York, NY 10019.

Basic Sailing, by M. B. George. Now in its fourteenth printing, this well-illustrated book provides authoritative lessons in the art of sailing. Price, $2.95. Motor Boating & Sailing Books, P.O. Box 2316, New York, N.Y. 10019.

Practical Sailing, by Tony Gibbs. Designed for self-teaching, class use, or brushing-up, this covers the essentials of handling, equipping, and sailing a modern sailboat, with emphasis of the theoretical as well as the practical. Lighting requirements and rules of the road are included. Price, $4.95. Motor Boating & Sailing Books, P.O. Box 2316, New York, N.Y. 10019.

SCHOOLS

Piloting And Seamanship

Boat Operators School, 535 Athol Ave., San Francisco, CA 94606.

Captain Van's prep schools for the CG motorboat, deck, engine, inland and ocean license exams; classroom or by mail. 1341 Proctor St., Port Arthur, TX 77640.

Coast Navigation School, 418 E. Canon Perdido, Santa Barbara, CA 93102.

National Small Craft Schools. For information write: American National Red Cross, Washington, D.C. 20006. See General Organizations listing, this section.

United States Coast Guard Auxiliary, Washington, D.C. 20591. See "General Organizations" listing for more details.

United States Power Squadrons, P.O. Box 345, 50 Craig Rd., Montvale, N.J. 07645. See "General Organizations" listing for more details.

Celestial Navigation

Coast Navigation School, 418 E. Canon Perdido, Santa Barbara, CA 93102.

The Lincoln Maritime Corp., Navigational Division, P.O. Box 1205, Pawtucket, R.I. 02862. J. D. Parker, Registrar.

Navigation Division, Motorboat Magazine, 38 Commercial Wharf, Boston, Mass. 02110. Meteorology, Coastwise Navigation, Celestial Navigation.

Weems & Plath, Inc., P.O. Box 1991, Annapolis, MD 21404.

Yacht Design

NAEBM-Westlawn School of Yacht Design, P.O. Box 779, Stamford, CT 06904. Jules G. Fleder, Director.

Yacht Design Institute, Brookline, Me. 04616. Contact R. E. Wallstrom.

United States Coast Guard District Offices

1st Coast Guard District, 150 Causeway St., Boston, MA 02114. Phone, 223-3634.

2d Coast Guard District, Federal Bldg., 1520 Market St., St. Louis, Mo. 63103. Phone, MA 2-4600.

3d Coast Guard District, Governors Island, New York, N.Y. 10004. Phone, 264-3311.

5th Coast Guard District, Federal Bldg., 431 Crawford St., Portsmouth, Va. 23705. Phone, 393-6081.

7th Coast Guard District, Rm. 1018 Federal Bldg., 51 Southwest First Ave., Miami, Fla. 33130. Phone, 350-5621.

Greater Antilles Section, U.S. Coast Guard, P.O. Box 2029, San Juan, P.R. 00903. Phone, 783-4075.

8th Coast Guard District, Customhouse, New Orleans, La. 70130. Phone, 527-6234.

9th Coast Guard District, Federal Office Bldg., 1240 E. 9th St., Cleveland, Ohio 44199. Phone, 522-3131.

11th Coast Guard District, Heartwell Building, 19 Pine Ave., Long Beach, Calif. 90802. Phone 437-2941.

12th Coast Guard District, Appraisers Building, 630 Sansome St., San Francisco, Calif. 94126. Phone, 556-2560.

13th Coast Guard District, Alaska Building, 618 Second Ave., Seattle, Wash. 98104. Phone, 624-2902.

14th Coast Guard District, 677 Ala Moana, Honolulu, Hawaii 96813. Phone, Honolulu, 5-88840.

17th Coast Guard District, Box 3-5000, Community Building, Juneau, Alaska 99801. Phone, 586-2680.

CHART SOURCES

Charts, Coast Pilots, Tide Tables, Tidal Current Tables and
other information published by U. S. Federal agencies (see listing on preceding pages) can be purchased prepaid by mail from
central offices, or directly from local authorized sales agents.

The major chart-issuing agencies publish catalogs of their products that list not only charts, but also related publications and
other information of value.

The National Ocean Survey publishes three catalogs: No. 1
covers the Atlantic and Gulf Coasts, No. 2 includes the Pacific
Coast and Islands, and No. 3 covers Alaskan waters. The Lake
Survey and the Canadian Hydrographic Service each publish a
catalog of the charts they issue. The Naval Oceanographic Office's
catalog has a three-part introduction and ten regional sections.

All catalogs are free, except those of the Naval Oceanographic
office. The catalogs are available upon request to the offices listed
below.

Central Offices

U.S. Coast Waters. Distribution Division, National Ocean Survey,
Washington, D.C. 20235.

Great Lakes (and New York State Canals). Lake Survey Center,
630 Federal Bldg., Detroit, Mich. 48226.

Mississippi River and Tributaries. U.S. Army Engineer District,
906 Olive St., St. Louis, Mo. 63101.

Canadian Waters. Canadian Hydrographic Service, 615 Booth St.,
Ottawa 4, Ont., Canada.

Other Foreign Waters. U. S. Naval Oceanographic Office, Washington, D.C. 20390.

Note: Lake Survey charts and the Great Lakes Pilot are sold over
the counter at Engineers' offices in Buffalo, N.Y.; Cleveland,
Ohio; Chicago, Ill.; Sault Ste. Marie, Mich., and Massena, N.Y.

INFORMATION

Mississippi River and Tributaries charts are sold at Engineers' offices in Chicago, Ill.; Omaha, Neb.; Cincinnati, Ohio; Nashville, Tenn.; and Vicksburg, Miss.

MUSEUMS AND RESTORATIONS

Maritime Museums
California
San Francisco Maritime Museum, Foot of Polk St., San Francisco, Calif. 94102.

Cabrillo Marine Museum, 3720 Stephen M. White Dr., San Pedro, CA 90731.

Connecticut
Mystic Seaport, Mystic, CT 06355. Village area with crafts, scrimshaw, models, paintings, prints, navigational instruments, Henry B. duPont Preservation Shipyard. See also Ship Exhibits listing.

District of Columbia
Smithsonian Institution, Constitution Ave., between 12th & 14th St., Washington, D.C. 20560.

Truxton-Decatur Naval Museum, 1610 H St., N.W., Washington, D.C. 20006.

U. S. Navy Memorial Museum, Building #76, Washington Navy Yard, Washington, DC 20374.

Maine
Bath Marine Museum, Sewall Mansion; Winter Street Center; Percy and Small Shipyard; the Apprenticeshop (boat building program); and the *Seguin,* oldest surviving wood tug; Bath, ME 04530.

Penobscot Marine Museum, Searsport, ME 04974. Six buildings with paintings, prints, American and Oriental furnishings, models of Maine-built vessels, tools, builders half-models, navigational instruments, small boats and nautical memorabilia. Open Memorial Day through October 15.

Maryland
U.S. Naval Academy Museum, Annapolis, MD 21402. Open 9

a.m. to 5 p.m. Tuesday through Friday; 11 a.m. to 5 p.m. Sunday. Closed Thanksgiving, Christmas and New Years Days, and every Monday.

Chesapeake Bay Maritime Museum, Navy Point, St. Michaels Harbor, Md. 21663.

Massachusetts

Museum of Science, Science Park, Charles River, Boston, MA 02114.

Francis Russell Hart Nautical Museum, Massachusetts Institute of Technology, 55 Massachusetts Ave., Cambridge, Mass. 02139.

Whaling Museum, Broad St., Nantucket, Mass. 02554. Full size brick try-works, completely rigged whale boat, scrimshaw, copper and blacksmith shops, whale skeletons, prints, portraits.

Whaling Museum, 18 Johnny Cake Hill, New Bedford, Mass. 02740.

Peabody Museum, 161 Essex St., Salem, Mass. 01970.

Michigan

Dossin Great Lakes Museum, Belle Island Park, Detroit, Mich.

Mason County Museum, 305 East Filer St., Ludington, Mich. 49431.

New York

East Hampton Town Marine Museum, Bluff Rd., Amagansett, L.I., N.Y. 11930.

Adirondack Museum, Blue Mountain Lake, NY 12812. Guide boats, canoes, small craft, some launches.

Thousand Islands Shipyard Museum, Clayton, N.Y. 13624. Antique pleasure boats, motors.

The Whaling Museum, Main St., Cold Spring Harbor, L.I., N.Y. 11724. Fully-rigged whale boat, dioramas of whaling scene, harbor

INFORMATION

scene; whaling gear; scrimshaw; ship and navigation gear; paintings. Open weekends all year, 11:30-5:30; and late June through Labor Day, Monday through Friday, 11:00-4:00.

Suffolk County Whaling Museum, Main St., Sag Harbor, L.I., N.Y. 11963.

Skenesborough Museum, Whitehall, N.Y. 12887.

Ohio
Ohio River Museum, Washington and Front Sts., Marietta, Ohio 45750. Indoor and outdoor exhibits of history of river life, commerce and travel.

Oregon
Columbia River Maritime Museum, Foot of 17th St., Astoria, OR 97103.

Pennsylvania
Civic Center Museum, 34th St. & Convention Ave., Philadelphia, Pa. 19104.

Philadelphia Maritime Museum, 321 Chestnut St., Philadelphia, Pa. 19106.

Vermont
Shelburne Museum, Shelburne, Vt. 05482. Exhibits include Colchester Reef Lighthouse, with collection of marine prints, paintings, scrimshaw; and Webb Gallery of American Art, with paintings. Admission charged. Free folder sent upon request. See also Ship Exhibit listing.

Virginia
The Mariners Museum, Newport News, Va. 23606.

Portsmouth Naval Shipyard Museum, 2 High St., Portsmouth, Va. 23709.

Washington
The Museum of History and Industry, 2161 E. Hamlin St., Seattle, WA 98112.

Ship Exhibits
California
Star of India, ferryboat *Berkeley,* and steam yacht *Medea,* a floating display of the Maritime Museum Association of San Diego, 1306 N. Harbor Dr., San Diego, CA 92101.

Alma, scow schooner; *C.A. Thayer*, lumber schooner; *Wapama*, steam schooner; *Eureka*, paddle wheel ferry; *Hercules*, tug; San Francisco Maritime State Historic Park, 2905 Hyde Street, San Francisco, CA 94109.

Balclutha, full-rigged ship; San Francisco Maritime Museum, Pier 43, Embarcadero, San Francisco, Calif. 94107.

Connecticut

Charles W. Morgan, whaler; *Joseph Conrad*, full-rigged ship; *L. A. Dunton, Emma C. Berry* and others, Mystic Seaport, Mystic, Conn. 06355.

Coast Guard Cutter Eagle, U. S. Coast Guard Academy, New London, Conn. 06320.

District of Columbia

Philadelphia, U.S. Museum of History and Technology, Smithsonian Institution, Washington, D.C. 20560.

Florida

H.M.S. Bounty Replica, 345 2nd Ave. N.E., St. Petersburg, Fla. 33701.

Hawaii

U.S.S. Arizona Memorial, and *U.S.S. Utah* Memorial, Pearl Harbor, Ha. 96610.

Maryland

U.S.S. Constellation, Constellation Dock, Pier 1; *U.S.S. Torsk*, Submariners Dock, Pier 3; USCG Lightship *Five Fathom*, and Schooner *Freedom*, Pier 3; Baltimore Seaport, Pratt St., Baltimore, Md.

J. T. Leonard, skipjack; *Edna E. Lockwood*, bugeye; *"Ole Barney"*, lightship, and others, Navy Point, St. Michaels, MD 21663.

Massachusetts

U.S.S. Constitution, oldest commissioned warship afloat, Charlestown, MA 02129.

Mayflower II, Replica, Box 1620, Plymouth, Mass. 02360.

U.S.S. Massachusetts, State Pier, Fall River, Massachusetts 02721. Open all year, 9 a.m. to 5 p.m. daily.

New York

Ambrose, lightship; *Wavertree*, full-rigged ship; *Mathilda*, Canadian tugboat; *Lettie G. Howard*, fishing schooner; *Maj. Gen. Wm. H. Hart*, ferryboat; *Aqua*, New York Harbor steam lighter; *Pioneer*, Delaware Bay freight schooner. South Street Seaport Museum, 16 Fulton St., New York, NY 10038.

North Carolina

U.S.S. North Carolina Battleship Memorial, Cape Fear River, Wilmington, N.C. 28401.

Ohio

W. O. Snyder, Jr., steamer, Muskingum River, Front and Washington Sts., Marietta, OH 45750.

Oregon

Columbia Lightship, Foot of 17th St., Astoria, OR 97103.

Pennsylvania

Gazela Primeire, 1883 barkentine. Philadelphia Maritime Museum, Foot of Vine St. at Delaware Ave., Philadelphia, PA 19106.

U.S.S. Olympia, Pier 11, N. Delaware Ave. & Race St., Philadelphia, Pa. 19106.

Texas

U.S.S. Texas, San Jacinto Battleground, P.O. Box 868, La Porte, Tex. 77571.

Vermont

S.S. Ticonderoga, U.S. Rt. 7, Shelburne, Vt. 05482.

Virginia

Godspeed, Discovery, Susan Constant, Jamestown Festival Park, Colonial Pkwy, Rt. 31, Jamestown, Va. 23081.

England

Cutty Sark, Greenwich, London.

H.M.S. Victory, Portsmouth, Hants.

Sweden

Wasa, Stockholm.

10.
GOVERNMENT REQUIREMENTS

Although you don't need a license (in most cases) to operate your boat, there are certain federal and state laws that govern its registration, equipment, and its use.

The major federal legislation is the Boating Act of 1971, which was signed into law on 10 August, 1971. It incorporates many provisions of the Motorboat Act of 1940, and the registration provisions of the Federal Boating Act of 1958.

The Motorboat Act of 1940 established a set of minimum equipment requirements (Table 10–1) for boats in each size category. The new act permits the Commandant of the Coast Guard to modify these or make additions that he deems necessary to promote safe boating. In any case, the requirements shown in Table 10–1 should be regarded as an absolute minimum. You should carry at least all the items required for award of the Coast Guard Auxiliary Courtesy Examination sticker, as listed in this section. Note that Table 10–2 shows the classification of fire extinguishers by size and type.

Boat registration, as required by the 1958 Act, is retained in the new legislation. State offices that handle the registration, and the fees required, are shown in Table 10–3.

GOVERNMENT

Table 10--1

Minimum Required Equipment

EQUIPMENT	CLASS A (Less than 16 feet)	CLASS 1 (16 feet to less than 26 feet)	CLASS 2 (26 feet to less than 40 feet)	CLASS 3 (40 feet to not more than 65 feet)
BACK-FIRE FLAME ARRESTOR	One approved device on each carburetor of all gasoline engines installed after April 25, 1940, except outboard motors.			
VENTILATION	At least two ventilator ducts fitted with cowls or their equivalent for the purpose of properly and efficiently ventilating the bilges of every engine and fuel-tank compartment of boats constructed or decked over after April 25, 1940, using gasoline or other fuel of a flashpoint less than 110° F.			
BELL	None.*	None.*	One, which when struck, produces a clear, bell-like tone of full round characteristics.	
LIFESAVING DEVICES	One approved life preserver, buoyant vest, ring buoy, special purpose water safety buoyant device, or buoyant cushion for each person on board or being towed on water skis, etc.		One approved life preserver or ring buoy for each person on board.	
WHISTLE	One hand, mouth, or power operated, audible at least ½ mile.		One hand or power operated, audible at least 1 mile.	One power operated, audible at least 1 mile.
FIRE EXTINGUISHER—PORTABLE — When NO fixed fire extinguishing system is installed in machinery space(s).	At least One B-I type approved hand portable fire extinguisher. (Not required on outboard motorboat less than 26 feet in length and not carrying passengers for hire if the construction of such motorboats will not permit the entrapment of explosive or flammable gases or vapors.)		At least Two B-I type approved hand portable fire extinguishers; OR At least One B-II type approved hand portable fire extinguisher.	At least Three B-I type approved hand portable fire extinguishers; OR At least One B-I type Plus One B-II type approved hand portable fire extinguisher.
When fixed fire extinguishing system is installed in machinery space(s).	None.	None.	At least One B-I type approved hand portable fire extinguisher.	At least Two B-I type approved hand portable fire extinguishers; OR At least One B-II type approved hand portable fire extinguisher.
	Fire extinguishers manufactured after 1 January 1965 will be marked, "Marine Type USCG Type —— Size —— Approval No. 162.028/EX . . .".**			

*NOTE.—Not required by the Motorboat Act of 1940; however, the "Rules of the Road" require these vessels to sound proper signals.

**NOTE.—Toxic vaporizing-liquid type fire extinguishers, such as those containing carbon tetrachloride or chlorobromomethane, are not accepted as required approved extinguishers on uninspected vessels (private pleasure craft).

Table 10-2   **FIRE EXTINGUISHERS**

Classification (type-size)	Foam (minimum gallons)	Carbon dioxide (minimum pounds)	Dry chemical (minimum pounds)	Freon (minimum pounds)
B-I	1¼	4	2	2½
B-II	2½	15	10	

Currently there are four sets of Rules of the Road that cover requirements for running lights on all types of vessels, and right-of-way under all possible situations. *Inland Water Rules* cover all bodies of water open to the sea or connected to it by navigable rivers and channels, except those where the Great Lakes Rules and Western Rivers Rules are in effect. *Great Lakes Rules* are applicable on the five Great Lakes, and their connecting and tributary waters as far east as Montreal. *Western Rivers Rules* apply to the Mississippi River from its source to the Huey P. Long Bridge at New Orleans, all tributaries emptying into the Mississippi River, and *their* tributaries. Also included are the Atchafalaya River above its junction with the Plaquemine-Morgan alternate waterway, and the Red River of the North.

International Rules cover the high seas outside of boundaries established at major harbors or other entrances, or along a series of offshore islands such as the Florida Keys. Boundary lines are described in detail in the "Navigation and Piloting" section of the *Boatman's Handbook.*

The Rules are all published by the U. S. Coast Guard, and are available free, as noted in the "Government Publications" section of the *Boatman's Handbook.*

Individual states often have equipment and operation requirements that supplement those given in the federal legislation, and state laws apply to waters that are not covered by federal acts, such as certain lakes wholly within a state.

Your best source of current information on state boating legis-

GOVERNMENT

STATE REGISTRATION REQUIREMENTS

NOTE: Under the Federal Boat Safety Act of 1971, all undocumented vessels equipped with propulsion machinery of any type, regardless of horsepower, must be numbered. States have until August, 1974 to bring their registration systems into conformity with this act, but may do so sooner if they wish.

STATE	BOATS AFFECTED	NUMBERING PERIOD	FEE	WHERE TO APPLY
ALABAMA	All motorboats, sailboats, boats for hire	1 year	Under 16', $4 16'-26', $6 26'-40', $12 Over 40', $24	Department of Conservation, State Administration Bldg, Montgomery, AL 36104.
ALASKA	All motorboats	3 years	$6	USCG Seventeenth District, P.O. Box 3-5000, Juneau, AK 99801.
ARIZONA	All watercraft	1 year	$2	Game & Fish Dept., 2211 W. Greenway Rd., Phoenix, AZ 85023.
ARKANSAS	Boats over 10 hp	1 year	Original, $2 Renewals, $1	County Revenue Collector.
CALIFORNIA	All motorboats except those with electric motors of less than 1 hp, and sailboats less than 8' in length	1 year	Original, $4 Renewals, $2	Department of Harbors and Watercraft, 1416 9th St., Room 1336, Sacramento, CA 95814.
COLORADO	All motorboats and sailboats	1 year	$3.50	Game, Fish & Parks Dept., 6060 Broadway, Denver, CO 80216.
CONNECTICUT	All motorboats	1 year	Under 16', $3 16'-26', $10 26'-40', $35 Over 45', $65	Town Clerk.

DELAWARE	All motorboats	1 year	$3	Office of Small Boat Safety, Department of Natural Resources & Environmental Control, D Street, Dover, DE 19901.
DISTRICT OF COLUMBIA	All motorboats	3 years	$6	USCG Fifth District, 431 Crawford St., Portsmouth, VA 23705.
FLORIDA	Boats over 10 hp	1 year	Under 12', $1 12'-16', $5 16'-26', $10 26'-40', $30 40'-65', $50 65'-110', $60 Over 110', $75 Fees are in lieu of personal property taxes	Office of County Tax Collector.
GEORGIA	Boats over 10 hp	3 years	Under 16', $5.25 16'-26', $7.75 26'-40', $10.25 Over 40', $15.25	State Game & Fish Commission, Room 710, Trinity-Washington Bldg., Atlanta, GA 30334.
HAWAII	All motorboats, sailboats over 8'	1 year	Under 16', $1 Over 16', $3 Renewals, $3 for first 12'; 25¢ each additional foot.	Habors Division, Dept. of Transportation, Box 397, Honolulu, HI 96809.
IDAHO	All motorboats	3 years	$2	Motor Vehicle Division, Dept. of Law Enforcement, P.O. Box 34, Boise, ID 83707.

Annual boat license: sum equal to 1% of boat length x hp of motor(s), but in no case less than $2.50. Sailboats, including auxiliaries, 50¢ per foot. Depreciation is a factor in license fees, and there are reduced rates for boats not within state for full year.

STATE	BOATS AFFECTED	NUMBERING PERIOD	FEE	WHERE TO APPLY
ILLINOIS	All motorboats, sailboats over 12'	2 years	$4	Conservation Dept., 400 S. Spring St., Springfield, IL 26706.
INDIANA	All motorboats	3 years	$3	Department of Natural Resources, 605 State Office Bldg., Indianapolis, IN 46209.
IOWA	All motorboats	2 years	$4	County Recorder
KANSAS	Boats 10 hp or more	3 years	$5	Forestry, Fish & Game Commission, P.O. Box 1028, Pratt, KS 67124.
KENTUCKY	All motorboats	1 year	Under 16', $3 16'-26', $5 26'-40', $8 Over 40', all inboards, $10	Circuit court clerk of county in which motorboat owner resides.
LOUISIANA	Boats over 10 hp	3 years	Original, $5 Renewals, $3	Wild Life & Fisheries Commission, Wild Life & Fisheries Bldg., 400 Royal St., New Orleans, LA 70130.
MAINE	Boats over 10 hp	3 years	$5	Bureau of Watercraft Registration & Safety, State Office Bldg., Augusta, ME 04330.
MARYLAND	Boats over 7½ hp & sailboats 25' or more in length	1 year	$5	Department of Natural Resources, 1825 Virginia St., Annapolis, MD 21401.
MASSACHUSETTS	Boats 5 hp or more	1 year	Original, $5 Renewals, $3	Division of Marine & Recreational Vehicles, Dept. of Public Safety, 64 Causeway St., Boston, MA 02114.

State	Coverage	Period	Fee	Agency
MICHIGAN	All motorboats	3 years	$5	Department of State, 2100 N. Larch St., Lansing, MI 48906.
	Private motorboats 16' or more in length cruising upon Great Lakes and connecting waters are licensed for 1 year at $5 to $75 or more depending on boat L.O.A. in addition to numbering fee.			
MINNESOTA	All watercraft	2 years	$1.50 puls 50¢ foot over 16'	Dept. of Conservation, 625 N. Robert St., St. Paul, MN 55101.
MISSISSIPPI	Boats over 10 hp	2 years	$2.25	County sheriff.
MISSOURI	Boats over 10 hp	3 years	$5 Outboard motors registered separately (one time only), $2	Boat Commission, P.O. Box 603, Jefferson City, MO 65101.
MONTANA	Boats over 8 hp	1 year	$1	Board of Equalization, Capitol Bldg., Helena, MT 59601.
NEBRASKA	All motorboats	1 year	Under 16' & under 5 hp, $2 Under 16' & over 5 hp, $5 16'-26', $8 26'-40', $15 Over 40', $25	State Game, Forestation & Parks Commission, Lincoln, NE 68509.
NEVADA	All motorboats	1 year	$3	Fish & Game Commission, P.O. Box 10678, Reno, NV 89501.
NEW HAMPSHIRE	All motorboats	3 years	$3	USCG First District, John F. Kennedy Federal Bldg., Government Center, Boston, MA 02203. Div. of Motor Vehicles, Dept. of Safety, 85 Loudon Rd., Concord, NH 03301.
	On non-tidal waters, outboard motors up to 5 hp, $3; 5½0 hp to 13⅗0 hp, $4; over 14 hp, $5; inboards 18' & under, $5; 18-26', $8; over 26', $10; 1 year.			

STATE	BOATS AFFECTED	NUMBERING PERIOD	FEE	WHERE TO APPLY
NEW JERSEY	All power vessels *Operator's license required on non-tidal waters.*	1 year	Under 16', $4 16'-26', $10 26'-40', $20 40'-65', $30 Over 65', $100	Bureau of Navigation, Motorboat Numbering, P.O. Box 250, Trenton, NJ 08625.
NEW MEXICO	All motorboats and sailboats	3 years	Original, $5 Renewals, $2	State Park & Recreation Commission, P.O. Box 1147, Santa Fe, NM 87501.
NEW YORK	All motorboats	3 years	Under 16', $3 16'-26', $6 Over 26', $10	Div. of Marine & Recreational Vehicles, Office of Parks & Recreation, South Mall, Albany, NY 12223.
NORTH CAROLINA	Boats over 10 hp	1 year	$3	Wildlife Resources Commission, Box 2919, Raleigh, NC 27602.
NORTH DAKOTA	Boats 10 hp or more	3 years	$3	State Game & Fish Dept., Bismark, ND 58501.
OHIO	All watercraft	1 year	Rowboat, canoe, barge, outboard hull, $1 Sailboat, $3 Inboard, under 100 hp, $7.50 Inboard, 100 hp or more, $10 Outboard motor, $3	Watercraft Div., Dept. of Natural Resources, 802 Ohio Department Bldg., Columbus, OH 43215.
OKLAHOMA	All watercraft and outboard motors over 10 hp *Plus annual license fee, in lieu of personal property tax.*	1 year	$1	State Tax Commission, 2101 N. Lincoln Blvd., Oklahoma City, OK 73105.

State	Covered	Term	Fees	Contact
OREGON	All motorboats and sailboats over 12'	1 year	Motorboats under 12, $3 Motor & Sail 12-16', $6 16-20', $8 Over 20', $8 plus $1 for each foot or fraction thereof	State Marine Board, Agriculture Bldg., 635 Capitol St. N.E., Salem, OR 97310.
PENNSYLVANIA	All motorboats	1 year	Under 16', $4 16' & over, $6	Miscellaneous License Div., Pennsylvania Dept. of Revenue, Harrisburg, PA 17101.
RHODE ISLAND	All motorboats	2 years	Under 16', $4 All others $10	Dept. of Natural Resources, Veterans Memorial Bldg., 38 Park St., Providence, RI 02903.
SOUTH CAROLINA	All motorboats	3 years	$5	Wildlife Resources Dept., P.O. Box 167 Columbia, SC 29202.
SOUTH DAKOTA	Boats 6 hp or more	3 years	$5	Dept. of Game, Fish & Parks, State Office Bldg., Pierre, SD 57501.
TENNESSEE	Boats over 5 hp All sailboats *Number good for as long as 3 years can be obtained by paying proportionally higher fee.*	1 year	Under 18', $2 18'-26', $4 26'-36', $6 36'-46', $8 46'-56', $10 56'-66', $12 66'-76', $14	State Game & Fish Commission, P.O. Box 9400, Ellington Agriculture Center, Nashville, TN 37220, or County Court Clerks or other authorized issuing agents.
TEXAS	All motorboats	2 years	Under 16', $6 16'-26', $9 26'-40', $12 Over 40', $15	State Parks & Wildlife Dept., John H. Reagan Bldg., Austin, TX 78701.
UTAH	All motorboats and sailboats	1 year	$5	Div. of Parks & Recreation, 132 S. Second West, Salt Lake City, UT 84101.

STATE	BOATS AFFECTED	NUMBERING PERIOD	FEE	WHERE TO APPLY
VERMONT	All motorboats	1 year	under 16', $2.50 16'-26', $5 26'-40', $10 Over 40', $25	Marine Div., Dept. of Public Safety, Montpelier, VT 05602.
VIRGINIA	All motorboats	3 years	$8	Boat Section, State Game & Fisheries Commission, P.O. Box 11104, Richmond, VA 23230.
WASHINGTON	All motorboats	3 years	$6	USCG Thirteenth District, 618 Second Ave., Seattle, WA 98104.
WEST VIRGINIA	Boats over 5 hp	1 year	Original, $5 Renewals, $2	Dept. of Natural Resources, State Office Bldg., Charleston, WV 25305.
WISCONSIN	All motorboats and sailboats over 12'	3 years	$3.25	Conservation Div., P.O. Box 450, Madison, WI 53701.
WYOMING	Boats over 5 hp	1 year	Under 16', $1.50 16'-26', $2 26'-40', $3 Over 40', $4	Game & Fish Commission, P.O. Box 1589, Cheyenne, WY 82001.
PUERTO RICO	—	—	—	Marine Operations Dept., Ports Authority, San Juan, Puerto Rico.
VIRGIN ISLANDS	—	—	—	Department of Commerce, Marine Div., Charlotte Amalie, St. Thomas Island, V.I.

lation is the *Handbook of Boating Laws* for your area, published by the Outboard Boating Club of America, 333 N. Michigan Ave., Chicago, Ill. 60601. The *Handbook* is available in four regional editions:

Northeastern States: Connecticut, Delaware, District of Columbia, Maine, Maryland, Massachusetts, New Hampshire, New Jersey, New York, Pennsylvania, Rhode Island, Vermont, West Virginia ($1.95).

Southern States: Alabama, Arkansas, Florida, Georgia, Louisiana, Mississippi, North Carolina, Oklahoma, South Carolina, Tennessee, Texas, Virginia ($1.95).

North Central States: Illinois, Indiana, Iowa, Kansas, Kentucky, Michigan, Minnesota, Missouri, Nebraska, North Dakota, Ohio, South Dakota, Wisconsin ($1.00).

Western States: Alaska, Arizona, California, Colorado, Hawaii, Idaho, Montana, Nevada, New Mexico, Oregon, Utah, Washington, Wyoming ($1.00).

It is recommended that you have and study the edition that covers your boating area.

ITEMS REQUIRED FOR USCG AUX DECAL

For a boat to receive the Auxiliary's Courtesy Motorboat Examination (CME) decal, it must, of course, first meet all of the legal requirements of the Motorboat Act of 1940 and related Coast Guard regulations. Further, some of the legal requirements are "beefed up" and made more stringent; additional items and conditions are imposed.

Lifesaving Equipment

An approved lifesaving device of the appropriate type is required for *each berth* on the boat; this may be a greater number than the legal requirement of one for each person on board at the time of a check. In addition, a boat with no bunks, or with only one, must still have a minimum of two lifesaving devices aboard.

GOVERNMENT

Fire Extinguishers

The Auxiliary standards for fire extinguishers on smaller boats are likewise more demanding than the law or regulations. Although a boat under 26 feet in length that is of "open construction," or one which has a built-in fire extinguisher system, need not carry an additional hand portable extinguisher to meet the legal minimum, it must have one for award of a CME decal.

Additional fire extinguishers—The prudent skipper considers whether he will be adequately safe with only the minimum required number of fire extinguishers. An important safety factor is the ready availability of an extinguisher close at hand when a fire emergency suddenly bursts forth. An extinguisher should be considered for *each* of the following locations: (1) the helm, where there is always someone when underway; (2) the engine compartment; (3) the galley; and (4) adjacent to the skipper's bunk, for quick reach at night. On smaller craft, the legally required minimum, or even the USCGAux requirements, may not be enough to provide one at all desirable locations.

Navigation Lights

The law does not require that a boat operated only in the daylight have navigation lights, but these must be fitted and in good working order to meet the Auxiliary's standards.

Distress Signals

At least one distress flare must be on a boat for it to pass the CME check, and preferably there should be several. Other emergency signalling equipment that is desirable includes smoke signals (better for day use than flares), dye marker (to aid aerial searches), a signalling mirror, and an orange flag or the new "Canadian" signal illustrated in fig. 101.

Anchor and Line

An anchor of suitable type and weight together with line of appropriate size and length is required for the CME decal. This is a valuable safety item should the engine fail and the craft be in danger of drifting or being blown into hazardous waters.

Smaller Craft Requirements

All Class A boats must have an oar or paddle, a manual pump or bailer, and a whistle meeting the legal requirements for Class 1 boats.

Installation Standards

In addition to requiring the above items of equipment, the CGAux program has established standards for the installation of fire extinguishers, fuel systems, electrical systems, and galley stoves. The following information is extracted from the *Courtesy Examiners Handbook,* CG-289.

Fire Extinguishers

Fire extinguishers are classified by letter and roman numeral according to the type of fire they are designed to put out and their size. The letter indicates the type of fire: "A" for combustible solids; "B" for flammable and combustible liquids; "C" for electrical fires. Motorboats are required to have either hand portable or semi-portable units capable of extinguishing fires involving flammable, liquids, and grease (class "B" fires). See Table 10-2.

Backfire Flame Control

The following are acceptable means of backfire flame control for gasoline engines:

(a) A backfire flame arrestor constructed in accordance with the specifications approved by the Commandant and listed in Equipment Lists (CG–190). The flame arrestor shall be suitably secured to the air intake with flame tight connections.

(b) An engine and fuel intake system which provides adequate protection from propagation of backfire flame to the atmosphere equivalent to that provided by an approved flame arrestor. A gasoline engine which has such an air and fuel intake system and

GOVERNMENT

which is operated without an approved flame arrestor shall be tested and labeled in accordance with detailed specifications and approved by the Commandant.

(c) Any attachment to the carburetor or locations of the engine air intake by means of which flames caused by engine backfire will be dispersed to the atmosphere outside of the vessel in such a way that the flames will not endanger the vessel or persons on board. All attachments shall be of metallic construction with flame tight connections and firmly secured to withstand vibration, shock and engine backfire.

Ventilation

All motorboats or motor vessels, except open boats, the construction or decking over of which is commenced after April 25, 1940, and which use fuel having a flash point of 110° F. or less, shall have at least two ventilator ducts, fitted with cowls or their equivalent, for the efficient removal of explosive or flammable gases from the bilges or every engine and fuel tank compartment. There shall be at least one exhaust duct installed so as to extend from the open atmosphere to the lower portion of the bilge and at least one intake duct installed so as to extend to a point at least midway to the bilge or at least below the level of the carburetor air intake. The cowls shall be located and trimmed for maximum effectiveness so as to prevent displaced fumes from being recirculated.

Ventilation systems installed in motorboats on which they are required by law must meet the following criteria:

a. There must be one or more intake ducts into each fuel and engine compartment, fitted with a cowl (scoop), extending from the open atmosphere to a level midway to the bilge (fuel compartment) or to at least below the level of the carburetor (engine compartment).

b. There must be one or more exhaust ducts from the lower portion of the bilge of each fuel and engine compartment to the free atmosphere, fitted with a cowl or an equivalent such as a wind actuated rotary exhauster or a power exhaust blower.

c. Normally, the intake cowl will face forward in an area of free underway airflow, and the exhaust cowl will face aft where a suction effect can be expected. They should be located with respect to each other so as to prevent the return of displaced vapors to any enclosed space, or to avoid the pickup of vapors from fuel filling stations.

d. There should be no constriction in the ducting system which is smaller than the minimum cross sectional area required for reasonable efficiency.

e. The lower end of the exhaust duct must not be so positioned in the bilge that it may be rendered ineffective by structural members or normal accumulations of bilgewater.

While the ventilation regulations are silent on the size prescribed for ducts, their intent is "for the efficient removal of explosive and flammable gases." The intent of the regulation for the *efficient* removal of gases is considered fulfilled if the ventilation duct installation in every compartment required to be ventilated conforms to either of the below tables. Values expressed in the tables are industry standards.

To determine the minimum cross sectional area of the air conduits (cowls and ducting) for motorboats having small engines and/or fuel tank compartments see Table 10-3, which is based on net compartment volume.

For most cabin cruisers and other large motorboats, Table 10-4, which is based on the vessel's beam, is a practical guide for determining the minimum cross sectional area of the air conduits (ducts and cowls).

Bell

The bell carried on Class 2 and 3 boats need be of no specific size as long as it produces a clear bell-like tone of full round characteristics. The bell may be carried inside the cabin, but provision should be made so that it may be mounted outside for use as a navigational warning when the boat is anchored under con-

GOVERNMENT

ditions of low visibility. This is of course only a recommendation, not a requirement. Motorboats engaged in a race which has been previously arranged or announced, or while tuning up for this race, need not carry a bell.

Owners and operators of Class A and Class 1 motorboats should be reminded that while the federal boating laws do not require a bell to be carried in these classes of motorboat, Rules of the Road will require its use if a signaling situation develops.

Whistle or Horn

Motorboats operating on the navigable waters of the United States shall be provided with an efficient whistle or other sound producing mechanical device as set forth in the following table except:

Motorboats engaged in a race which has been previously arranged or announced, or while engaged in such navigation as is incidental to the tuning up of the motorboat and engines for the race, need not carry the devices required by Table 10–1.

Owners and operators of Class A motorboats should be reminded that while a whistle is not required by the federal boating laws on this class motorboat, Rules of the Road will require its use if a signaling situation develops.

Galley Stoves

Galley stoves used in or installed aboard motorboats must meet the following standards in order for the craft to be eligible for award of the decal:

a. Galley stoves must be designed and manufactured for marine use.

b. Stoves must be so positioned and shielded that no flammable material is in close proximity or could be ignited. Portable stoves are acceptable, provided that they may be securely fixed in position when in use and when in the stowed position. Permanently installed stoves must be securely fastened in place.

c. With exceptions of gasoline, Naphtha, or Benzene fuels, any of the common fuels may be employed. A removable or accessible liquid tight drip pan at least ¾-inch deep must be provided under all burners of stoves using liquid fuel.

d. Gravity tanks should not be of more than 2 gallons capacity and must be located so that they will be protected from heat from the stove. A readily accessible cut-off valve shall be located in the line between the gravity or pressure tank so that it is not necessary to reach over the stove to close it. Gravity tanks must be securely fixed in place.

e. Liquefied Petroleum Gas—LPG, also known as "bottled gas" —cooking appliances must be approved by the American Gas Association Laboratories. The LPG container, high pressure piping and reducing regulator valve must be substantially secured in place, readily accessible, and located outside the vessel on the weather deck, cabin top, or other such position outside cockpits or semi-enclosures, so that escaping vapor cannot reach enclosed spaces in the vessel, and installed so as to be protected from climatic extremes. Piping must be routed so that it is protected from physical damage and against vibration. Wherever lines pass through decks or bulkheads, they should be protected by close fitting ferrules of nonabrasive material. The entire system must be free from leaks. DO NOT FLAME TEST. A master cut-off valve for all burners must be located in the manifold of the stove. Each LPG container must have a manually operated cut-off valve fitted with a securely attached hand wheel located directly at the container outlet.

f. If the construction of the vessel renders it impracticable to conform to the standards of paragraph e., above, the container, regulating equipment and all high pressure piping may be installed in a vapor tight housing located above the waterline in an open cockpit. This housing must be constructed or lined with corrosion resistant material, must open only from the top with the cover seated on a gasket and tightly latched. This cover must be constructed so as to be conveniently and quickly opened for access to the valve hand wheel. The housing must be fitted with a vent line of not less than ½-inch inside diameter leading from the bottom of the housing through the hull side below the housing bottom and above the waterline in order to disperse the gas harmlessly outside the vessel in event of failure to any part of the high pressure system.

g. The compartment in which a galley stove is located must be adequately ventilated. Ventilation standards comparable to that required for engine and fuel tank compartments is required for appliances employing jellied, liquid or LPG fuels.

Appliances which use gasoline as fuel are not acceptable for the purpose of award of the decal. In addition, appliances using fuels which are derivatives or distillates of Naphtha or Benzene are not acceptable. These latter fuels have a wide range in flashpoint, but all are extremely flammable and explosive. LPG appliances which employ an integral or caddy-pack fuel container which fastens directly to the appliance (that is, do not comply with paragraphs e or f above) are not acceptable.

It is recommended that a hand portable fire extinguisher be located in the same compartment with the galley stove readily accessible for emergency use.

Permanently Installed Fuel Tanks

Tanks should be located in a dry space, one which is preferably easily accessible. Tanks must be adequately supported, braced and held down so as to prevent movement, installed so as to be clear of the bottom or floorboards or any other structure in order to permit free circulation of air.

There can be no drain cock or other device for draining the tank located on the bottom of the tank. There can be no clean out hand hole located at any position on the tank. Tank top surfaces must be constructed so that they cannot hold accumulations of moisture.

The tank must be free from evidence of leaks at any point in its surface or connecting fittings, and must be free of distortion, creasing or gouging or evidence of corrosion.

The tank, if metallic, must be bonded to a common ground in the vessel. If other than metallic, the metal fittings for fuel piping to the engine must be bonded to a common ground.

While not a requisite for the award of the decal, the boatman should be advised that tanks exceeding 30 inches in horizontal measurement should contain baffle plates for control of surge.

Fuel piping leading from the tank to inboard engines should be run with as few connections as practicable and protected against mechanical damage from chafing or vibration. Fuel piping should be routed so that in event of a break in the line there will be no siphoning of fuel. A shutoff valve should be installed in the fuel line as close as practicable to the tank connection. Under no circumstances should a cock be used instead of a valve in the fuel line. The fuel line should be installed so as to be readily accessible for servicing or inspection. The parts of fuel piping secured to hull members should be separated from the part leading to the engine by a flexible section. Fuel piping must be free from leaks.

Fuel Tank Fill Pipe

Every permanently installed fuel tank must be fitted with a fuel tank fill pipe so arranged that it fits tightly to a fill plate located on deck outside the cockpit. The fill plate must be so located and arranged that any fuel spills are directly overboard and that vapors from fueling do not flow into enclosed spaces. On runabouts or other craft not constructed with a coaming around the cockpit there must be a lip on the inboard side of the fill plate to prevent fuel spillage from flowing into the boat. Fill pipes which terminate on the deck of a self-bailing cockpit are acceptable. Fill plates must be equipped with a tight cap. The connections between the fill plate and the fill pipe, and the fill pipe and the tank must be tight so as to prevent leakage of fuel into the interior of the vessel. The fill plate must be tightly secured to the deck so that spilled fuel cannot leak into the boat around the fill plate. Fill plate to fuel tank electric continuity must be maintained. If the fill plate is connected to the tank by means of a nonmetallic hose, then the fill plate must be bonded to the fill pipe fitting on the tank and thence to a common ground.

While not a condition for award of the decal, boatmen should be advised that the best marine practice calls for the fuel tank fill pipe to extend directly into the tank and terminate within one half of its diameter from the bottom of the tank.

Fuel Tank Vents

Every permanently installed fuel tank must be equipped with an adequate vent pipe leading from the top of the tank to a point overboard to permit displaced fumes to be conveyed safely outside the boat. Under no circumstances may tank vents terminate inside the boat.

While not a condition for award of the decal, boatmen should be advised that tank vents should be equipped with a fire screen flame arrestor to prevent flash back from any possible source of ignition.

Portable Fuel Tanks and Spare Fuel Containers

Tanks and containers of greater than seven gallon capacity shall not be considered portable tanks and do not come under the provisions of this article. All fuel tanks and spare fuel containers of greater than seven gallon capacity must meet the criteria for permanently installed fuel tanks, vent and fill pipe in order to be eligible for the decal.

Portable fuel tanks and spare fuel containers must meet the following standards in order to be eligible for the decal:

a. The tank must be free of holes, dents (other than shallow dishing), distortion, rust, corrosion, scoring, or gouging.

b. The tank must not leak at its seams, fittings when fuel lines are in place and when not in place, fill cap, gauge, or around the handle or other projection.

c. The tank vent if installed shall be capable of being closed when the tank is not in use.

d. The tank construction must be sufficiently sturdy so that the tank will withstand ordinary usage without distortion or leakage of fuel.

e. Tanks or containers may not be made of glass or any other breakable material.

f. Spare fuel containers on board a boat must be fitted with a vapor tight, leak proof cap. A vent if installed must be capable of being closed.

g. Fuel tanks and containers shall be stowed in a rack, secured with a strap or other device, or so positioned in the boat that they will not go adrift.

h. All fuel tanks or containers carried in a boat shall be stowed in an accessible location in well-ventilated spaces outside enclosed living accommodations.

Carburetors and Carburetor Drip Collectors

In order to be eligible for the decal every carburetor must be of a marine type. This provision shall also apply to the carburetors installed on auxiliary generators.

Carburetors, other than down draft carburetors, must have an integral drip collector or properly connected drip collector (drip pan) of adequate capacity to contain flooding spillover. Down draft carburetors are identified by the fact that the combustible air-fuel mixture flows downward through a vertical carburetor throat into the engine manifold. In this type carburetor any flooding surplus fuel is directed down the throat into the engine intake manifold and not into the bilge. Up draft and side draft carburetors are identified by the fact that the air-fuel mixture is directed upwards, or sidewards, respectively, through the carburetor throat into the engine manifold. Leakage or flooding spillover will settle away from the manifold in either of these types and drain into the bilge unless preventive devices are employed.

One method provides that the carburetor air intake be turned upward at approximately 45° to provide a substantial sump. Alter-

GOVERNMENT

nately, a drip collector is attached. Either of these methods provides a reservoir to collect excess gasoline, and both must be drained by a connection to the intake manifold which provides for automatic return of drip by means of the vacuum. If the Examiner is convinced that the protective device on the carburetor will eliminate leakage into the bilge, he may waive the requirement for a drip pan. All other updraft and sidedraft carburetors must have a drip pan installed beneath the carburetor in order to qualify for a decal. This pan must be equipped with a fine mesh wire screen to prevent the possibility of the gasoline in the pan catching fire. A thin tube leading from the lowest point of this pan to the intake manifold will automatically empty this pan when the engine is in operation. If the drip pan is not so equipped, the owner should be cautioned to empty the pan at frequent intervals to prevent accumulation of gasoline.

Electrical Installation

Wiring installations should be routed as high as possible above the bilge. Individual wires and harnessed wires should be supported with clamps or straps at frequent intervals, and protected against chafing at supports and where it passes through bulkheads or structural members. Wiring and insulation should be of sufficient size to carry the load of the circuit it serves. Wiring, electrical equipment and fittings shall be in good condition and installed to minimize danger of short circuits and resultant fires. All circuits must be protected by fuses or circuit breakers of the appropriate rating. Self-resetting circuit breakers are not acceptable. Open knife switches shall not be located in the bilge. Switchboards, fuse boxes and terminal blocks should be located so that they are protected from rain and spray, unless enclosed in watertight boxes. Wiring insulation must be intact and in good condition, and the electrical circuits of all equipment must be insulated from the exposed metallic parts. On metal boats battery chargers which may be installed for use with commercial shore power should be designed with an isolating transformer.

LIGHTS FOR VARIOUS TYPES OF VESSELS—INLAND RULES

Table 10-5

Note: Vessels lighted according to the International Rules are not required to change their lights when navigating waters subject to other Rules of the Road.

		Bow (Foremast or Forward)	Side	Range	Remarks or Additional Lights
1	MOTOR BOATS Class A—under 16' Class 1—16' to less than 26'	None	Combination red and green each color showing 10 pts.*	White 32 pt.[1] Visible 2 mi.	[1]Placed higher than combination *Visible 1 mi.
2	Class 2— 26' to less than 40'	White—20 pts.	Red—10 pt. Green—10 pt. Screened so as not to show across bow. Visible 1 mi.	White—32 pt. Visible 2 mi. Placed higher than bow light.	
3	Class 3— 40' to 65'	Visible 2 mi.			
4	Motorboats and auxiliaries driven by *sail only*, show the colored lights appropriate to their class, and fixed white 12 pt. stern light showing aft, visible 2 miles, carried as nearly as possible at the level of the side lights. Motorboats and auxiliaries, under *motor and sail*, are lighted as motorboats of their respective classes. In bad weather, small boats may, if necessary, show an electric torch or lighted lantern to overtaking vessels. Small sailing vessels under way in bad weather, if they cannot keep their side lights fixed, may keep their side lights at hand ready to show in time to avert collision. Note:—Under Motor Boat Act, motorboats of any class, may, optionally, carry lights prescribed by International Rules while operating on other than the high seas; on the high seas they must carry such lights. (See pages				
5	Sailing vessel or vessel in tow (except barges, canal boats, scows, etc.	None	Red—10 pt. Green—10 pt.	None	*12 pt. white showing aft, visible 2 mi., at level of side lights (See comments in item above regarding bad weather)
6	Steam or motor vessels over 65' in length (except those vessels falling in classifications noted below)	White 20 pt. Vis. 5 mi.	Red—10 pt. Green—10 pt. Vis. 2 mi. 36 in. screen	White 32 pt.[2]	[2]At least 15 feet higher than foremast light (On *sea-going* vessel, horizontal spacing must be at least as great as vertical separation)
7	Double-ended[3] ferry boat	White 32 pt.[4] Vis. 2 mi.	Red—10 pt. Green—10 pt. Vis. 2 mi. Three-foot screens	White—32 pt.[4]	[3]If not of double-ended type, carries same lights as inland steamer [4]On both ends at same height. Special light amidships may designate line

Table 10-5 (continued)

#	Vessel				
8	Steam pilot vessel on station[5] on pilotage duty and underway[6]	None	Red—10 pt. Green—10 pt. Three-foot screens[6]	None	White 32 pt. at masthead 8' above red 32 pt., each vis. 2 mi. Shows flares at intervals of not more than 15 min. [5]If not on station, carries same lights as other steam vessels [6]On station at anchor, side lights are extinguished
9	Fishing vessel underway engaged in commercial fishing[7]	None	None	None	Red 32 pt. 6' to 12' above white 32 pt. not more than 10' apart horizontally. White vis. 3 mi. red 2 mi. [7]If underway, but not fishing carries usual lights of her class except vessel under 10 gross tons may show combination red and green lantern in lieu of fixed side lights
10	Inland[10] tug without tow[8]	White 20 pt. Vis. 2 mi. if not over 56'; vis. 5 mi. over 65'	Red—10 pt. Green—10 pt. Three-foot screens	White 32 pt.[9]	[8]Lighted same as ordinary inland steam vessel [9]At least 15' higher than foremast light [10]For lights of ocean-going tug on inland waters, see International Rules, Table 4-5
11	Inland[10] tug with tow alongside or pushed ahead	Two white 20 pt. vertically arranged, at least 3' apart or lights mentioned in fourth column. Vis. same as item 10, above	Red—10 pt. Green—10 pt. If side light is obstructed by vessel towed, light is transferred to outside of tow.	Two white 32 pt. vertically arranged, at least 3' apart or foremast lights mentioned in second column	With 20-pt. towing lights forward, may carry 32-pt. white range light aft. May carry small white light aft for tow to steer by, not visible forward of beam. With 32-pt. towing light aft, may carry 20-pt white light forward.
12	Inland[10] tug with tow astern	Three white 20 pt. vertically arranged, at least 3' apart or lights mentioned in fourth column. Vis. same as item 10, above	Red—10 pt. Green—10 pt.	Three white 32 pt. vertically arranged, at least 3' apart or foremast lights mentioned in second column	When pushing tow ahead and using 20 pt. white towing lights forward, carries two amber 12 pt. lights aft vertically arranged
13	Rowboat (under oars or sail)	None	None	None	White light shown on approach of another vessel

Table 10-5 (continued)

		Bow (Foremast or Forward)	Side	Range	Remarks or Additional Lights
14	Vessels working on a wreck	White 32 pt. (each outside vessel) at least 6' above decks	None	White 32 pt. stern light (each outside vessel) at least 6' above decks	Two red 32 pt. in vertical line, 3' to 6' apart, at least 15' above decks
15	Dredge (held in position by moorings or spuds)	None	None	None	White 32 pt. each corner at least 6' above deck. Two red 32 pt. in vertical line 3' to 6' apart, at least 15' above deck. Scows moored alongside show white 32 pt. on each outboard corner, at least 6' above deck
16	Dredge (self-propelling suction type, underway, with suction on bottom)	White 20 pt. Vis. 2 mi. if not over 65'; vis. 5 mi. over 65'	Red—10 pt. Green—10 pt.	White 32 pt.	Two red 20 pt. under the white 20 pt. foremast light, 3' to 6' apart. Upper red light 4' to 6' below white light. At stern two red 4 pt. showing aft, in vertical line 4' to 6' apart
17	Vessel towing wreck	Carries lights same as described for inland tug with tow astern (see No. 12) except that in lieu of the regular 3 white towing lights she shows 4 lights vertically arranged, 3' to 6' apart, upper and lower white, two middle lights red, 20-point if carried on the foremast, 32-point if carried aft			
18	Naval and other U.S.	12	12		[12] Both the Inland and International Rules provide, in Article 13, that these rules shall not interfere with special rules made by the Government of any nation with respect to additional station and signal lights for two or more ships of war or for vessels sailing under convoy, or with exhibition of recognition signals adopted by ship owners, properly authorized by their respective Governments
19	At anchor—vessel under 150' in length	One white 32 pt. forward, vis. 2 mi. where best seen	None	None	In specially designated anchorage areas, vessels under 65' need no anchor light.
20	at anchor—vessel 150' in length or over	One white 32 pt. forward at least 20' above hull. Vis. 2 mi.	None	None	One white 32 pt. aft. at least 15' lower than forward light. Vis. 2 mi.

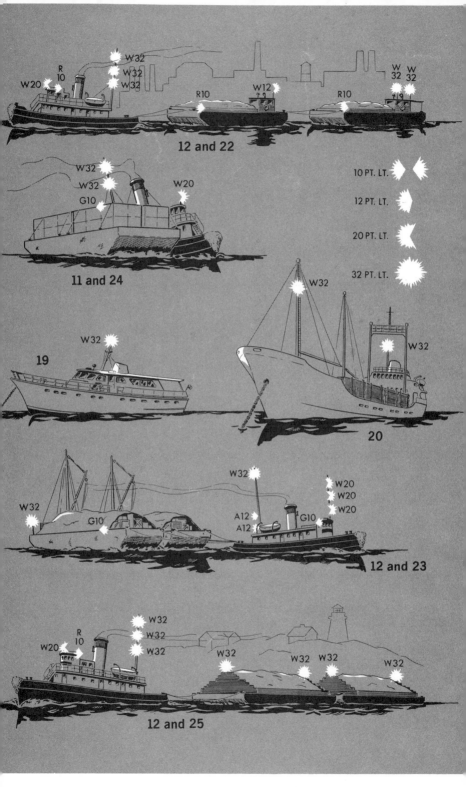

Table 10-6

LIGHTS FOR BARGES, CANAL BOATS AND SCOWS IN TOW ON INLAND WATERS

Except Great Lakes, east to Montreal—Red River of the North—Mississippi River and tributaries above Huey P. Long Bridge—that part of the Atchafalaya River above its junction with the Plaquemine-Morgan City alternate waterway—Gulf Intracoastal Waterway and certain waters connecting waters, from the Rio Grande to Cape Sable—Hudson River (Troy to Sandy Hook)—East River and Long Island Sound—Narragansett Bay— Lake Champlain—and other tributaries.

		Bow	Side	Stern	Remarks or Additional Lights
21	One barge or canal boat towed astern of tug	None	Green—10 pt. Red—10 pt. Vis. 2 mi.	Two white 32 pt. athwartship horizontal. At least 5' apart and at least 4' above deckhouse	None
22	More than one barge or canal boat towed astern in tandem	None	Green—10 pt. Red—10 pt. Vis. 2 mi.	[13]One white—12 pt. Vis. 2 mi.	[13]Except last vessel of tow which carries instead two 32 pt. white athwartship horizontal at least 5' apart and at least 4' above deckhouse
23	More than one barge or canal boat towed astern abreast (one tier)[14]	None	Green—10 pt. Red—10 pt. Vis. 2 mi. (carried at outer sides of bows of outside boats)	[14]One white—32 pt. on each outside boat	[14]If more than one tier, white stern lights are placed on outside boats of last tier only
24	Barges, canal boats or scows towed alongside of tug	None	Colored side lights carried on outer side of outside barge if side lights of towing vessel are obstructed by barge	None	None
25	Scows towed singly or tandem	White 32 pt.[15] Vis. 5 mi.	None	White 32 pt.[15] Vis. 5 mi.	[15]Lights to be carried at least 8' above surface of water.
26	Scows massed in tiers, two or more abreast, astern	White 32 pt. on outer side of all outside scows. Vis. 5 mi.[15]	None	White 32 pt. on outer side of outside scows last tier only. Vis. 5 mi.[15]	[15]Lights to be carried at least 8' above surface of water.

NOTE:—When barges, canal boats or scows are *pushed ahead* of the tug, head boat carries red 10-pt. side lights on outer bows, or if more than one abreast, they are shown from outer bow of outside boats.

Table 10-7 **LIGHTS FOR VARIOUS TYPES OF VESSELS—INTERNATIONAL RULES**

		Bow (Foremast or Forward)	Side	Range	Remarks or Additional Lights
27	Power-driven vessels less than 65 feet in length[17] NOTE—Small power-driven boats may carry white light forward at height less than 9 feet but it must be carried not less than 3 feet above the side lights or combination red and green light.	White—20 pt. at least 9' above gunwale. Vis. 3 mi.	Red—10 pt. Green—10 pt. Vis. 1 mi. or combination red and green, each color showing 10 pts. At least 3' below foremast light	None	12-pt. white showing aft. [17]Instead of the lights called for here these vessels may optionally carry those lights intended for larger power-driven vessels (see item 31)
28	Vessels under oars or sails under 40 feet	None	Combination red and green, each color showing 10 pts. shown to approaching vessels	None	
29	Rowboats, under oars or sails	None	None	None	Show electric torch or lighted lantern to prevent collision
30	Sailing vessel or vessel in tow	None	Red—10 pt. Green—10 pt. Vis. 2 mi. 36 in. screens	None	12 pt. white light showing aft. Vis. 2 mi. Sailboats may optionally carry on top of foremast two 20 pt. lights, upper red, lower green, visible 2 mi., sufficiently separated for distinction
31	Power-driven vessels generally (ocean liners, sea-going yachts, etc.)	White 20 pt. 20' to 40' above hull. Vis. 5 mi. Both (see "range") 20-pt. white lights must be in line with, and over, the keel	Red—10 pt. Green—10 pt. Vis. 2 mi. Three-foot inboard screens	White 20 pt. at least 15' higher than foremast light vis. 5 mi. Optional on vessels under 150 feet. Horizontal distance between white lights at least 3 times the vertical distance	White 12 pt. showing astern. Vis. 2 miles. Carried at, or near, level of side lights
32	Pilot vessels (power-driven	On station, under way, carry white 32-pt. masthead light not less than 20 ft. above the hull, and 8 feet below it a red 32-pt. light, both vis. 3 mi.	Normal red and green side lights only when underway	Normal stern light when underway	Show flare or intermittent 32-pt. white light at intervals of not more than 10 minutes. Normal anchor lights if at anchor
33	Vessels engaged in trolling	[18]	[18]	[18]	[18]Show only lights appropriate for power-driven or sailing vessel

#	Vessel			
34	Vessels engaged in fishing but not trolling or trawling	None[19]	When making way through the water same side lights as under items 27, 28, or 31 above	Two vertical 32-pt. lights, upper red, lower white, 4' to 12' apart. Boats under 40' may show the white 3' under red and not less than 9' above gunwale; larger craft must show it at height above side lights of at least twice distance between vertical lights[19]	12-pt. white stern light. If outlying gear extends more than 500', another 32-pt. white light 6' to 20' away from vertical lights toward outlying gear and neither higher than white light nor lower than side lights [19]When not actually engaged in fishing, show normal lights of vessel their size
35	Vessels engaged in trawling	None[19]	Same as item 34	Same as item 34 except that upper of two vertical lights is green[19]	Same as item 34
36	Vessels at anchor	32-pt. white light at or near bow, vis. 2 mi. On ships 150 feet or more, at least 20' above hull, vis. 3 mi.	None	None	At or near stern of vessels 150' or more, a 32-pt. white light at least 15' lower than forward one and vis. for 3 mi. After light is optional for vessels under 150' in length
37	Vessel aground	Same as in item 36	None	None	Same as in item 36 plus two red vertical 32 pt, at least 6' apart. Vis. 2 mi.
38	Vessel not under control	None	None, unless under way on, when side and stern lights are carried	None	Two red 32 pt. in vertical line at least 6' apart. Vis. 2 mi.
39	Cable-laying vessel	Three 32-pt in vertical line at least 6' apart. Upper and lower red; middle white. Vis. 2 mi.	None, unless under way on, when side and stern lights are carried	None	Same rules apply to vessels laying or picking up a navigation mark, or engaged in surveying or underwater operations
40	Power-driven vessel with one vessel in tow, or more, if tow is 600' or less in length from stern of tug	Two white 20 pt. in verticle line not less than 6' apart. Lower light must be not less than 14' above the hull.	Red—10 pt. Green—10 pt. Vis. 2 mi. three-foot screens	White 20 pt. (optional if tug is less than 150' in length)	Must show either the fixed white 12-pt. stern light, or small white light aft for tow to steer by, not visible forward of beam
41	Power-driven vessel with tow over 66' in length	Three white 20 pt. in vertical line at least 6' apart. Lower light may be not less than 14' above hull	Red—10 pt. Green—10 pt. Vis. 2 mi. three-foot screens	White 20 pt. (optional if tug is less than 150' in length)	Must show either the fixed white 12-pt. stern light, or small white light aft for tow to steer by, not visible forward of beam

EQUIPMENT REQUIRED FOR
USCG AUX FACILITIES

The CME checklist also contains a number of items recommended for the proper operation of a craft or for its safety, items beyond those required for award of the decal. The actual selections of items from this list will vary with the size and use of the particular boat involved.

This list of generally recommended items includes many that are *required for "Facilities,"* the boats of members of the Auxiliary that have been brought to higher standards for use in their programs of search and rescue, regatta patrolling, etc.

Anchors

The carrying of a second anchor is recommended in addition to the one required to pass the CME check. This additional anchor may be a lighter one for non-emergency daytime use.

It is recommended that a length of chain be used between the anchor and the nylon line. Shackles used on either end of this chain should have their pins secured with safety wire.

Bilge Pumps

One or more mechanical or electrical bilge pumps are recommended for all boats, and these should, of course, always be in good working order. Facilities of Class 2 or 3 should have at least two such pumps, and their bilges must be clean and free of any oil or grease; wood chips or other debris that could clog pumps and limber holes must be removed.

Lines

Every boat should have mooring (dock) lines suitable in length and size to that particular craft. These should be of several different lengths for convenience in use. No generalization can be made as to the lengths, but the diameter should roughly correspond to that of storm or working anchor rodes.

A heaving line of light construction is desirable if the craft is large enough to require the use of heavy mooring lines. The use of polypropylene line, or other material that is brightly colored and will float, is recommended for this purpose.

Life Rings

A ring life buoy with a length of light line attached is recommended for rendering assistance to swimmers or accident victims in the water. This can also be used to float a heavier line across to a stranded boat. If of an approved type, this ring buoy can count as one of the lifesaving devices required to be on board. A water light (a device which automatically lights up in contact with the water) enhances the use of a ring buoy at night.

Operational Equipment

Recommended operational equipment includes fenders in appropriate sizes and numbers for the craft involved. Not only will these be used in normal berthing, they are also necessary if two craft must make fast to each other while underway or at anchor. A boathook will be found very useful for fending off, placing lines over piles, picking up pennants of mooring buoys, recovering articles dropped over the side, and many other uses.

A searchlight—installed on larger craft, hand-held on smaller boats—serves both as a routine aid in night piloting and as an emergency signalling device. A multicell flashlight or electric lantern can serve these functions, but not so well as a searchlight.

Navigation publications and charts should be carried aboard boats in accordance with their use. Compasses are desirable on almost any boat for emergency if not regular use. Piloting and plotting instruments are also recommended.

A hand-held lead line is a useful back-up to the more complicated electronic depth sounder; one is particularly handy when one must probe around a stranded boat in search of deeper water.

An emergency supply of drinking water—and perhaps food, too—should be carried on all craft. It may never be used, but

GOVERNMENT

when needed it can literally be a "lifesaver." Supplies of this nature should be periodically freshened or replaced to ensure acceptable quality when needed. Distilled water should be carried for periodic replenishment of any storage batteries on board; this can, of course, serve as an emergency source of drinking water.

A first aid kit is an essential item of safety equipment. The kit should be accompanied with a manual or separate book of instructions.

The list of tools and spare parts to be carried aboard must be developed by each skipper individually for his craft. The items will be governed by the type of boat, its normal use, and the capabilities of the crew to use them. An item required on USCGAux Facilities is one or more spare bulbs for the navigation lights. Items for all craft include simple tools, plugs, cloth, screws, nails, wire, tape, and other objects for the execution of emergency repairs at sea. Mechanical and electrical spares will be highly individualized by the particular boat and skipper.

Further Operational and Safety Items

A sea anchor or drogue is an essential item of safety equipment for boats operating in many areas, but one is not legally required. As noted above, life rafts, preferably with a canopy, are much needed safety items in many waters.

Electric windshield wipers are excellent items of equipment when running into rainy or rough weather; safety is often much improved by their availability and use. The installation of washers that squirt fresh water on windshields will help greatly when spray, particularly of salt water, is intermittently received over the bow.

Many electronic items will add to operational safety. These include radiotelephones, electronic depth sounders, radio direction finders (RDFs), and fuel vapor detectors for engine rooms and bilges of gasoline-powered craft. Alarm systems are available to alert the skipper of dangerous conditions of engine overheating, low oil pressure, or high water in the bilge. Electric bilge exhaust blowers will add to the safety of the required ventilation systems for all engine and fuel tank compartments. All of these are in the "desirable," or even "necessary," category.

Pollution control equipment is rapidly moving from the operationally desirable to the necessary category. All skippers should be looking forward to their needs and problems in this area.

Cleaning gear may not be "glamorous," but it is certainly operational. Specific lists will vary from boat to boat, but all may be expected to contain a swab (mop), bucket, sponges, chamois, metal polish and rags, and similar items.

Sailboats

Sailboats without mechanical power, either installed or detachable, do not come within the equipment requirements of the Motorboat Act, nor are they checked as a part of the Courtesy Motorboat Examination program. Such craft over 16 feet in length are, however, eligible to become Auxiliary Facilities and must meet certain prescribed standards. These requirements can serve as a guide to all owners of sailing craft as to desirable safety equipment above the legal requirements.

Sailing Facilities under 26 feet in length are required to have one B-1 hand fire extinguisher and larger craft must have on board two such units. These sailboats must meet the CME standard of one approved lifesaving device on board for each berth, with a minimum of two such devices. Further, such craft must meet all standards for motorboats other than those relating to propulsion machinery, fuel systems, and ventilation of related compartments. This would leave in the requirements such items as an anchor with line, distress flare, galley stove installation and general electrical system—all matters appropriate to the safe operation of any sailboat.

GOVERNMENT

11.
USEFUL TABLES

One way to convey a lot of useful information quickly and easily is through the use of tables. Here are those covering time, speed and distance problems; nautical mile-statute mile conversions; propeller selection for inboard and outboard propulsion; cable, rope, and chain strengths and uses; metric conversions; strengths of metals and woods, and weights and measures.

Table 11-1

SPEED COMPARISON

km./h	m.p.h.	meters/sec.	knots
10	6.22	2.78	5.4
20	12.4	5.56	10.8
30	18.7	8.34	16.2
40	24.9	11.1	21.6
50	31.1	13.9	27.0
60	37.4	16.7	32.4
70	43.6	19.4	37.8
80	49.8	22.2	43.2
90	56.0	25.0	48.6
100	62.2	27.8	54.0
120	74.7	33.3	64.8
140	87.1	38.9	75.6
160	99.5	44.5	86.4
180	112	50.0	97.2
200	124	55.6	108
220	137	61.2	119
240	149	66.7	130
260	162	72.3	140
280	174	77.8	151
300	187	83.4	162

Table 11-2

TIME-SPEED-DISTANCE

	Time taken to travel 1 nautical mile (or statute mile)								
Min.	**1**	**2**	**3**	**4**	**5**	**6**	**7**	**8**	**9**
Sec.	Speed of boat in knots (or statute miles per hour)								
0	60.00	30.00	20.00	15.00	12.00	10.00	8.57	7.50	6.67
2	58.06	29.51	19.78	14.88	11.92	9.95	8.53	7.47	6.64
4	56.25	29.03	19.56	14.75	11.84	9.89	8.49	7.44	6.62
6	54.55	28.57	19.36	14.63	11.76	9.84	8.45	7.41	6.59
8	52.94	28.13	19.15	14.52	11.69	9.78	8.41	7.38	6.56
10	51.43	27.69	18.95	14.40	11.61	9.73	8.37	7.35	6.54
12	50.00	27.27	18.75	14.29	11.54	9.68	8.33	7.32	6.52
14	48.65	26.87	18.56	14.17	11.47	9.63	8.29	7.29	6.50
16	46.37	26.47	18.37	14.06	11.39	9.57	8.26	7.26	6.48
18	46.15	26.09	18.18	13.95	11.32	9.52	8.22	7.23	6.45
20	45.00	25.71	18.00	13.85	11.25	9.47	8.18	7.20	6.43
22	43.90	25.35	17.82	13.74	11.18	9.42	8.15	7.17	6.41
24	42.86	25.00	17.65	13.64	11.11	9.38	8.11	7.14	6.38
26	41.86	24.66	17.48	13.53	11.04	9.33	8.07	7.12	6.36
28	40.90	24.32	17.31	13.43	10.98	9.28	8.04	7.09	6.34
30	40.00	24.00	17.14	13.33	10.91	9.23	8.00	7.06	6.32
32	39.13	23.68	16.98	13.24	10.84	9.18	7.97	7.03	6.29
34	38.30	23.38	16.82	13.14	10.78	9.14	7.93	7.00	6.27
36	37.50	23.08	16.67	13.04	10.71	9.09	7.90	6.98	6.25
38	36.74	22.79	16.51	12.95	10.65	9.05	7.86	6.95	6.23
40	36.00	22.50	16.36	12.85	10.59	9.00	7.83	6.92	6.21
42	35.29	22.22	16.22	12.77	10.53	8.96	7.79	6.90	6.19
44	34.62	21.95	16.07	12.68	10.47	8.91	7.76	6.87	6.16
46	33.96	21.69	15.93	12.59	10.40	8.87	7.73	6.84	6.14
48	33.33	21.43	15.79	12.50	10.35	8.82	7.69	6.82	6.12
50	32.73	21.18	15.65	12.41	10.29	8.78	7.66	6.79	6.10
52	32.14	20.93	15.52	12.33	10.23	8.74	7.63	6.77	6.08
54	31.58	20.69	15.38	12.25	10.17	8.70	7.60	6.74	6.06
56	31.03	20.45	15.25	12.16	10.11	8.65	7.56	6.72	6.04
58	30.51	20.23	15.13	12.08	10.06	8.61	7.53	6.69	6.02
60	30.00	20.00	15.00	12.00	10.00	8.57	7.50	6.67	6.00

TABLES

Table 11-3

CONVERSION TABLES—NAUTICAL AND STATUTE MILES

Nautical	Statute	Nautical	Statute	Nautical	Statute	Statute	Nautical	Statute	Nautical	Statute	Nautic
1.00	1.151	8.75	10.075	16.50	18.999	1.00	0.868	9.00	7.815	17.00	14.76
1.25	1.439	9.00	10.363	16.75	19.287	1.25	1.085	9.25	8.032	17.25	14.98
1.50	1.729	9.25	10.651	17.00	19.575	1.50	1.302	9.50	8.249	17.50	15.19
1.75	2.015	9.50	10.939	17.25	19.863	1.75	1.519	9.75	8.467	17.75	15.41
2.00	2.303	9.75	11.227	17.50	20.151	2.00	1.736	10.00	8.684	18.00	15.63
2.25	2.590	10.00	11.515	17.75	20.439	2.25	1.953	10.25	8.901	18.25	15.84
2.50	2.878	10.25	11.803	18.00	20.727	2.50	2.171	10.50	9.118	18.50	16.06
2.75	3.166	10.50	12.090	18.25	21.015	2.75	2.387	10.75	9.335	18.75	16.28
3.00	3.454	10.75	12.378	18.50	21.303	3.00	2.604	11.00	9.552	19.00	16.50
3.25	3.742	11.00	12.666	18.75	21.590	3.25	2.821	11.25	9.769	19.25	16.71
3.50	4.030	11.25	12.954	19.00	21.878	3.50	3.038	11.50	9.986	19.50	16.93
3.75	4.318	11.50	13.242	19.25	22.166	3.75	3.256	11.75	10.203	19.75	17.15
4.00	4.606	11.75	13.530	19.50	22.454	4.00	3.473	12.00	10.420	20.00	17.36
4.25	4.893	12.00	13.818	19.75	22.742	4.25	3.690	12.25	10.638	20.25	17.58
4.50	5.181	12.25	14.106	20.00	23.030	4.50	3.907	12.50	10.855	20.50	17.80
4.75	5.469	12.50	14.393	20.25	23.318	4.75	4.124	12.75	11.072	20.75	18.02
5.00	5.757	12.75	14.681	20.50	23.606	5.00	4.341	13.00	11.289	21.00	18.23
5.25	6.045	13.00	14.969	20.75	23.893	5.25	4.559	13.25	11.507	21.25	18.45
5.50	6.333	13.25	15.257	21.00	24.181	5.50	4.776	13.50	11.724	21.50	18.67
5.75	6.621	13.50	15.545	21.25	24.468	5.75	4.994	13.75	11.941	21.75	18.88
6.00	6.909	13.75	15.833	21.50	24.757	6.00	5.211	14.00	12.158	22.00	19.10
6.25	7.196	14.00	16.121	21.75	25.045	6.25	5.428	14.25	12.376	22.25	19.32
6.50	7.484	14.25	16.409	22.00	25.333	6.50	5.645	14.50	12.593	22.50	19.53
6.75	7.772	14.50	16.696	22.25	25.621	6.75	5.862	14.75	12.810	22.75	19.75
7.00	8.060	14.75	16.984	22.50	25.909	7.00	6.079	15.00	13.027	23.00	19.97
7.25	8.348	15.00	17.272	22.75	26.196	7.25	6.296	15.25	13.244	23.25	20.19
7.50	8.636	15.25	17.560	23.00	26.484	7.50	6.513	15.50	13.461	23.50	20.40
7.75	8.924	15.50	17.848	23.50	27.000	7.75	6.730	15.75	13.678	23.75	20.62
8.00	9.212	15.75	18.136	24.00	27.636	8.00	6.947	16.00	13.895	24.00	20.84
8.25	9.500	16.00	18.424	24.50	28.212	8.25	7.164	16.25	14.112	24.25	21.06
8.50	9.787	16.25	18.712	25.00	28.787	8.50	7.381	16.50	14.329	24.50	21.27
—						8.75	7.598	16.75	14.546	25.00	21.71

1 nautical mile=1.151 statute miles
1 statute mile=0.869 nautical mile

Fig. 1101 Propeller dimensions are diameter and pitch. The diameter is that of a circle described by the outermost point of a propeller blade. Pitch is the distance a propeller would move in one revolution (dotted line) if it operated as a screw being driven through solid material. Actual movement is less than the theoretical pitch distance, and the difference between actual movement (solid line) and pitch distance is the propeller slip. Slip is expressed as a percentage of pitch distance. Depending on the type of boat, slip varies between about 10% and 35%.

TABLE 11–4. INBOARD PROPELLER SELECTION— DIAMETER

Table prepared by Columbian Bronze can be used to determine approximate diameter of normal three-blade propeller that will best match engine horsepower and propeller shaft speed.

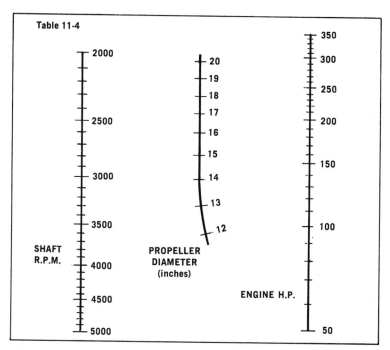

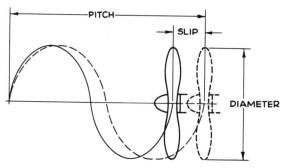

Table 11-5

INBOARD ENGINE PROPELLER SELECTION

r.p.m.	slip	PITCH 8 in.	10 in.	12 in.	14 in.	16 in.	18 in.
700	10%	4.16	5.18	6.22	7.27	8.31	9.32
	20%	3.68	4.61	5.53	6.45	7.38	8.28
	30%	3.23	4.03	4.83	5.64	6.46	7.27
800	10%	4.76	5.92	7.12	8.32	9.48	10.64
	20%	4.20	5.28	6.32	7.36	8.44	9.48
	30%	3.68	4.60	5.52	6.44	7.40	8.32
900	10%	5.35	6.66	8.00	9.35	10.68	11.98
	20%	4.73	5.93	7.11	8.29	9.49	10.65
	30%	4.15	5.18	6.21	7.49	8.31	9.35
1,000	10%	5.94	7.41	8.88	10.38	11.85	13.32
	20%	5.27	6.58	7.90	9.22	10.55	11.83
	30%	4.62	5.76	6.91	8.06	9.23	10.38
1,200	10%	7.13	8 89	10 65	12 46	14 22	15 98
	20%	6.32	7 90	9 48	11 06	12 66	14 20
	30%	5.54	6 91	8 29	9 67	11 08	12 46
1,400	10%	8.32	10.37	12.43	14.54	16.59	18.64
	20%	7.37	9.22	11.06	12.09	14.77	16.57
	30%	6.46	8.06	9.67	11.52	12.93	14.54
1,600	10%	9.51	11.85	14.21	16.52	18.96	21.30
	20%	8.42	10.54	12.64	14.74	16.88	18.94
	30%	7.38	9.21	11.05	13.13	14.78	16.62
1,800	10%	10.70	13.33	15.99	18.70	21.33	23.96
	20%	9.47	11.86	14.22	16.58	18.99	21.31
	30%	8.30	10.36	12.43	14.74	16.63	18.70
2,000	10%	11.89	14.81	17.77	20.78	23.70	26.62
	20%	10.52	13.18	15.80	18.42	21.10	23.68
	30%	9.22	11.51	13.82	16.12	18.46	20.76
2,200	10%	13.08	16.29	19.55	22.86	26.07	29.28
	20%	11.57	14.50	17.38	20.26	23.21	26.05
	30%	10.14	12.66	15.20	17.73	20.31	22.84
2,400	10%	14.27	17.77	21.33	24.94	28.44	31.94
	20%	12.62	15.87	18.96	22.10	25.32	28.42
	30%	11.06	13.81	16.58	19.34	22.16	24.92
2,600	10%	15.46	19.25	23.11	27.02	30.81	34.60
	20%	13.67	17.19	20.54	23.94	27.43	30.79
	30%	11.98	14.96	17.96	20.95	24.01	27.00
2,800	10%	16.65	20.73	24.89	29.10	33.18	37.26
	20%	14.72	18.51	22.12	25.78	29.54	33.16
	30%	12.90	16.11	19.34	22.56	25.86	29.08
3,000	10%	17.84	22.21	26.67	31.18	35.55	39.92
	20%	15.77	19.83	23.70	27.62	31.65	35.53
	30%	13.82	17.26	20.72	24.17	27.71	31.16

TABLE 11–5. INBOARD PROPELLER SELECTION— PITCH

The table, opposite, can be used to determine the approximate pitch a propeller should have to permit a boat to operate at its optimum cruising speed, or the approximate speed that will result from use of a propeller of a given pitch. Propeller shaft rpm and the boat's slip factor must be known. Light, fast racing boats have a slip of about 10%; runabouts, 12%-20%; fast cruisers, 18%-30%; and heavy cruisers, 20%-35%. Shaft speed is engine rpm divided by any reduction gear ratio present.

Table 11-6

INBOARD ENGINE PROPELLER SHAFT SELECTION						
SHAFT DIAMETER (inches)			ENGINE DISPLACEMENT (cu. in.)/ REDUCTION GEAR RATIO			
Naval or Tobin bronze	Monel, stainless steel, or aluminum bronze	1:1 (direct drive)	1.5:1	2:1	2.5:1	3:1
$\frac{7}{8}$	$\frac{3}{4}$	100-175				
1	$\frac{7}{8}$	175-250	100-175			
$1\frac{1}{8}$	1	250-325	175-250	100-175		
$1\frac{1}{4}$	$1\frac{1}{8}$	325-400	250-325	175-250	100-175	
$1\frac{3}{8}$	$1\frac{1}{4}$	400-500	325-400	250-325	175-250	100-175
$1\frac{1}{2}$	$1\frac{3}{8}$		400-500	325-400	250-325	175-250
$1\frac{5}{8}$	$1\frac{1}{2}$			400-500	325-400	250-325
$1\frac{3}{4}$	$1\frac{5}{8}$				400-500	325-400
2	$1\frac{3}{4}$					400-500

These figures are for gasoline engines. For diesel engines, add $\frac{1}{8}$″ diameter to all shaft size recommendations.

TABLE 11–7. OUTBOARD PROPELLER SELECTION

The following information is based on service manual material provided by major outboard motor manufacturers. As loads and applications may not match those shown, it may be necessary to test several propellers to find the one best suited to your needs.

TABLES

Table 11-7

OUTBOARD ENGINE PROPELLER SPECIFICATIONS

Motor Year(s)	Model	HP/RPM	PROPELLER Dia.	Pitch	Bl.	APPLICATION Approximate Gross Loads	Approximate Boat Length	Transom Height Stand.	Long	Speed Range (mph)
75		135/	13″	23″	3	Up to 1200	Up to 16′			48-60
		4500–	13″	21″	3	1100-1600	15′-17′			45-60
		5500	13″	19″	3	1400-1900	15′-17′			40-55
			13″	18″	3	1700-2200	16′-20′			35-45
			13″	17″	3	2000-2500	16′-20′			30-45
			13″	16″	3	2300-3200	17′-22′			27-37
			13″	15″	3	2600-3500	17′-22′			25-33
			13″	14″	3	3100-4000	18′-23′			19-27
			13″	13″	3	3600-4500	19′-24′			18-25
			13″	11″	3	Cruisers, Houseboats, workboats				15-22
			13″	11″	3″	3000-4000				
			14″	14″	3	Houseboats, Workboats				1-20
			14″	12″	3	Houseboats, Workboats				1-16
75		120/	13″	23″	3	Up to 1100	Up to 15′			49-58
		5000–	13″	21″	3	Up to 1200	14′-16′			45-55
		5500	13″	19″	3	1100-1600	15′-18′			41-49
			13″	18″	3	1200-1600	16′-20′			39-46
			13″	17″	3	1400-2000	16′-20′			34-44
			13″	16″	3	1700-2500	17′-22′			32-39
			13″	15″	3	2000-2900	17′-22′			25-35
			13″	14″	3	2300-3200	17′-22′			24-32
			13″	13″	3	2600-3400	18′-23′			22-29
			13″	11″	3	3000-4000	18′-23′			19-25
			14″	14″	3	Houseboats, Workboats				1-19
			14″	12″	3	Houseboats, Workboats				1-15
75		105/	13″	23″	3	Up to 1000	Up to 15′			40-50
		4500–	13″	21″	3	900-1200	14′-16′			38-48
		5500	13″	19″	3	1000-1400	15′-17′			36-46
			13″	18″	3	1200-1300	16′-18′			33-43
			13″	17″	3	1400-2200	16′-18′			31-41
			13″	16″	3	1600-2500	17′-20′			27-37
			13″	15″	3	1800-2900	17′-20′			26-36
			13″	14″	3	2000-3000	17′-20′			24-34
			13″	13″	3	2200-3200	18′-22′			20-30
			13″	11″	3	2400-3400	18′-22′			20-30
			14″	14″	3	Houseboats, Workboats				1-13
			14″	12″	3	Houseboats, Workboats				1-14
75		90/	13″	23″	3	Up to 1000	Up to 14′			38-50
		4500–	13″	21″	3	1000-1600	13′-15′			37-48
		5500	13″	19″	3	1100-1800	14′-17′			35-45
			13″	18″	3	1300-2000	15′-18′			33-43
			13″	17″	3	1500-2200	15′-18′			29-39
			13″	16″	3	1700-2500	16′-19′			25-35
			13″	15″	3	1800-2600	16′-19′			24-34
			13″	14″	3	2000-2800	16′-19′			21-31
			13″	13″	3	2200-3000	17′-20′			18-28
			13″	11″	3	2400-3200	17′-20′			18-28
			14″	14″	3	Houseboats, Workboats				1-18
			14″	12″	3	Houseboats, Workboats				1-15

Table 11-7 (continued) **OUTBOARD ENGINE PROPELLER SPECIFICATIONS**

Motor Year(s)	Model	HP/RPM	PROPELLER Dia.	PROPELLER Pitch	Bl.	APPLICATION Approximate Gross Loads	APPLICATION Approximate Boat Length	Transom Height Stand.	Transom Height Long	Speed Range (mph)
75	75/ 4400– 5100		13"	23"	3	Up to 900	Up to 14'			39-48
			13"	21"	3	800-1100	13'-15'			37-47
			13"	19"	3	1000-1600	14'-16'			35-45
			13"	18"	3	1200-1800	14'-16'			33-43
			13"	17"	3	1400-2000	15'-17'			27-37
			13"	16"	3	1600-2200	15'-17'			23-33
			13"	15"	3	1800-2400	16'-19'			22-32
			13"	14"	3	2000-2700	16'-19'			19-29
			13"	13"	3	2200-2900	16'-19'			17-26
			13"	11"	3	2400-3100	17'-20'			17-26
			14"	14"	3	Houseboats, Workboats				1-17
			14"	12"	3	Houseboats, Workboats				1-13
75	60/ 5000– 5500		10½"	15"	2	Up to 850	Up to 14'			35-45
			11"	13"	3	800-1400	14'-16'			26-38
			11½"	12"	3	1000-1800	14'-17'			24-34
			10⅜"	11½"	3	1200-2200	15'-19'			22-32
			10⅜"	10"	3	1400-2600	16'-20'			20-30
			10½"	7"	3	Houseboats, Workboats				1-15
75	55/ 5000– 5500		10½"	15"	2	Up to 700	Up to 14'			35-45
			10⅜"	14½"	3	500-1100	13'-15'			29-39
			10⅜"	13½"	3	500-1100	14'-16'			27-37
			10⅜"	12½"	3	700-1400	14'-17'			25-35
			10⅜"	11½"	3	900-1700	15'-17'			23-33
			10⅜"	10"	3	1100-2100	16'-19'			19-27
			10½"	7"	3	Houseboats, Workboats				1-15
75	45/ 4500– 5500		10½"	15"	2	Up to 700	Up to 14'			32-42
			10⅜"	14½"	3	500-1000	13'-15'			28-38
			10⅜"	13½"	3	600-1100	14'-16'			26-36
			10⅜"	12½"	3	700-1300	14'-17'			22-32
			10⅜"	11½"	3	900-1500	15'-18'			20-30
			10⅜"	10"	3	1100-1900	16'-19'			18-28
			10½"	7"	3	Houseboats, Workboats				1-15
75	35/ 4400– 5100		10½"	15"	2	Up to 600	Up to 14'			30-40
			10⅜"	14½"	3	300-800	13'-15'			27-37
			10⅜"	13½"	3	400-1100	13'-15'			25-35
			10⅜"	12½"	3	500-1200	13'-17'			21-31
			10⅜"	11½"	3	600-1400	15'-18'			19-29
			10⅜"	10"	3	700-1800	16'-19'			17-27
			10½"	7"	3	Houseboats, Workboats				1-15
75	30/ 4500– 5500		10½"	15"	2	Up to 500	Up to 14'			28-38
			10⅜"	14½"	3	300-700	12'-15'			24-34
			10⅜"	13½"	3	400-900	13'-16'			20-30
			10⅜"	12½"	3	500-1100	14'-17'			18-28
			10⅜"	11½"	3	600-1300	14'-18'			16-26
			10⅜"	10"	3	700-1500	15'-19'			14-24
			10½"	7"	3	Houseboats, Workboats				1-15

TABLES

Table 11-7 (continued) **OUTBOARD ENGINE PROPELLER SPECIFICATIONS**

Motor Year(s)	Model	HP/RPM	PROPELLER Dia.	Pitch	Bl.	APPLICATION Approximate Gross Loads	Approximate Boat Length	Transom Height Stand. Long	Speed Range (mph)
75	25/ 4500– 5500		8½"	11"	2	Up to 500	Up to 14'		20-30
			8½"	11"	3	400-600	12'-15'		19-29
			8½"	10"	3	500-900	12'-15'		17-27
			8½"	8½"	3	600-1000	13'-16'		15-25
			8½"	7½"	3	700-1500	13'-17'		13-23
			8½"	6"	3	Workboats, auxiliaries			1-14
75	20/ 4500– 5500		8½"	11"	2	Up to 500	Up to 14'		18-28
			8½"	11"	3	400-600	12'-15'		17-27
			8½"	10"	3	500-900	12'-15'		16-26
			8½"	8½"	3	600-1000	12'-15'		15-25
			8½"	7½"	3	1200+	13'-17'		13-23
			8½"	6"	3	Workboats, auxiliaries			1-14
75	15/ 4600– 5600		8"	9"	3	Up to 400	Up to 14'		18-28
			8⅛"	8¼"	3	Up to 600	11'-14'		18-28
			8¼"	8¾"	2	500-700	11'-14'		18-28
			8"	8"	3	500-700	12'-15'		16-26
			8¼"	8¼"	2	600-900	12'-15'		14-24
			8¼"	6"	2	900+	15'+		13-23
			8¼"	6"	3	Workboats, auxiliaries			1-15
			8¼"	4½"	3	Workboats, auxiliaries			1-15
75	10/ 4300– 5200		8"	9"	3	Up to 300	Up to 14'		15-25
			8⅛"	8¼"	3	Up to 400	Up to 14'		15-25
			8¼"	8¾"	2	300-500	Up to 14'		15-25
			7"	8"	3	300-500	11'-14'		14-24
			8¼"	8¼"	2	400-600	11'-14'		14-24
			8¼"	6"	2	500-900	12'-15'		11-19
			8¼"	6"	3	900+	12'-15'		1-15
			8¼"	4½"	3	Workboats, auxiliaries			1-15
75	8/ 4500– 5500		7½"	6½"	2	Up to 500	Up to 14'		10-20
			8"	5"	2	400-600	11'-15'		8-18
			8"	5"	2	400-700	11'-15'		8-18
			7"	4¾"	2	500-800	11'-15'		5-15
			8"	3½"	2	Workboats, auxiliaries			1-10
75	6/ 4500– 5500		7½"	6½"	2	Up to 400	Up to 14'		9-19
			8"	5"	2	300-600	11'-15'		7-17
			7"	4¾"	2	Workboats, auxiliaries			1-10
			8"	3½"	2	Workboats, auxiliaries			1-10
75	5/ 4250– 5250		7½"	6"	2	Up to 700	10'-14'		5-15
			7½"	4½"	3	700+			1-10
			7½"	3"	3	Workboats, auxiliaries			1-10
75	3.5/ 4000– 5000		7½"	4½"	2	All	All		

Table 11-7 (continued) OUTBOARD ENGINE PROPELLER SPECIFICATIONS

Motor Year(s)	Model	HP/RPM	PROPELLER Dia.	Pitch	Bl.	APPLICATION Approximate Gross Loads	Approximate Boat Length	Transom Height Stand.	Long	Speed Range (mph)
OMC (EVINRUDE & JOHNSON)										
73-75		135	12¾"	23"	3	High performance				48-65
			13¾"	23"	2	High performance				48-62
			12¾"	21"	3		15'18'			42-56
			13¾"	21"	2		15'-18'			42-54
			13"	19"	3		17'-19'			35-50
			13⅜"	17"	3		19'-22'			29-42
			13¼"	17"	3		19'-22'			29-40
			13¾"	15"	3	Planing houseboats, large cruisers				20-36
			14"	13"	3	Displacement boats, large houseboats				12-24
			14"	11"	3	Barge or workboats				1-14
71-73	Thru-hub exhaust	125	12¾"	23"	3	High performance				46-62
			13¾"	23"	2	High performance				46-62
73		115	13¾"	21"	2		15'-18'			42-52
			12¾"	21"	3		15'-18'			42-52
			13"	19"	3		17'-19'			33-45
			13⅜"	17"	3		19'-22'			27-38
			13¼"	17"	3		19'-22'			27-38
			13¾"	15"	3	Large boats, planing houseboats				18-32
			14"	13"	3	Displacement boats, houseboats				10-22
			14"	11"	3	Barges, workboats				1-12
71-75	Thru-hub exhaust	100	12¾"	23"	3	High performance				50-62
			13¾"	23"	2	High performance				50-62
69-72		115	13¾"	21"	2	Light, fast boats	13½'-16½'			42-52
			12¾"	21"	3		13½'-16½'			42-52
			13"	19"	3		15½'-18'			33-45
			13⅜"	17"	3		17½'-19'			27-38
			13¼"	17"	3		17½'-19'			27-38
			13¾"	15"	3	Large boats, planing houseboats				18-32
			14"	13"	3	Displacement boats, large houseboats				10-22
			14"	11"	3	Barges, workboats				1-12
69-74	Thru-hub exhaust	85	13¾"	23"	2	High performance			Long	47-59
			12¾"	23"	3	High performance			Long	47-59
			13¾"	21"	2		13'-16½'			40-52
			12¾"	21"	3		13'-16½'			40-52
			13"	19"	3		14'-17'			36-46
			13⅜"	17"	3		16'-18'			30-41
			13¼"	17"	3		16'-18'			30-41
			13¾"	15"	3		17½'-20'			24-35
			14"	13"	3	Large boats, planing houseboats				15-27
			14"	11"	3	Displacement boats, houseboats				6-18
			14"	9"	3	Barges, workboats				1-8
Thru 68		100	13¼"	20"	2		12'-15'		Long	
			13"	18"	2		12'-15'		Long	38-46
			12½"	18"	3		13'-16'			27-35
			12½"	16"	3		14'-17'			22-30
			13"	14"	3		16'-18'			18-26
			14"	12"	3		18'-20'			16-23
			14"	11"	3	Houseboats				12-19
			14¼"	10"	3	Barges, workboats				5-12
All Thru 68		60	10"	12"	3	General Purpose				
		65	10⅛"	11"	3	General Purpose				
		75	10"	9¼"	3	General Purpose				
		80								
		85								
		90								

TABLES

Table 11-7 (continued) ## OUTBOARD ENGINE PROPELLER SPECIFICATIONS

Motor Year(s)	Model	HP/RPM	PROPELLER Dia.	Pitch	Bl.	APPLICATION Approximate Gross Loads	Approximate Boat Length	Transom Height Stand.	Long	Speed Range (mph)
68-74		55	13¾"	23"	2	High performance boats			Long	43-55
		60	12¾"	23"	3	High performance boats			Long	43-55
	Thru hub exhaust	65	13¾"	21"	2	Fast boats	13'-15'			36-45
			12¾"	21"	3	Fast boats	13'-15'			36-48
			13"	19"	3		14'-16'			31-38
			13⅜"	17"	3		15½'-17'			26-33
			13¼"	17"	3		15½'-17'			26-33
			13¾"	15"	3		15½'-19'			20-28
			14"	13"	3	Large boats	17'-21'			15-22
			14"	11"	3	Large boats, planing houseboats				10-17
			14"	9"	3	Barges, displacement houseboats				1-12
71-74	Thru-hub exhaust	50	13¾"	21"	2	Light fast boats	12'-14'		Long	36-42
			12¾"	21"	3	High speed boats	12'-14'			36-42
			13"	19"	3		13'-15'			32-28
			13⅜"	17"	3		14'-16'			27-34
			13¼"	17"	3		14'-16'			27-34
			13¾"	15"	3		15'-18'			24-30
			14"	13"	3	Large boats				18-26
			14"	11"	3	Large boats, planing houseboats				13-20
			14"	9"	3	Large displacement boats				1-15
58-59		50	12⅛"	14"	3	General purpose				
51-56 All		25	10⅜"	14"	3	Light loads	13'-15'			26-35
		28	10½"	13"	3		14'-17'			24-32
		30	10½"	12"	3		16'-18'			22-29
		33	10⅜"	11½"	3		17½'-20'			18-26
		35	12¾"	11"	3		17½'-20'			18-26
		40	11"	9"	3	Heavy duty, large boats houseboats				1-20
57-75		15	9"	10"	3	Extremely weedy	12'-14'			20-30
			9"	10"	3	General purpose	12'-16'			20-30
All		18	9"	9"	3	Heavy loads	14'-16'			10-22
		20								
69-73		25								
51-57		10	9"	9"	3	General purpose	12'-14'			
56-57		10	9"	8"	3	General purpose	12'-14'			
58-63		10	8⅛"	8"	3	General purpose	12'-14'			
64-75		9½	8⅛"	8"	3	General purpose				
50-58		7½	8"	8½"	2	General purpose				
54-75		6	8"	7¼"	2	General purpose				
54-65		5½"	8"	7¼"	2	General purpose				
65-73		5	8"	7½"	3	General purpose				
64-72	Right angle	3	8"	5½"	3	General purpose				
		4	8"	4½"	3	Heavy loads				
73	Right angle	3	7½"	6"	3	General purpose				
		4								

Table 11-7 (continued) **OUTBOARD ENGINE PROPELLER SPECIFICATIONS**

Motor Year(s)	Model	HP/RPM	PROPELLER Dia.	Pitch	Bl.	APPLICATION Approximate Gross Loads	Approximate Boat Length	Transom Height Stand.	Long	Speed Range (mph)
52-70	Weedless	3 4	6⅛"	6¼"	2	General purpose				
71-72	Weedless	3 4	6⅜"	5½"	3	General purpose				
68-73		1½ 2	7¼"	4½"	3	General purpose				
MERCURY MARINE										
73-75	Merc 1500	150/ 4800- 5800	13"	25"	3	Up to 1300	Up to 17'	All	All	51-60
			13"	23"	3	1000-1800	Up to 18'	15	20"	48-56
			13"	21"	3	1500-2300	16'-19'			40-50
			13¾"	19"	3	1800-2600	17'-20'			37-45
			14"	17"	3	2100-3500	18'-21'			26-42
			14"	15"	3	3000 plus	20'-25'			15-29
			14"	13"	3	Workboats, houseboats				1-15
72	Merc 1400	140/ 4800- 5800	13"	25"	3	Up to 1200	Up to 17'	All	All	48-60
			13"	24"	2	Up to 1200	Up to 17'	15	20"	48-60
			13"	23"	3	Up to 1400	Up to 18'			44-52
			13"	22"	3	Up to 1400	Up to 18'			44-52
			13"	21"	3	1300-2100	16'-19'			39-46
			13"	20"	2	1300-2100	16'-19'			39-46
			13"	19"	3	1600-2400	16'-20"			37-41
			13"	17"	3	1700-3000	17'-21'			26-38
			14"	15"	3	6000 plus	20'-25'			15-28
			14"	13"	3	Workboats, houseboats				1-15
70-71	Merc 1350	135/ 4800- 5300	13"	24"	2	Up to 1200	Up to 17'	All	All	51-63
			13¾"	23"	2	Up to 1400	Up to 18'	15	20"	49-57
			13"	22"	2	Up to 1400	Up to 18'			52-60
			13¾"	21"	2	1200-2000	16'-19'			44-51
			13"	21"	3	1200-2000	16'-19'			44-51
			13"	20"	2	1200-2000	16'-19'			47-54
			13¾"	19"	2	1600-2400	17'-21'			39-46
			13"	19"	3	1600-2400	17'-21'			39-46
			13"	17"	3	2000-2800	19'-23'			33-41
			14"	15"	3	2400-3200	21'-25'			27-35
			14"	13"	3	3000-4500	23'-28'			20-29
			14"	11"	3	Houseboats				12-22
			14"	9½"	3	Workboats				1-14
73-75	Merc 1150	115/ 4800- 5300	13"	25"	3	Up to 1300	Up to 16'	All	All	51-56
			13"	23"	3	1000-1800	Up to 17'	15	20"	44-52
			13"	21"	3	1200-2100	16'-19'			40-47
			13"	19"	3	1500-2500	17'-20'			35-43
			13"	17"	3	2000-2800	18'-21'			31-39
			14"	15"	3	2300-3600	19'-24'			27-36
			14"	13"	3	3000-5000	20'-27'			18-31
			14"	11"	3	Houseboats, workboats				1-22
70-72	Merc 1150	115/ 4800- 5300	13"	23"	3	Up to 1300	Up to 16'	All	All	50-55
			13"	22"	2	Up to 1300	Up to 16'	15	20"	52-56
			13"	21"	3	1200-2000	16'-19'			44-51
			13"	20"	2	1200-2000	16'-19'			47-54
			13"	19"	3	1600-2400	17'-21'			39-46
			13"	17"	3	2000-2800	19'-23'			33-41
			14"	15"	3	2400-3200	21'-25'			27-35
			14"	13"	3	3000-4500	23'-28'			20-29
			14"	11"	3	Houseboats				12-22
			14"	9½"	3	Workboats				1-14

Table 11-7 (continued) **OUTBOARD ENGINE PROPELLER SPECIFICATIONS**

Motor Year(s)	Model	HP/RPM	PROPELLER Dia.	Pitch	Bl.	APPLICATION Approximate Gross Loads	Approximate Boat Length	Transom Height Stand.	Long	Speed Range (mph)
73	Merc 850	85/ 4800- 5500	13″	25″	3	Up to 1200	Up to 16′	All	All	45-52
			13″	23″	3	1000-1800	Up to 17′	15″	20″	41-48
			13″	21″	3	1200-2200	15′-18′			38-44
			13″	19″	3	1400-2300	16′-19′			34-41
			13″	17″	3	1800-2600	17′-20′			29-36
			14″	15″	3	2200-3200	19′-24′			25-32
			14″	13″	3	2400-4000	20′-26′			21-28
			14″	11″	3	Houseboats				15-23
			14″	9½″	3	Workboats				1-18
69-72	Merc 800	80/ 4800- 5300	13″	25″	3	Up to 950	Up to 15′	All	All	42-49
			13″	24″	2	Up to 950	Up to 15′	15″	20″	44-51
			13″	23″	3	Up to 1000	Up to 16′			36-44
			13″	22″	2	Up to 1000	Up to 16′			38-46
			13″	21″	3	1000-1800	15′-17′			34-42
			13″	20″	2	1000-1800	15′-17′			35-40
			13″	19″	3	1600-2200	16′-18′			32-36
			13″	17″	3	1900-2600	17′-19′			28-34
			14″	15″	3	2000-2800	19′-21′			24-29
			14″	13″	3	2000-3600	21′-23′			18-24
			14″	11″	3	Houseboats				13-20
			14″	9½″	3	Workboats				1-15
72-73	Merc 650 (3 cyl)	65/ 4800- 5300	10¾″	17″	3	Up to 750	Up to 14′	Al	All	43-50
			10¾″	16″	3	Up to 850	12′-14′	15″	20″	41-46
			11″	15″	3	Up to 950	13′-15′			38-43
			11¼″	14″	3	700-1300	14′-16′			35-40
			11½″	13″	3	950-1500	15′-17′			32-37
			11¾″	12″	3	1100-1700	16′-18′			27-34
			12″	11″	3	1300-2000	18′-20′			23-30
			12¼″	10″	3	1500-2500	20′-23′			19-27
			12¼″	9″	3	1700-3000	21′-25′		—	1-20
63-71	Merc 650 (4 cyl)	65/ 4800- 5300	13″	24″	2	Up to 1000	Up to 15′	All	All	43-50
			13¾″	23″	2	Up to 1000	Up to 16′	15″	20″	39-45
			13″	22″	2	Up to 1000	Up to 17′			40-46
			13¾″	21″	2	900-1300	15′-17′			35-41
			13″	21″	3	900-1300	15′-17′			35-41
			13″	20″	2	900-1300	15′-17′			36-42
			13″	19″	3	1000-1800	16′-19′			31-37
			13″	17″	3	1200-2000	18′-21′			26-33
			14″	15″	3	1800-2600	19′-22′			21-28
			14″	13″	3	2000-3000	20′-23′			16-23
			14″	11″	3	2200-3500	21′-24′			11-18
			14″	9½″	3	Houseboats				1-13
70-73	Merc 500	50/ 4800- 5500	10¾″	19″	3	Up to 1000	Up to 15′	All	All	37-44
			10¾″	17″	2	900-1200	14′-16′	15″	20″	32-39
			10¾″	17″	3	900-1200	14′-16′			32-39
			10¾″	15″	2	1000-1800	14′-16′			28-35
			10¾″	15″	3	1000-1800	14′-16′			28-35
			11″	13″	2	1200-2000	15′-17′			24-32
			10¾″	13″	3	1200-2000	15′-17′			24-32
			11″	12″	2	1400-2100	15′-17′			22-31
			10¾″	12″	3	1400-2100	15′-17′			22-31
			11″	11″	2	1600-2200	16′-18′			19-30
			10¾″	11″	3	1600-2200	16′-18′			19-30
			10¾″	10″	3	1800-2500	17′-20′			15-26
			10¾″	9″	3	2400 plus	20′ plus			1-16

Table 11-7 (continued) **OUTBOARD ENGINE PROPELLER SPECIFICATIONS**

Motor Year(s)	Model	HP/RPM	PROPELLER Dia.	Pitch	Bl.	APPLICATION Approximate Gross Loads	Approximate Boat Length	Transom Height Stand.	Long	Speed Range (mph)
72-73	Merc 402	40/ 4800- 5300	10¾"	17"	2	Up to 900	12'-14'	All	All	32-38
			10¾"	17"	3	Up to 900	12'-14'	15	20"	32-38
			10¾"	15"	2	700-1100	12'-15'			28-34
			10¾"	15"	3	700-1100	12'-15'			28-34
			11"	13"	2	800-1200	14'-16'			24-30
			10¾"	13"	3	800-1200	14'-16'			24-30
			11"	12"	2	1200-1700	15'-17'			22-28
			10¾"	12"	3	1200-1700	15'-17'			22-28
			11"	11"	2	1500-1800	16'-19'			19-26
			10¾"	11"	3	1500-1800	16'-19'			19-26
			10¾"	10"	3	1600-2000	18'-22'			15-23
			10¾"	9"	3	Workboats, auxiliaries				1-16
63-73	Merc 200	20/ 4800- 5500	9⅞"	11"	2	Up to 1000	12'-15'	All	All	22-23
			9⅞"	9"	3	850-1600	15' plus	15"	20"	13-24
			9⅞"	7"	3	Workboats, auxiliaries				1-14
68-73	Merc 110	9.8/ 4500- 5500	9"	10"	2	Up to 700	11'-14'	All	All	15-26
			9"	9"	2	400-700	12'-15'	15"	20"	15-20
			8¾"	7"	3	Workboats, auxiliaries				1-15
69-73	Merc 75	7.5/ 4500- 5500	9"	9"	2	Up to 450	8'-13'	15"	20"	15-20
			8¾"	7"	3	General purpose		15"	20"	3-16
75	Merc. 45	4/ 4500- 5500	8¼"	6"	2	General purpose		15"	20"	
69-74	Merc. 40	4/ 4500- 5500	8¼"	6"	2	General purpose		15"	20"	

Table 11-8

WEIGHT AND STRENGTH — MANILA, NYLON, AND CHAIN

	APPROX. WEIGHT OF 100' IN AIR				ROPE—Breaking Strength		CHAIN—Proof Test	
Diameter	Nylon Rope	Manila Rope	BBB Galv. Chain	6 x 19 Fiber Core Wire Rope	Nylon Yacht Rope	Manila Yacht Rope	BBB Gal. Coil Chain	High Strength Alloy Chain
1/4	1.6	1.9	76	100	1,300	650	2,700	6,500
5/16	2.6	3.2	115	160	2,000	1,150	3,700	. . . . .
3/8	3.8	4.0	170	230	2,900	1,550	4,600	13,000
7/16	5.2	5.1	225	310	3,900	1,900	6,200	. . . . .
1/2	6.9	6.5	295	400	5,000	2,900	8,200	22,000
9/16	8.8	8.5	350	510	6,200	3,800	10,200	. . . . .
5/8	10.8	11.2	430	630	7,500	4,800	12,500	33,000
3/4	15.8	13.8	600	900	10,700	5,900	17,700	46,000
7/8	21.8	20.8	810	1230	14,200	8,400	24,000	. . . . .
1	28.5	25.2	1050	1600	18,500	9,900	31,000	. . . . .

TABLES

Table 11-9

WEIGHT AND STRENGTH OF WIRE ROPE (Black

Size Circumference.	Flexible Steel Wire Rope 6 Strands, each 12 Wires			Extra Flexible Steel Wire Rope 6 Strands, each 24 Wires		Special Extra Flexible Steel Wire Rope. 6 Strands, each 37 Wires		Bullivant's Special Make.	Size Circumference
	Weight per Fathom Approx.	Guaranteed Breaking Strain.	Diameter of Barrel or Sheave round which it may be at a slow speed worked	Weight per Fathom Approx.	Guaranteed Breaking Strain	Weight per Fathom Approx.	Guaranteed Breaking Strain	Guaranteed Breaking Strain	
Inches	Lbs.	Tons	Inches	Lbs.	Tons	Lbs.	Tons	Tons	Inches
I	.63	1.75	6	.88	2.95	1.0	—	—	I
1¼	1.06	2.5	7½	1.31	4.45	1.56	—	—	1¼
1½	1.44	4.0	9	1.88	6.7	2.0	7.25	—	1½
1¾	2.0	5.5	10½	2.5	8.75	2.88	10.0	—	1¾
2	2.44	7.0	12	3.5	11.85	4.0	13.0	—	2
2¼	3.37	9.0	13½	4.5	14.6	4.88	15.75	—	2¼
2½	4.19	12.0	15	5.44	18.55	5.88	19.75	—	2½
2¾	5.25	15.0	16½	6.25	21.95	7.0	24.0	—	2¾
3	6.25	18.0	18	7.63	25·7	8.25	29.0	—	3
3¼	7.06	22.0	19½	9.37	30.8	10.38	33.5	—	3¼
3½	8.25	26.0	21	10.75	35.2	11.5	38.5	—	3½
3¾	9.87	29.0	22½	12.19	41.1	13.38	44.5	—	3¾
4	11.25	33.0	24	13.62	46.3	15.25	51.0	—	4
4¼	12.35	36.0	25½	15.69	52.9	17.12	58.0	—	4¼
4½	13.44	39.0	27	17.75	58.6	19.0	63.5	—	4½
4¾	—	—	—	19.98	66.4	21.69	71.25	—	4¾
5	—	—	—	22.5	74.2	24.38	79.25	—	5
5¼	—	—	—	23.25	82.88	27.69	87.75	—	5¼
5½	—	—	—	24.5	91.55	31.0	96.75	—	5½
5¾	—	—	—	—	—	33.75	103.75	—	5¾
6	—	—	—	—	—	36.5	113.75	—	6
6½	—	—	—	—	—	42.5	132.0	—	6½
7	—	—	—	—	—	48.5	154.0	—	7
7½	—	—	—	—	—	55.0	178.5	—	7½
8	—	—	—	—	—	63.0	198.0	202	8
9	—	—	—	—	—	79.0	250.0	257	9
10	—	—	—	—	—	98.5	305.0	318	10
11	—	—	—	—	—	120.0	—	381	11
12	—	—	—	—	—	142.0	—	455	12

Table 11-10   FIBER CORDAGE — TYPICAL WEIGHTS AND MINIMUM BREAKING STRENGTHS (POUNDS)

NOMINAL SIZE (inches)		MANILA Fed. Spec. TR 605			NYLON (High Tenacity—M.T.)			DU PONT DACRON or H.T. POLYESTER			POLYOLEFINS (M.T.) (Polypropylene and/or Polyethylene)			DOUBLE NYLON BRAID			POLYESTER/POLYOLEFIN DOUBLE BRAID		
Dia.	Circ.	Net Wt. 100'	Ft. per lb.	Breaking Strength	Net Wt. 100'	Ft. per lb.	Breaking Strength	Net Wt. 100'	Ft. per lb.	Breaking Strength	Net Wt. 100'	Ft. per lb.	Breaking Strength	Net Wt. 100'	Ft. per lb.	Breaking Strength	Net Wt. 100'	Ft. per lb.	Breaking Strength
3/16	5/8	1.47	68	450	1	100	1,000	1.3	77	1,000	.73	137	750	NA	NA	NA	.75	133	900
1/4	3/4	1.96	51	600	1.5	66.6	1,700	2.1	47.5	1,700	1.24	80	1,250	1.66	60.3	2,100	1.7	60.2	1,700
5/16	1	2.84	35	1,000	2.5	40	2,650	3.3	30	2,550	1.88	53	1,850	2.78	36	3,500	2.6	38.4	2,600
3/8	1 1/8	4.02	25	1,350	3.6	28	3,650	4.7	21.3	3,500	2.9	34.5	2,600	3.33	30	4,200	3.5	28.5	3,500
7/16	1 1/4	5.15	19.4	1,750	5	20	5,100	6.3	15.9	4,800	3.9	25.5	3,400	5.0	20	6,000	5.1	20	5,100
1/2	1 1/2	7.35	13.6	2,650	6.6	15	6,650	8.2	12.2	6,100	4.9	20.4	4,150	6.67	14.9	7,500	6.8	15	6,800
9/16	1 3/4	10.2	9.8	3,450	8.4	11.9	8,500	10.2	9.8	7,700	6.2	16	4,900	8.33	12	9,500	NA	NA	NA
5/8	2	13.1	7.6	4,400	10.5	9.5	10,300	13.2	7.6	9,500	7.8	12.8	5,900	11.1	9	12,000	11	9	11,000
3/4	2 1/4	16.3	6.1	5,400	14.5	6.9	14,600	17.9	5.6	13,200	11.1	9	7,900	15.0	6.7	17,000	15	6.7	15,000
7/8	2 3/4	22	4.55	7,700	20	5	19,600	24.9	4	17,500	15.4	6.5	11,000	20.8	4.8	23,700	20	5	20,000
1	3	26.5	3.77	9,000	26	3.84	25,000	30.4	3.3	22,000	18.6	5.4	13,000	25.0	4	28,500	28	3.6	28,000
1 1/8	3 1/2	35.2	2.84	12,000	34	2.94	33,250	40.5	2.5	26,500	24.2	4.1	17,500	35.0	2.8	39,000	35	2.8	35,000
1 1/4	3 3/4	40.8	2.45	13,500	39	2.56	37,800	46.2	2.16	30,500	27.5	3.6	20,000	40.0	2.5	44,000	40	2.5	40,000
1 5/16	4	46.9	2.13	15,000	45	2.22	44,500	53.4	1.87	34,500	31.3	3.2	23,000	45.0	2.2	49,500	45	2.2	45,000
1 1/2	4 1/2	58.8	1.7	18,500	55	1.8	55,000	67	1.5	43,000	39.5	2.5	29,000	60.0	1.6	65,000	60	1.6	60,000

NOTE:—The figures on synthetics, above, are an average of those available from four large cordage manufacturers. Those for the rope you buy should be availabe at your dealers. Check them carefully. Also check the rope. In general a soft, sleazy rope may be somewhat stronger and easier to splice but it will not wear as well and is more apt to hockle or unlay than a firm, well "locked-up" rope. Blended ropes, part polyolefins and part other fibers, may be found. Multifilament (fine filament) polypropylene looks like nylon—don't expect it to be as strong or do the job of nylon. (It floats, nylon doesn't.) Spun, or stapled, nylon and Dacron are not as strong as ropes made from continuous filaments but are less slippery and easier to grasp. Sometimes used for sheets on sailing craft.

*Du Pont registered trademark.

TABLES

Table 11-11

ROPE AND FIBER COMPARISON CHART

	MANILA	NYLON	DACRON	POLY-OLEFINS
Relative Strength	1	4	3	2
Relative Weight	3	2	4	1
Elongation	1	4	2	3
Relative Resistance to Impact or Shock Loads	1	4	2	3
Mildew and Rot Resistance	Poor	Excellent	Excellent	Excellent
Acid Resistance	Poor	Fair	Fair	Excellent
Alkali Resistance	Poor	Excellent	Excellent	Excellent
Sunlight Resistance	Fair	Fair	Good	Fair
Organic Solvent Resistance	Good	Good	Good	Fair
Melting Point	380° (Burns)	410°F.	410°F.	about 300°F.
Floatability	Only when new	None	None	Indefinite
*Relative Abrasion Resistance (*Depends on many factors— whether wet or dry, etc.)	2	3	4	1
KEY TO RATINGS: 1 Lowest—4 Highest				

Table 11-12

RECOMMENDED ROPE FOR VARIOUS USES

	Tie-Up or Mooring Lines	Anchor Ropes or Mooring Pennants	Sheets and Halyards	Flag Halyards	Seizing and Whipping	Bolt Rope Synthetic Sails	Towing	Water Skiing
MANILA	✓	✓	✓	✓			✓	
NYLON	✓	✓		✓			✓	
DACRON	✓		✓	✓		✓		
POLYOLEFIN	✓						✓	✓
BRAIDED DACRON			✓	✓				
BRAIDED NYLON	✓	✓		✓	✓		✓	
WIRE (Stainless)		Pennants	✓					
BRAIDED COTTON				✓	✓			
NYLON SEINE TWINE					✓			
LINEN or FLAX			✓	✓	✓			

Table 11-13   **METRIC CONVERSIONS**

1 mile.................1.609 km	1 km.................0.621 miles
1 nautical mile..........1.852 km	1 m.................1.094 yards
1 yard.................0.914 m	1 m.................3.281 feet
1 foot.................0.305 m	1 cm.................0.394 inches
1 inch.................25.4 mm	1 cm².................0.155 sq. in.
1 sq. in.................6.452 cm²	1 m².................10.76 sq. ft.
1 sq. ft.................0.836 m²	1 cm³.................0.061 cu. in.
1 cu. in.................16.39 cm³	1 m³.................35.315 cu. ft.
1 cu. ft.................0.283 m³	1 m³.................1.307 cu. yd.
1 gallon (US)..........3.785 litres	1 litre.............0.264 gallons
1 pint (US)............0.472 litres	1 litre.............2.119 pints
1 ounce..............28.35 grams	1 kg.................35.27 ounces
1 pound.................0.454 kg	1 kg.................2.205 pounds
1 lb. ft.................0.138 kgm	1 kgm.................7.233 lb. ft.
1 mile per hour......1.609 km/hour	1 km/hour.............0.621 mph
1 gallon per mile 235.2 litres/100 km	10 litres/100 km........0.042 gpm

Table 11-14   **WEIGHT AND STRENGTH OF METALS**

METAL	Specific Gravity	Lb. in a Cu. Ft.	Tearing Force	Crushing Force	Modulus of Elasticity
			Lb. on Sq. in.	Lb. on Sq. in.	Lb. on Sq. in.
Aluminum, cast........	2.560	160.0	—	—	—
Aluminum, sheet	2.670	166.9	—	—	—
Brass, cast..........	8.396	524.8	18,000	10,300	9,170,000
Brass, sheet	8.525	532.8	31,360	—	—
Brass, wire	8.544	533.0	49,000	—	14,230,000
Bronze.............	8.222	513.4	—	—	—
Copper, bolts........	8.850	531.3	36,000	—	—
Copper, cast	8.607	537.9	19,000	—	—
Copper, sheet	8.785	549.1	30,000	—	—
Copper, wire	8.878	548.6	60,000	—	—
Iron, cast, average	7.125	445.3	16,500	112,000	17,000,000
Iron, wrought, average .	7.680	480.0	60,000	36,000	28,000,000
Lead, cast...........	11.352	709.5	1,792	6,900	—
Lead, sheet..........	11.400	712.8	3,328	—	720,000
Nickel, cast.........	7.807	487.9	—	—	—
Steel, hard..........	7.818	488.6	103,000	—	42,000,000
Steel, soft..........	7.834	489.6	121,700	—	29,000,000
Zinc, cast	7.028	439.3	8,500	—	13,500,000
Zinc, sheet	7.291	455.7	7,111	—	12,650,000

TABLES

Table 11-15

STAINLESS STEEL, MONEL, & COPPER-NICKEL IN MARINE USE.

Material	Application	Yield Strength	Tensile Strength	Elongation % in 2"
302 S.S.)	rails, trim, cable, hardware,	40 KSI	90 KSI	50
304 S.S.)	galley equipment	42 KSI	84 KSI	55
305 S.S.	bolts, nuts, screws, fasteners	35 KSI	85 KSI	50
316 S.S.	general use, preferred choice in salt spray	42 KSI	84 KSI	50
316L S.S.	preferred choice for welding	34 KSI	81 KSI	50
17-4 PH S.S.	propeller shafts	175 KSI	205 KSI	15
Monel Alloy 400	pump parts, water boxes, valves, tubing, fasteners	35 KSI	80 KSI	45
Money Alloy K-500	valves, pump shafts, high strength applications	130 KSI	160 KSI	22
70/30 Copper-Nickel	pipe, tubing, water boxes, etc.	25 KSI	60 KSI	45
90/10 Copper-Nickel	pipe, tubing, water boxes, etc.	16 KSI	44 KSI	42

Table 11-16

WEIGHT OF WATER

Fresh Water

A cubic foot=.0312 ton=62.39 lb.=998.18 avd. oz.=7.481 gal.
A cubic inch=.0362 lb.=.5776 avd. oz.=.0043 gal.
A gallon=.00417 ton=8.340 lb.=133.44 avd. oz.=.1336 cu. ft.
A ton=32.054 cu. ft.=2000 lb.=239.79 gal.
Weight of fresh water=weight of salt water × .9740.

Salt Water

A cubic foot=.0320 ton=64.05 lb.=1024.80 avd. oz.=7.481 gal.
A cubic inch=.0371 lb.=.5930 avd. oz.=.0043 gal.
A gallon=.00428 ton=8.561 lb.=136.97 avd. oz.=.1336 cu. ft.
A ton=31.225 cu. ft.=2000 lb.=233.59 gal.

Table 11-17

WEIGHT AND STRENGTH OF TIMBER

Name.	Specific Gravity.	Lbs. in a Cub. Ft.	Tearing Force.	Crushing Force.	Breaking Force.	Modulus of Elasticity
			Lbs. on Sq. In.	Lbs. on Sq. In.	Lbs. on Sq. In.	Lbs. on Sq. In.
Acacia	.710	44.4	16,000	—	—	—
Alder	.555	34.6	14,186	6,895	9,540	1,087,000
Apple	.793	49.5	19,500	6,499	—	—
Ash	.753	47.0	17,000	9,000	12,200	1,645,000
Beech	.700	43.8	11,500	9,363	9,336	1,354,000
Birch	.750	46.9	15,000	6,402	11,671	1,645,000
Box	.1000	62.5	20,000	10,299	—	—
Cedar	.486	30.8	11,400	5,800	7,420	486,000
Chestnut	.535	33.4	13,300	—	10,656	1,137,000
Cypress	·655	41.0	6,000	—	—	—
Ebony	1.279	79.4	—	19,000	136,00	1,300,000
Elder	.695	43.4	10,230	8,467	—	—
Elm	.544	33.8	13,489	10,331	6,078	700,000
Fir, larch	.496	31.0	10,220	5,568	5,943	1,363,000
" pitch-pine	.660	41.2	7,818	—	9,792	1,226,000
" red pine	.577	36.1	14,300	5,375	8,844	1,458,000
" spruce	.512	32.0	10,100	6,500	12,346	1,804,000
" yellow pine	.461	28.8	—	5,445	—	1,600,000
Greenheart	1.001	62.5	—	—	16,654	2,656,000
Hawthorn	.910	56.8	10,500	—	—	—
Hazel	.860	53.7	18,000	4,600	—	—
Hornbeam . . -	.760	47.4	20,240	7,289	—	—
Laburnum	.920	57.4	10,500	—	—	—
Lancewood	.675	42.1	—	6,614	17,354	812,000
Lignum-vitae	1.333	83.2	11,800	9,921	11,400	558,000
Lime	.760	47.4	23,500	—	11,202	1,152,000
Mahogany, Australian	.952	59.4	—	9,921	20,238	1,157,000
" Honduras . . .	.560	35.0	—	—	11,475	1,593,000
" Spanish	.853	53.2	21,800	8,198	7,560	1,255,000
Oak, British	.934	58.3	10,000	10,055	10,032	1,451,000
" Dantzic	.756	47.2	12,780	7,723	8,742	1,191,000
" red	.872	64.4	10,253	5,987	10,596	2,149,000
" Riga	.688	43.0	—	—	12,888	1,610,000
Poplar	.511	31.9	7,200	5,124	10,260	1,134,000
Sycamore	.590	36.8	13,000	—	9,630	1,036,000
Teak, African	.983	61.3	21,000	9,320	14,976	2,305,000
" Indian	.880	55.0	15,000	—	14,600	2,800,000
Walnut	.671	41.8	8,130	6,645	8,000	—
Willow	.405	25.3	—	—	6,570	—
Yew	.807	50.3	8,000	—	—	—

TABLES

Table 11-18

WEIGHT OF LIQUID FUELS

Fuel	Average Pounds Per Gallon
Diesel fuel	7.1
Gasoline	6.0

Table 11-19

VISIBILITY AT SEA

Approx. distance of sea horizon from height above sea level:

Height in feet	Distance naut. miles	Height in feet	Distance naut. miles
4	2.3	100	11.5
10	3.6	120	12.6
15	4.4	140	13.6
20	5.1	150	14.1
30	6.3	200	16.25
40	7.25	250	18.2
50	8.1	300	19.9
60	8.9	350	21.5
70	9.6	400	23.0
80	10.3	450	24.4
90	10.9	500	25.7

Table 11-20

VELOCITY OF SOUND

In miles for intervals from one to twenty seconds, at average Summer temperature.

Interval, Seconds	Distance, Miles	Intervals, Seconds	Distance, Miles
1	.21	11	2.33
2	.42	12	2.54
3	.63	13	2.75
4	.85	14	2.96
5	1.06	15	3.18
6	1.27	16	3.40
7	1.48	17	3.61
8	1.70	18	3.82
9	1.91	19	4.03
10	2.12	20	4.24

Table 11-21

TECHNICAL VALUES AND FORMULA

1 horsepower=33,000 foot pounds per minute.

1 atmosphere (technical expression for pressure)=14.223 lb./sq. in.=1 kg/cm²=water column of 10 metres.

The circumference of a circle=Diameter × 3.1416.

The diameter of a circle=Circumference × 0.3183.

The area of a circle=Radius × radius × 3.1416 (πr^2).

The area of a cylinder=Circumference × height + end areas as determined above.

The area of an ellipse=$\dfrac{\text{Largest length} \times \text{largest width}}{2}$ × 3.1416

The area of parallelogram=Base × vertical height.

The area of a parallel trapezoid=Half the total length of the parallel sides × vertical height.

The volume of a sphere=Diam. × diam. × diam. × 0.5236 $\left(\text{or }\dfrac{4\pi r^3}{3}\right)$

The area of a sphere=Diam. × diam. × 3.1416 (or $4\pi r^2$).

The area of a triangle=Base × vertical height divided by two.

The volume of a cube = Base × side × side. (Also applies to a right angled parallelepiped.

The volume of a pyramid=Side × height divided by three.

The volume of a cone=Radius × radius × height × 3.1416 divided by three.

Table 11-22

GALVANIC SERIES OF METALS IN SEA WATER

ANODIC
OR LEAST NOBLE
— ACTIVE

Magnesium and magnesium alloys
CB75 aluminum anode alloy
Zinc
B605 aluminum anode alloy
Galvanized steel or galvanized wrought iron
Aluminum 7072 (cladding alloy)
Aluminum 5456, 5086, 5052
Aluminum 3003, 1100, 6061, 356
Cadmium
2117 aluminum rivet alloy
Mild steel
Wrought iron
Cast Iron
Ni-Resist
13% chromium stainless steel, type 410 (active)
50-50 lead tin solder
18-8 stainless steel, type 304 (active)
18-8 3% NO stainless steel, type 316 (active)
Lead
Tin
Muntz metal
Manganese bronze
Naval brass (60% copper—39% zinc)
Nickel (active)
78% Ni.-13.5% Cr.-6% Fe. (Inconel) (Active)
Yellow brass (65% copper—35% zinc)
Admiralty brass
Aluminum bronze
Red brass (85% copper—15% zinc)
Copper
Silicon bronze

CATHODIC
OR MOST NOBLE
—PASSIVE

  5% Zn.—20% Ni.—75% Cu.
90% Cu.—10% Ni.
70% Cu.—30% Ni.
88% Cu.— 2% Zn.—10% Sn. (composition G-bronze)
88% Cu.— 3% Zn.—6.5% Sn.—1.5% Pb
                         (composition M-bronze)
Nickel (passive)
78% Ni.—13.5% Cr.—6% Fe. (Inconel) (Passive)
70% Ni.—30% Cu.
18-8 stainless steel type 304 (passive)
18-8 3% Mo. stainless steel, type 316 (passive)
Hastelloy C
Titanium
Platinum

TABLES

Table 11-23   THE DECIMAL EQUIVALENTS OF THE DIVISIONS OF THE FOOT.

In.	0	1/16	1/8	3/16	1/4	5/16	3/8	7/16	1/2	9/16	5/8	11/16	3/4	13/16	7/8	15/16
0		.0052	.0104	.0156	.0208	.0260	.0313	.0365	.0417	.0469	.0521	.0573	.0625	.0677	.0729	.0781
1	.0833	.0885	.0937	.0990	.1042	.1094	.1146	.1198	.1250	.1302	.1354	.1406	.1458	.1510	.1563	.1615
2	.1667	.1719	.1771	.1825	.1875	.1927	.1979	.2031	.2083	.2135	.2188	.2240	.2292	.2344	.2396	.2448
3	.2500	.2552	.2604	.2656	.2708	.2760	.2813	.2865	.2917	.2969	.3021	.3073	.3125	.3177	.3229	.3281
4	.3333	.3385	.3437	.3490	.3542	.3594	.3646	.3698	.3750	.3802	.3854	.3906	.3958	.4010	.4063	.4115
5	.4167	.4219	.4271	.4323	.4375	.4427	.4479	.4531	.4583	.4635	.4688	.4740	.4792	.4844	.4896	.4948
6	.5000	.5052	.5104	.5156	.5208	.5260	.5313	.5365	.5417	.5469	.5521	.5573	.5625	.5677	.5729	.5781
7	.5833	.5885	.5937	.5990	.6052	.6094	.6146	.6198	.6250	.6302	.6354	.6406	.6458	.6510	.6563	.6615
8	.6667	.6719	.6771	.6823	.6875	.6927	.6979	.7031	.7083	.7135	.7187	.7240	.7292	.7344	.7396	.7448
9	.7500	.7552	.7604	.7656	.7708	.7760	.7813	.7865	.7917	.7969	.8021	.8073	.8125	.8177	.8229	.8281
10	.8333	.8385	.8437	.8490	.8542	.8594	.8646	.8698	.8750	.8802	.8854	.8906	.8958	.9010	.9063	.9115
11	.9167	.9219	.9271	.9323	.9375	.9427	.9479	.9531	.9583	.9635	.9688	.9740	.9792	.9844	.9896	.9948

Table 11-24   **ASTRONOMICAL DISTANCES**

---

1 light-second=186,000 miles.
1 light-minute=11 million miles.
1 light-year=5.88 $\times$ 10^{12} miles.
1 parsec=3.26 light-years.
The distance from the earth to the nearest solar system=4.3 light-years.
The distance of the sun from the earth=8.3 light-minutes=approx. 93 million miles=
    108 sun diameters.
The distance of the moon from the earth=1.25 light-seconds=approx. 240,000 miles.
The diameter of the earth=7,928 miles.
The diameter of the sun=864,000 miles.
The diameter of the moon=2158 miles.
The volume of the earth=approx. 259 $\times$ 10^9 miles.
The area of the earth=197 million square miles.
Land area of earth=29% of total area.
Sea area of earth=71% of total area.
The mass of the earth=6.6 $\times$ 10^{21} tons.
The average density of the earth=5.52.
The mass of the sun=approx. 333,000 times that of the earth.
The mass of the moon=1/81 of that of the earth.

12.

MAINTENANCE

Some skippers find that half the fun of boating is the work they put into it. Whether it's cleaning, painting, or engine adjustments, they take pride in their ability to do the job; they enjoy using their hands; they have confidence in the results of their efforts.

Whether you find it fun or not, maintenance is as much a part of boat ownership as is the use of the boat. Whether for spring fitting out, or for upkeep of a vessel that's in use all year long, there are jobs that should be part of your yachting routine.

Here is the basic information you need on cleaning and painting, engine maintenance, care of electrical systems, plumbing, and trailers; tool lists. For your convenience, maintenance procedures are presented in check-list form wherever possible.

TOOLS FOR TUNING AND SPRUCING UP

Basic Ashore-and-Afloat Tool Kit

Hammer	*Screw Driver*	*Knife*	*Chisel*
Pliers	*Drill & Bits*	*Adjustable Wrench*	

Maintenance Tools

Basic Afloat-Ashore Kit plus:

Cross-cut Saw   Hack Saw   *Brace with bits up to 1" dia.*
Set of Screwdrivers with insulated handles,
large models with square shafts
½" *and 1" Chisels   Oval Rasp   Assorted Files*
Set of open-end Wrenches   Adjustable Plumber's Wrench
Needle and Snub-nose Pliers   Metal Snips   Plane
Plug Cutter   Vise-grip Pliers   Yankee Screwdriver
with regular and Phillips head bits   Plus your own favorites.

Power Tools

Paint Remover Heaters   Shop Vacuum Cleaners
Soldering Guns & Irons   Disc, Belt & Orbital Sanders
Circular and Sabre Saws
Hand Drills—with accessories such as: router and expansion bits, screwdriver, angle & speed reduction heads with slip clutch, drill press, oversize chucks & bits, water pump

Non-Tools for Your Tool Box

Oil Can   Fid   Whetstone   Tarpaulin   Magnet
Flashlight   Tape   Whipping Thread   Rags
Plastic Drop Cloth   Monel Wire   Rigger's Apron
Roll of Paper Towels   Staple Gun & Monel Staples
Can of Silicone Lubricant   Can of Bedding & Sealing Compound
Epoxy Putty & Glue   Marline
Stainless Steel Cotter Rings & Pins
Stainless Shackles & Hose Clamps
Trouble Lamp & Extension Cord
Current Checker & Continuity Tester
Pencils   Pad   Tape Measure

CLUES TO SHIPSHAPE CLEAN-UP

by John Duffett

Basic Clean-up Kit

- *50 feet of hose*
- *soap and scouring cleanser*
- *rust remover and old rags*
- *large sponge and long-handled mop*
- *bilge cleaner compound*
- *metal polish and wax*
- *scouring pads, steel or bronze wool*
- *wet-or-dry sandpaper*
- *rubber gloves*
- *small selected kit of these to also keep aboard*

Topsides

With all covers and bracing removed, first hose down to wash off all traces of salt, dust, loose grime. Scrub with a trisodium phosphate based cleaner, available from paint, hardware and building supply outlets. Stubborn spots can be treated with scouring powder, though this may remove gloss. Areas dulled by scouring are buffed to renew gloss.

Bottom

Growth, scum, and waterline weeds along the boot topping that were not removed when the boat was hauled will have hardened and are twice as hard to get off. Marine stores locally may stock compounds particularly suitable for loosening the barnacles or pollutants that attack boats secured afloat all season. As with bottom paints, your most effective mix may vary from harbor to harbor.

- Hose bottom to wash off or soften any growths.
- Attack barnacles with a metal scraper.
- Use power sander on stubborn spots.

MAINTENANCE

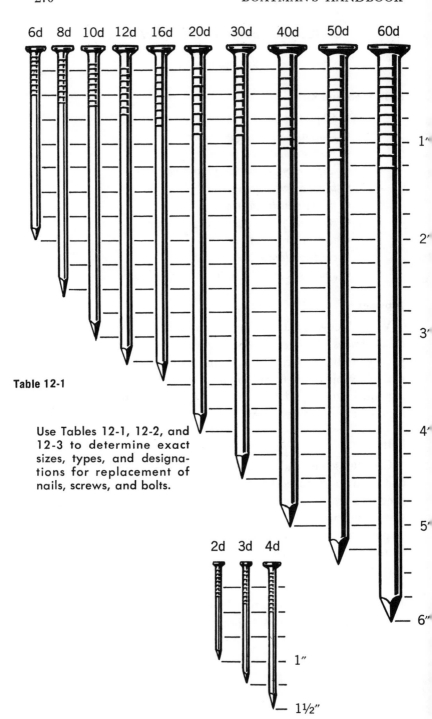

Table 12-1

Use Tables 12-1, 12-2, and 12-3 to determine exact sizes, types, and designations for replacement of nails, screws, and bolts.

Table 12-2

Screw sizes (gauge): 2, 3, 4, 5, 6, 7, 8, 9, 10, 11, 12, 14, 16

Length scale: ½", 1", 1½", 2"

LAG SCREW (SQUARE HEAD)

FILLISTER HEAD

OVAL HEAD

ROUND HEAD (R.H.)

FLAT HEAD (F.H.)

SHANK SIZE (GAUGE)

PLAIN SLOTTED HEADS

PHILLIPS HEAD

MAINTENANCE

• Keep wetting bottom to avoid breathing toxic dust if anti-fouling paint has been used.

• Note seams or gouges that will require sealant or pointing up before painting.

• Recall and note down, if possible, brand of bottom paint previously used. Application of new type may not bond to old formulation. If in doubt, cleaning down to bare hull may be necessary.

Bilge

Hose out and pump out bilges, checking freedom of limber holes and pumps at same time. Rewash with bilge cleaner compound or soap concentrate.

If boat normally has some rain water, spray or leakage collecting in the bilge, consider putting in one of the bilge cleaner additives that slosh around and maintain clean condition while boat is underway.

Engines

Exterior: use a marine or automotive cleaner that can degrease and remove any caked dirt from engine so that condition of paint and excessive rusting, chafing hoses, or loose control linkage can be observed.

Interior: run automotive solvent through carburetor to dissolve any gum formation. Add water-inhibitor to gas tank as well.

Lines

Give all cordage fresh water washing while examining for chafes. Switch end for end to equalize wear, and replace if in doubt.

Spot check by untwisting lay to examine for interior sand that could be chafing the line. Do not use pressure hose in washing since this also might force in cutting grit.

Interiors

• Wash down bulkheads with soap and water, or a cleaner such as Nautabrite.

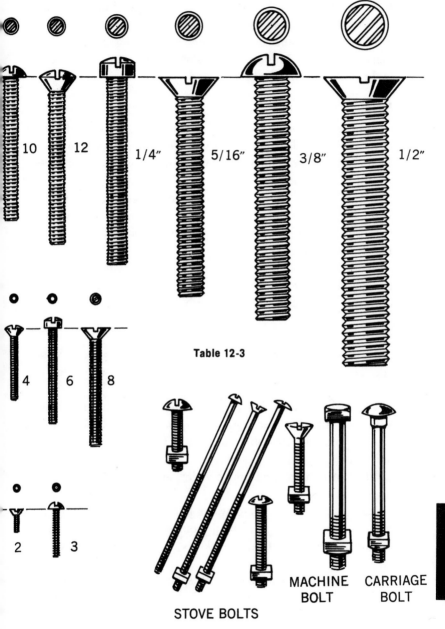

10   12   1/4"   5/16"   3/8"   1/2"

4   6   8

Table 12-3

2   3

STOVE BOLTS   MACHINE BOLT   CARRIAGE BOLT

● Treat forepeak and cuddy corners that get little ventilation with anti-dryrot compounds aboard wood boats.

● After washing and airing, use one of the fungus control treatments like MDR Mildew & Anti-Rot Spray to inhibit must and mold in cabinets and lockers.

Metals

Aluminum: Remove oil and grease with cleaning fluid. A cleaner-wax-polish combination will treat bare aluminum.

For painted aluminum, use mild soap and water or auto body paint polish-cleaner.

Brass, Bronze, Chrome: Regular metal cleaners and polishes will remove tarnish. Use a heavy duty compound like ABC Metal Cleanser for tougher corrosion. Spray coatings or waxes will help metals keep shine.

Stainless, Iron, Monel: Scouring pads and powder can remove surface rust. Use products like Rust-Away or Naval Jelly for extensive rust. Polish with wire brush. Rinse down.

Plastics

Fiberglass, Formica, Royalite: Various products are now sold specifically for fiberglass cleaning, or use mild detergent and water.

Gel coat stains can be scoured, though buffing afterward with a product like DuPont White Compound may be necessary to renew gloss plus matching color. Wax for fiberglass can protect surface.

Vinyl: A detergent will remove dirt, and vinyl paint can renew appearance.

Plexiglas: Mild soap and water but no scouring powder. Salt crystals can be washed off with compound like Travaco's Sea-2 Liquid Concentrate. It also works as wash fluid with windshield wipers.

Scratches can be removed with special Plexiglas buffing compounds.

PVC (Polyvinyl Chloride): Wood alcohol can be used sparingly, but will soften surface if overdone.

Sails

Coastal sailors should wash out salt when sailboat is hauled. Mild sudsing with soap (no detergents) plus fresh water rinse is best spring treatment.

Wood

Painted Surfaces: Washing down with cleaning fluid like Soilax is sufficient. For cabinets, mix in anti-fungus additive.

Varnished Surfaces: Wash down, though breaks in varnish surface of mahogany may have allowed discoloration to start that will require bleaching before revarnishing.

Teak: Use one of special teak cleaners. Then restore color with compound like Kuhls Teak Oil.

MARINE PAINTS

by John L. Duffett

Painting Principles

- Read the instructions on the can.
- Clean and prepare surface carefully.
- Remove loose flakes of previous coat, and all of it if in doubt about its compatibility with new paint.
- Use same brands, if possible, for each coat.
- Observe specified temperature and humidity requirements.
- Note if boat should be launched while bottom paint is still wet.
- Clean brushes before they dry.

Aluminum

Your boat builder can probably recommend the proper paints and tell you which brands were previously used. Vinyl-based paints are usually satisfactory. Prepare previously unpainted aluminum by washing with an etching cleaner. Then rinse and let dry before applying vinyl-base primer.

Before applying anti-fouling bottom paint, start with vinyl primer-undercoater. Final coats should be vinyl base with Tri-butyl-Tin Oxide as the active toxic agent and called TBTO or Bio-Met. Use of copper or red lead paints is not recommended.

Canvas

Paint coats year after year on canvas decks can build up layers that accelerate cracking. One answer is to use low cost house paint that chalks and wears off during the season. Synthetic resin paints are also suitable, and sand or grit compound can be added to final coat for non-skid surface.

Treat flexible canvas tops and covers with primer and one of the new liquid vinyl coatings.

Engines

Paints that resist high heat are used, and fire-retardant paints or additives can be employed to paint engine compartment.

Fiberglass

Unpainted surface should first be washed with solvent to remove any wax or mold-release substance. Cracks, dents, or orange-peel hairlines can be filled with surfacing compound recommended by paint manufacturer. For use on fiberglass, Alkyd, Alkyd Acrilic, Alkyd Polyurethane, Polyurethane, Polyester Silicone, Epoxy and Vinyl paints are all satisfactory.

Tinted epoxy and polyester resins are now available with pigments to match breaks in the gel coat or areas that have weathered and changed color so that molded-in hue can be matched.

Boats that are hauled out after every use may need no bottom paint, but could use a hard gloss containing no anti-fouling properties for speed.

For anti-fouling treatment, no primer may be needed after the solvent wash to remove any wax. Copper, lead, or tin-bearing anti-fouling paints may be used with any base except the alkyds.

Lower Drive Units

Stern drive and outboard motor shafts that stick down into the water may be treated with anti-corrosive enamels and, in some cases, anti-fouling compounds. Engine builders and paint manufacturers can make recommendations. Original colors can usually be matched.

Steel

Once the metal has been properly prepared, paints used on wood, fiberglass, or aluminum, as well as those with special rust inhibitors, can be employed. First sand blast or use an etching-type wash. Prime with zinc chromate, red lead, or other rust inhibitor.

Before applying anti-fouling on the bottom, two coats of barrier non-metallic paint should go over the primer beneath the final anti-fouling. Galvanic corrosion could result if copper-bearing paint came in contact with the steel. Some paint producers provide a system of compatible paints for steel hull use.

Vinyl

Cushions, seat covers and curtains as well as tops and cockpit covers of vinyl can be renewed with liquid vinyl coatings available in many colors.

Wood

Suitable for application on wood are Alkyd, Alkyd Acrilic, Alkyd Polyurethane, Polyurethane, Polyester Silicone, Epoxy, Latex Liquid Rubber, and Vinyl. Success, however, will depend on how well the wood surface has been cleaned, sanded, and prepared. Priming and fillers should usually be of the non-oily type and preferably of the same brand as the final paint. A wood bottom may be treated with any of the anti-fouling paints or with

MAINTENANCE

a hard non-toxic racing surface if the boat will not be left in the water.

Varnishes, whether tung oil and phenolic resin types or the newer synthetics and two-part epoxy systems, require careful application. Follow instructions as to surface sanding and bleaching if brightwork has weathered. Then, on a nearly windless day with the right temperature, apply the needed number of coats.

HOW MUCH PAINT DO YOU NEED?

From the Woolsey booklet, *How to Paint Your Boat,* Copyright 1967 by Woolsey Marine Industries, Inc. Reprinted by permission.

In estimating the amount of material needed for a specific job, you may assume that one gallon of paint or enamel will cover 500 sq. ft. for one coat on the average painted surface. Over new wood, use the figure of 325 sq. ft. per gallon. One gallon of varnish will cover 750 sq. ft. average on recoat work, and 500 sq. ft. on new wood. Paint and varnish remover may take several applications and consequently can be expected to soften only about 200–250 sq. ft. per gallon.

Some Useful Formulas

Here are some formulas based on practical experience. They should help you in determining how much paint you will need. The results are stated in gallons.

Spars (Varnished)

Multiply the greatest diameter (in feet) by the length (in feet) and multiply the result by 2.5. For new wood divide the result by 500 and for previously finished wood divide by 750 to obtain the gallonage required.

For example, suppose you have a new spar 8″ in diameter and 40′ long. Then $\dfrac{8/12 \times 40 \times 2.5}{500} = \dfrac{67}{500}$ or approximately ⅛ gallon

PAINT LOG for ...

Surface	Color	Product Used	1975		1976		1977	
			Amount	Cost	Amount	Cost	Amount	Cost
Spars								
Decks								
Bright-work								
Cabins								
Interior								
Topsides								
Boot-topping								
Bottom								
Engine								
Dinghy								
Seams								

MAINTENANCE

(1 pint) for the priming coat. For refinishing work, a pint is enough for about 1½ coats. To determine the requirements for painted spars, change the coverage factor to 325 for new work and to 500 for previously painted wood.

Cabins or Deck Houses

Multiply the height of the deck house (in feet) by the girth (in feet). Deduct the area of any large areas such as windows and doors. If the deck house is to be painted, divide the result by 325 for the priming coat and 500 for each finishing coat. If it is to be varnished, divide by 500 for the first coat and 750 for the following coats.

Decks

Multiply the length of the boat (in feet) by its greatest beam (in feet) and then multiply the result by 0.75. From this deduct the area of cabin houses, hatches, etc. Divide the remainder by 325 to obtain gallons required for priming coat and by 500 for each finishing coat of color.

If the deck is to be coated with Cawspar Varnish, divide the figure by 500 and 750 respectively.

Topsides

Multiply the length over all (in feet) by the greatest freeboard (in feet). Multiply the result by 1.5. Divide by 325 for new work and by 500 for old work to obtain the gallonage.

The Bottom

Multiply the waterline length by the draft (in feet). For a keel boat multiply by 3.5 and for a centerboard boat multiply by 3.0. Divide the result by 300 for priming new work, and by 400 for subsequent coats, to give the required gallonage.

SEALANTS & BEDDING COMPOUNDS

by John Duffett

Spring used to be the time of year when seams were caulked and then the boat launched and watched carefully to see if the seams would swell shut before the boat took on too much water and started to sink. Fortunately raking out old dried compound and refilling the seams of wooden boats is no longer a major part of fitting-out. But keeping water outside the boat where it belongs is still the job of a variety of sealants.

The old oil-base putty type of seam compounds are still available, but when used in wood boat seams the seams should be primed first to prevent absorption of the oil from the compound into the wood so quickly that the caulking promptly dries up. Deep seams were first filled with cotton and sometimes packed so tightly by amateurs that fastenings and planking let go as the wood tried to expand once in the water.

Bedding compound used under deck fittings to keep water from leaking through the bolt holes and moisture from starting rot in the wood would also dry out and harden in a year or so. It is still used, however, to bed through-hull fittings below the water line when a toxic mixture is needed to repel barnacles. But now most bedding and sealing chores are handled by the rubber-type products that keep their elasticity indefinitely, do not dry out or harden, and do not use an oil that keeps paint from bonding. Only in the bilge around the engine, where gasoline and oil can get at them, are the rubber-base types less than ideal.

These new compounds can be divided into polysulfide (Thiokol), polyurethane, and silicone compounds. These synthetic rubbers are available in two-part systems that combine the sealant with a catalyst to cure it, or one part products that take moisture from the air to cause the curing and are usually slower acting.

All are available in a variety of colors and are suitable for bonding a fitting that is being bolted to the deck, repairing a leak

MAINTENANCE

around a windshield gasket, or stopping the dribble of water seeping from a through-hull fitting. Seams, of course, are usually sealed once and for all, if the wood is first carefully primed, since the material has great adhesion plus stretch and sheer strength.

Treatment of electrical connections to provide insulation and protection from corrosion is also easy with some of the silicones. GE's new RTV (room temperature vulcanizing) Silicone Rubber Adhesive Sealant can be applied directly to electrical junction box connections. In its transparent form, terminals and wiring can be seen right through it but are protected from vibration and corrosion. No pre-mixing is required with RTV, and it air-cures with minimum shrinkage.

Fortunately boat builders are using these same new sealants in quantity as well so that a new boat is less likely to require much corrective treatment at fitting-out time. But when a new fitting or locker is installed, a through-hull fitting added, or a leak noted around an engine connection, chances are one of the new polysulfide, polyurethane, or silicone compounds, under a variety of trade names, can cure the problem quickly and permanently with the squeeze of a tube. Read the directions on each to make the most suitable choice.

OUTBOARD MOTOR

Item	Operation
Spark plugs	Replace with fresh, correctly gapped ones.
Ignition wiring	Inspect. Relace "tired" looking high voltage wires. Tighten all connections.
Distributor or magneto cap	Remove, clean, inspect for chips or cracks. Replace unless perfect. Wipe with dielectric moisture-fighting spray.

Item	Operation
Distributor or magneto rotor	Remove and inspect for cracks or burning. Replace unless perfect. Wipe with dielectric spray.
Ignition points	Inspect. Replace if pitted. Adjust to specs. Readjust after 10 hours of operation.
Ignition timing	Adjust "by the book" after points are set.
Condenser	Check connections and mounting hardware.
Fuel tank	Empty out stale gas. Flush.
Fuel line	Inspect for tightness.
Fuel filter	Drain. Clean. Replace element.
Carburetor	Send it to the shop if it gave trouble last season. Otherwise, tighten hold-down nuts; check control linkages and lubricate them.
Oil cups	Inspect the motor and its accessories, looking for oil cups. Put a few drops of oil in any that are found.
Lower unit	Drain all oil from the lower unit. Refill with fresh lubricant of specified grade and viscosity.
Cooling system	Flush out the cooling system with clean fresh water. Alternately, run the motor in a tank or barrel of fresh water to purge it and allow you to watch the water pump operate.
Propeller	Inspect the propeller critically. If it's nicked or dented, replace it. Keep it for a spare.
Anticorrosion	Install new sacrificial anodes on the lower unit. Sometimes these are combined with a trim tab.
Oil film	Wipe down the entire power head and lower unit with an oily cloth. Alternately, spray with rust proofing compound.

MAINTENANCE

Table 12-4   **INBOARD ENGINE RECOMMENDATIONS**

Engine make, model	Fuel	Lubricant
AERO MARINE		
AM 165 CR, AM 240, AM 265, AM 320,	Regular	Marine SAE 30
AM 375, AM 455, AM 600	Premium	Marine SAE 30
D301, 4 R 1010, 6 R 1010	Diesel Fuel	Marine SAE 30
BARR		
FDX 220, FDY 330	Diesel Fuel	20W-20
Toro Flow 478	Diesel Fuel	Marine SAE 30
BRENNAN		
Imp	Regular	Marine SAE 30
E4, 100, 125, Gold Cup	Regular	40
CATERPILLAR DIESEL		
All Models	Diesel Fuel	Mobil Delvac 1330 or equiv.
CHRIS CRAFT		
All Models	Regular	Marine SAE 30
CHRYSLER		
Chrysler 235, 335, Fury 235	Premium	Marine SAE 30 or
Golden Lion 325, Hatteras Special		Special
Imperial 325, Volvo 110 Aquamatic		
Volvo 110 Commando		
Golden Lion Special, Hemi 525	Consult Manufacturer	40
All Other Models	Regular	Marine SAE 30 or
		Special
CRUSADER		Marine SAE 30 or
Gasoline Engines	Regular	Special
Diesel Engines	Diesel Fuel	Marine SAE 30
CUMMINS DIESEL		
All Models	Diesel Fuel	20W-20
DAYTONA		
Gasoline Engines	Regular	Special
Gasoline Engines—Turbo Charged	Premium	Special
Diesel Engines	Diesel Fuel	Marine SAE 30
DETROIT DIESEL		
Series 53, 71, 110	Diesel Fuel	Marine SAE 30
FAGEOL	4	4 stroke cycle
(Crofton)		engine, oil not
		mixed with
		gasoline. Use
		Marine SAE 30.
FLAGSHIP (Brunswick Corp.)		
V8, 185, 225	Regular	20W-20
GALE OMC	Regular	Special
GRAYMARINE	Regular or	20W-20
V8CH-280, Model 232	Premium	
V8CH-238, V8CF-238,	Premium	Marine SAE 30
V8CH-220, V8CF-220		
V8CH-195, V8CF-195,	Regular or	Marine SAE 30
V8CH-185, V8CF-185,	Premium	
Model 80, Four-162,		
Four-112, Seascout-91		
Seascout Diesel	Diesel Fuel	Marine SAE 30

Table 12-4 (Continued) INBOARD ENGINE RECOMMENDATIONS

Engine make, model	Fuel	Lubricant
HOLMAN AND MOODY	Premium ....Marine SAE 30	
INTERCEPTOR MARINE		
300, 330, 400 ....Premium ....Special		
All Other Models ....Regular ....Marine SAE 30		
INTERNATIONAL-PALMER		
Gasoline Engines ....Regular ....Marine SAE 30		
Diesel Engines ....Diesel Fuel ....Mobil Delvac 1330 or equiv.		
LATHROP		
Gasoline Engines ....Regular ....Marine SAE 30		
Diesel Engines ....Diesel Fuel ....Marine SAE 30		
LEHMAN ECON-O-POWER		
Gasoline Engines ....Premium ....Marine SAE 30		
Diesel Engines ....Diesel Fuel 20W-20		
LISTER-BLACKSTONE		
Diesel Engines ....Diesel Fuel ....Marine SAE 30		
M W M		
Diesel Engines ....Diesel Fuel 20W-20		
MERCEDES-BENZ		
Diesel Engines ....Diesel Fuel ....Marine SAE 30		
MER CRUISER I, II, III	Regular or 20W-20	
4-Cycle Gasoline Engines ....Premium		
Diesel Engines ....Diesel Fuel ....Marine SAE 30		
OSCO	Regular or 20W-20	
Gasoline Engines ....Premium		
Diesel Engines ....Diesel Fuel 20W-20		
PACEMAKER		Marine SAE 30
All Models ....Regular ....Special		
PERKINS DIESEL		
Naturally Aspirated ....Diesel Fuel ....Marine SAE 30		
Turbocharged ....Diesel Fuel ....Mobil Delvac 1320 or equiv.		
REVLEY	Regular ....Marine SAE 30 or	
		Special
SEAMASTER		
SM 300 ....Regular ....Special		
Others ....Regular ....Marine SAE 30		
STARRETT		
Diesel Engines ....Diesel Fuel ....Marine SAE 30		
UNIVERSAL		
4 Cylinder & V-8 ....Regular ....Marine SAE 30		
Super Sabre V-6 ....Regular ....20W-20 or		
		Special
WESTERBEKE	Diesel Fuel ....Marine SAE 30	
WESTERBEKE-VIRE (2 cycle)	Regular ....Outboard	
		2/5 pint oil/gal gas
WISCONSIN		
THDM, VH4DM ....Regular ....Marine SAE 30		
YAMAHA	3, 5, 7.5	3/4 11.1
YANMAR DIESEL	Diesel Fuel ....Marine SAE 30	

Table 12-5

OUTBOARD ENGINE RECOMMENDATIONS

1. Mobiloil Outboard oil or equivalent is recommended for use in the following outboard engines requiring a gasoline/oil fuel mixture. The recommended ratio of gasoline to oil is shown in each case. In many instances, the engine manufacturers recommend a richer oil ratio (i.e., more oil per gallon of gasoline) for break-in, or commercial use, in which case this recommendation should be followed.

2. Use Mobilube 47 or equivalent for the underwater gears except where an asterisk is shown with the model number. Mobilgrease No. 2 or equivalent should be used where an asterisk appears.

3. Models which were discontinued prior to 1955 have not been included.

Make	Model	B H P	Number of Cyl.	Pints Oil Per Gal Gas	Gasoline to Oil Ratio
AERO MARINE	4	4	1	1/5	40:1
	5, 7.5	5, 7.5	2	1/5	40:1
BRITISH SEA BEE	Minor	1½	1	2/5	
	3, Super 3	3	1	2/5	20:1
BRITISH SEAGULL	Forty Featherweight	2	1	3/4	
	Forty Plus	3	1	3/4	
	Century	4	1	3/4	11:1
	Century Plus	5	1	3/4	
CHIEF (Clinton Engines, Inc.)	J9	3.5	1	1/4	30:1
CHRYSLER	3.5	3.5	1	1/2	16:1
	3.6	3.6	1	1/6	50:1
	4.4, 5, 6.6, 7	4.4, 5, 6.6, 7	2	1/6	50:1
	6, 7.5	6, 7.5	2	1/2 (1/3 1966 + after)	16:1 24:1
	9.2	9.2	2	1/3	24:1
	9.9	9.9	2	1/6	50:1
	12	12	2	1/2 (1/3 1961 + after)	16:1 24:1
	20, 35, 45, 50	20, 35, 45, 50	2	1/3 (1/6 1965 + after)	24:1 50:1
	55	55	2	1/6	
	70, 75, 85	70, 75, 85	3	1/6	50:1
	80	80	4	1/3 (1/6 1965 + after)	24:1 50:1
	105, 120	105, 120	4	1/6	50:1
COMMANDO (Commanco, Inc.)	*Sport 300, *Sport Deluxe, 305	2.5	1	1/2	
	*Husky, *Commando V	4.0	1	1/2	
	*Commando VI	4.5	1	1/2	16:1
	*Commando VII	4.5	1	1/2	
ELGIN and SEARS	2, 3.5	2, 3.5	1	1/6	
	6, 7.5, 9	6, 7.5, 9	2	1/6	
	12, 14	12, 14	2	1/6	
	25, 28, 35	25, 28, 35	2	1/6	50:1
	40, 45	40, 45	2	1/6	
	60, 75	60, 75	3	1/6	

Table 12-5 (cont.)   Outboard Engine Recommendations

Make	Model	B H P	Number of Cyl.	Pints Oil Per Gal Gas	Gasoline to Oil Ratio
ESKA	1703, 1705, 1707	3, 5, 7,	1	1/2	16:1
EVINRUDE	Mate	1½	1	1/6	
	Lightwin, Ducktwin, Yachtwin	3	2	1/6	
	Angler	5	2	1/6	
	Fisherman	6	2	1/6	
	Sportwin	9½	2	1/6	
	Fastwin	18	2	1/6	
	Sportster	25	2	1/6	
	Ski-Twin, Ski Twin Electric	33	2	1/6	50:1
	Big Twin, Big Twin Electric, Lark	40	2	1/6	
	Triumph	55, 60	3	1/6	
	Sportfour, Sportfour (Heavy Duty)	60, 65	4	1/6	
	Speedifour, Starflite	80, 85	4	1/6	
*(Use 1/3 pint for 1963 and earlier models)	Starflite 100-S, 115-S	100, 115	4	1/6	
FIRESTONE (discontinued)	*2 HP, 3.6 HP	2, 3.6	1	1/2	
	5 HP, 7.5 HP, *8 HP	5, 7.5, 8	2	1/2	
	10 HP	10	2	1/2	16:1
	*12 HP, *40 HP (Prior to 1960)	12, 40	2	1/2	
	*12 HP, *40 HP	12, 40	2	1/3	24:1
	16 HP, 35 HP	16, 35	2	1/2	16:1
GALE (Buccaneer, Sovereign) (discontinued 1963)	*3D, *3S	3	1	1/3	
	5D, 5S, 5DL	5	2	1/3	
	12D, 12S	12	2	1/3	
	*15D, *15DL	15	2	1/3	
	22D, 22DE	25	2	1/3	24:1
	25D Series	25	2	1/3	
	35D Series	35	2	1/3	
	40D Series	40	2	1/3	
	60D Series	60	4	1/3	
GUPPY (Lancaster Pump & Mfg. Co.)	30A	2½	1	1/2	16:1
HIAWATHA (Gamble-Skogmo, Inc.) (discontinued 1961)	*3.6 HP	3.6	1	1/2	
	5 HP, 16HP	5, 16	2	1/2	16:1
	7.5 HP, 12HP	7.5, 12	2	3/8	
	25 HP	25	2	3/8	
	40 HP Series	40	2	3/8	21:1
	60 HP Series	60	3	3/8	
HOMELITE (Fisher-Pierce Co., Inc.)	460-A1, 460-A2, Bearcat 55	55	4	4 stroke cycle engine, oil not mixed with gasoline. Oil capacity 2¼ qts. Use Marine SAE 30.	
JOHNSON	JW/JH, CD, AD	3, 5.5, 7.5	2	**1/3	
	MQ, QD, FD, RX	9.5, 10, 18, 28	2	**1/3	
	RD, RDS	30, 40	2	**1/3	24:1
	RK, VX	40, 60	4	**1/3	
	V4	50	4	1/3	
	V4A, V4S	75	4	**1/3	
	V4M	90	4	1/6	
	All 1966 and Later Models	1½ to 115	1, 2, 3 or 4	1/6	50:1
**1/6 for 1964 and Later Models					
McCULLOCH	4	4	1	1/5	
	7.5, 9, 14	7.5, 9, 14.1	2	1/5	
	28, 45	28, 45	2	1/5	
	75	75	3	1/5	40:1
	OX140	14.1	2	1/5	
	OX450	45	2	1/5	

(continued)

MAINTENANCE

Table 12-5 (cont.)   Outboard Engine Recommendations

Make	Model	B H P	Number of Cyl.	Pints Oil Per Gal Gas	Gasoline to Oil Ratio
MERCURY**	Merc 39, 40	3.9, 4	1	3/8	
	*Mark 6A, *Merc 60,	6	2	3/8	
	Merc 75	6, 7.5			
	*Merc 100, *Merc 110	10, 9.8	2	3/8	
	*Mark 15A, *Merc 150	15	2	3/8	
	*Merc 200	20	2	3/8	
	*Merc 250, Mark 25				
	*Merc 350	25, 35	2	3/8	
	*Mark 30, *Mark 35A,				
	*Merc 300	30, 35	4	3/8	21:1
	*Mark 55	40	4	3/8	
	Mark 58, Merc 400,				
	Merc 450	45	4	3/8	
	Merc 500, Merc 650,				
	Merc 800	50, 65, 80	4	3/8	
	Merc 600	60	6	3/8	
	Merc 700, Merc 800,				
	Merc 850	70, 80, 85	6	3/8	
	Mark 78, Merc 900,				
**Manufacturer prefers	Merc 950, Merc 1000	90, 95, 100	6	3/8	
gear lubricant similar	Merc 1100, Merc 1250	110, 125	6	3/8	
to Mobilube 46 SAE 90	For 1966 and Later				
for non-grease lubricated	Models			1/6	50:1
underwater gears.					
MONO	M-50	5	1	1/2	16:1
(Mono Mfg. Co.)	M-75	7.5	1	1/2	16:1
NEPTUNE	*AA1-A Mighty Mite,	1.7	1	1/2	16:1
(Muncie Gear Works)	*WC-1				
OLIVER	J-4, Mohawk J-5,				
	Mohawk J-6	6	2	3/8	
	K-4, Ranger K-5,				
	Ranger K-6	16	2	3/8	21:1
	B-2, Olympus B-3,				
	Bulldog B-4	35	2	3/8	
PEERLESS	J9	3.5	1	1/4	
(Clinton Engines, Inc.)	J10	9.9	2	1/4	30:1
PERKINS	4.5 HP, 6.5 HP	4.5, 6.5	2	3/8	
	18 HP	18	2	3/8	21:1
	30 HP, 40 HP	30, 40	2	1/3	24:1
SEA KING	3 HP, 3.5 HP	3, 3.5	1	1/2	16:1
(Montgomery Ward)	5 HP, 8 HP, 12 HP	5, 8, 12	2	**1/3	24:1
	6 HP, 9.2 HP	6, 9.2	2	1/3	
	20 HP, 25 HP, 35 HP	20, 25, 35	2	***1/3	24:1
	40 HP, 45 HP, 50 HP	40, 45, 50	2	***1/3	
**1/2 for Engines Built	55 HP	55	2	1/6	50:1
Prior to 1959.	80 HP	80	4	1/6	
***1/6 for 1966 and later					
models.					
VIKING	3½	3½	1	1/2	16:1
(T. Eaton Co., Ltd.)	6, 9.2	6, 9.2	2	1/3	24:1
	15, 20, 35	15, 20, 35	2	1/6	50:1
	50, 55	50, 55	2	1/6	
WEST BEND	*2 HP, *3.5 HP	2, 3.5	1	1/2	
(Some Models	*6 HP, *7.5 HP, *8 HP	6, 7.5, 8	2	1/2	16:1
Named Commodore)	10 HP, *12 HP	10, 12	2	1/3	24:1
(discontinued 1964)	*16 HP	16	2	1/2	16:1
	*18 HP, 20 HP, *25 HP	18, 20, 25	2	1/3	
	30 HP, 35 HP	30, 35	2	1/3	
	40 HP, 45 HP	40, 45	2	1/3	24:1
	"500"	50	2	1/3	
	"800", Shark-O-Matic	80	4	1/3	
WIZARD	3.5, *3.6	3.5, 3.6	1	1/2	16:1
(Western Auto)	6, 9	6, 9	2	**1/3	24:1
	20	20	2	1/6	50:1
	15, 25, 35, 40	15, 25, 35, 40	2	3/8	
	60	60	4	3/8	21:1
	**For Engines Built				
	Prior to 1965			1/2	16:1

Table 12-6

OIL-FUEL MIXTURES—MIXING PROCEDURE

Correct mixture ratios for engines using oil-fuel blends are very important to assure proper engine operation and protection along with maximum economy of both fuel and oil. The ratios of oil to gasoline shown in the accompanying chart are those recommended by the various manufacturers for their individual makes and models. They are for average conditions of use, and it is recommended for special situations (racing, for example) that the Engineering Department of the outboard engine manufacturer be consulted.

Outboard engine manufacturers caution against adding any special chemicals or compounds to gasoline in an attempt to secure greater power output.

Correct mixture ratios also depend on thorough blending of the oil and gasoline portions. First, measure the ingredients accurately; next put a small amount of the fuel in the mixing can or tank, and then add the lubricating oil and the remainder of the gasoline. Shake well, or otherwise agitate to assure thorough mixing.

GASOLINE TO OIL RATIO TABLE

		Pints when applied to				
Pints of Oil Per Gal. of Gas	ACTUAL RATIO	2 GAL.	3 GAL.	4 GAL.	5 GAL.	6 GAL.
1/12	96:1	1/6	1/4	1/3	5/12	1/2
1/6	48:1	1/3	1/2	2/3	5/6	1
1/5	40:1	2/5	3/5	4/5	1	1⅕
1/3	24:1	2/3	1	1⅓	1⅔	2
3/8	21:1	3/4	1⅛	1½	1⅞	2¼
1/2	16:1	1	1½	2	2½	3
3/4	11:1	1½	2¼	3	3¾	4½

NOTE: In some cases, it may be more convenient to mix by the ounce rather than by the pint. Graduations on the container are given in both pints and ounces. There are 16 fluid ounces to the pint.

INBOARD ENGINE MAINTENANCE

Item	Operation
IGNITION Spark plugs	Remove. Crank engine to clear cylinders of excess oil. Clean and gap plugs or, preferably, replace them.
Ignition wiring	Inspect. Replace if insulation is cracked or chafed. Tighten all connections. Wipe with anti-moisture dielectric spray.

MAINTENANCE

Table 12-7

STERN DRIVE LUBRICATION

Make & Model	Lubricant Recommendations (Normal Operation)
BRENNAN Imp	Upper Unit, Gear Lube HD 90 Lower Unit, Outboard Gear Grease
CHRYSLER Drive 90 Shark-O-Matic Volvo 250	Gear Lube HD 90 Outboard Gear Oil EP 90 Havoline Super Premium 10W-40 or equiv.
EATON Powernaut Interceptor Mod. 200 to #219752 Interceptor Mod. 200 after #219752	Gear Lube HD 90 Texaco Gear Oil 3450 or equiv. Havoline Super Premium 10W-40 or equiv.
BRUNSWICK Exeter Combord	Mobilube 47 or equiv.
GRAYMARINE	Mobilube HD 80-90 or equiv.
HARNISCHFEGER (Napco) Powerhawk	Outboard Gear Oil EP 90
HOLMAN & MOODY	Havoline Super Premium 10W-40 or equiv.
MERCURY MARINE MerCruiser I, II, III	Outboard Gear Oil EP 90
MUNCIE Flexidrive "500"	Mobilube 47 or equiv.
OMC	Mobilube 47 or equiv.
OSCO	Gear Lube HD 90
PERKINS	Texaco Gear Oil 3450 or equiv.
RANGER	Universal Gear Lube EP 90
SEA HAWK	Mobilube 47 or equiv.
UNIVERSAL Sabre V6	Mobilube 47 or equiv.
WESTERN Sea Power	Mobilube 46 SAE 90 or Mobilube 47 or equiv.

Item	Operation
Distributor cap	Remove, clean, inspect for chips or cracks. Replace unless perfect, unblemished. Wipe with dielectric spray.
Distributor rotor	Remove and inspect for cracks or burning. Replace unless perfect. Wipe with dielectric spray.
Distributor points	Inspect. Replace if pitted. Adjust to specification using a dwell meter if possible. Re-adjust after first 10 hours.
Ignition timing	Adjust to spec after points are properly set. Use a timing light if possible.
Coil	Snug up mounting hardware and connections. Wipe down with dielectric spray.
Ignition switch	Test all connections. Looseness here is a frequent cause of "unexplained" engine miss.
Condenser	Check connections and mounting hardware.

FUEL SYSTEM

Item	Operation
Fuel tank	Inspect mountings for security. Pour in several cans of gum-dissolving solvent to fight tar which may have formed.
Vents	Uncover and blow clear. Inspect for integrity to tank and that vent spills overboard.
Fuel valves	Open all.
Fuel lines	Inspect all connections for leaks. Be sure lines are secure and tight.
Fuel pump	Snug up mounting cap screws. Drain and clean filter if pump has one. Replace the pump (or rebuild) if it's four seasons old or older.

MAINTENANCE

Item	Operation
Filter	Drain. Replace the element.
Flame arrester	Remove and clean thoroughly.
Carburetor	Send it to the shop for rebuild if it gave trouble last season. Otherwise, tighten hold-down nuts, check connections, and, if possible, pour a few ounces of gasoline into the float bowl vent tube as a pre-start prime. Careful with the gas!

LUBRICATION

Item	Operation
Distributor	Put a few drops of oil on the felt under the rotor. If there's an oil cup on the distributor body, squirt in a few drops of engine oil.
Generator	Look for oil cups. Put several drops of oil in cups that are found.
Crankcase	Warm the engine, change the oil.
Oil filter	Replace with fresh element.
Transmission:	Warm the engine. Change the transmission lubricant.
Block & Head	Wipe the entire engine down with rust proofing oil.

COOLING
SYSTEM

Item	Operation
Drain plugs, cocks	Replace those removed for lay-up. Close all cocks.
Hoses	Carefully inspect. Replace cracked and rotten looking hoses.
Clamps	Look for rusty clamps. Replace "tired" ones with good stainless steel ones. Tighten all.

Item	Operation
Water pump	Install a new drive V-belt. Re-adjust this belt after first hour or two of operation. If possible, hand prime pump before first start-up.
Sea cocks	Test for functioning. Lubricate if applicable. Test hose connections.

EXHAUST SYSTEM

Transom pipe	Remove plugs or tape from outlet.
Fittings	Replace rusted clamps, preferably using double clamps. Inspect entire system for gas-tight integrity.

AFTER STARTUP

Cooling	Immediately after the first startup, see that the cooling water pump is functioning.
Instruments	Watch the "pins" to see that there is oil pressure, that the generator is charging, and that engine temperature settles at the correct point.

POWER TRAIN MAINTENANCE

Transmission	Warm the transmission by running the engine; then change the lubricant. Follow manufacturer's specs as to grade of oil.
Alignment	Align the engine/transmission assembly exactly with the propeller shaft *after* the boat has been afloat several days.
Outdrive	Service and lubricate the outdrive lower unit according to specs.

MAINTENANCE

Item	Operation
Propeller	Inspect the prop minutely. If it is even slightly nicked or dented, send it to the shop for rework and balancing.
Prop shaft	Inspect the shaft, looking for bends or scoring.
Struts	Physically shake the prop shaft struts, making sure they are secure and tight to the hull.
Strut bearings	Shake the prop shaft in the strut bearings, seeking excess looseness. Some clearance is OK. If you're in doubt, get expert opinion.
Prop Replacement	Mount prop hub on taper snugly; don't let it ride up on the key and get off center.
Shaft log	Be sure the shaft log is well bedded to the hull and secured to the boat's bottom. Tighten the fastenings; they often loosen as the bedding compresses.
Stuffing box	If the box dribbles, tighten the gland nuts slightly. Don't over do.
Zincs	Install fresh new protective zinc anodes on the struts and prop shaft.

CONTROLS MAINTENANCE

Steering gear	Test the control for full starboard and port rudder (or outboard swing). Clear possible obstructions.
Steering lubrication	Oil or grease all working parts of the steering mechanism.
Throttle adjustment	Definitely see that when the hand lever is closed (idle) the throttle stop is against the adjusting

Item	Operation
	screw on the carburetor. Also see that the throttle opens wide as required for full bore operation.
Throttle lubrication	Work oil or thin grease through the throttle linkage and cable until action is smooth and free.
Throttle friction	Adjust the friction device in the throttle quadrant, if necessary, to prevent the throttle from creeping.
Choke	Lubricate the choke control and adjust as described for the throttle. Be *sure* choke opens wide.
Clutch	Disconnect from clutch lever on transmission. Work the control, making sure there is adequate travel for forward and reverse. Lubricate.
Trim	If the boat has trim tabs, lubricate and adjust the controls according to specs.
Zinc	Install a fresh new zinc protective anode on the rudder, outdrive, or outboard, as applicable.

ELECTRICAL SYSTEM

Wiring	Inspect all visible wires. Watch for frayed insulation, poor connections. Repair or replace as required.
Main switch board	Check every connection for tightness. Do same for distribution panels.
Bonding	Make sure that tanks, engine, all electrical accessories are bonded together with heavy wire.

MAINTENANCE

INBOARD ENGINE MAINTENANCE LOG

☐ STARBOARD ENGINE   ☐ PORT ENGINE

DATE

ENGINE HOURS

Column headers (repeated): Inspect / Adjust / Lubricate / Replace

IGNITION SYSTEM
- Spark Plugs
- H. T. Wiring
- Distributor Cap
- Points / Rotor
- Condenser
- Coil
- Switch(s)
- Alternator / Gen.

FUEL SYSTEM
- Filler Pipes & Cap
- Fuel Tank(s)
- Shut-off Valve(s)
- Lines
- Pump(s)
- Filter(s)
- Carburetor
- Flame Arrestors

COOLING SYSTEM
- Water Pump (Fresh)
- Water Pump (Sea)
- Hoses and Clamps
- V Belt(s)
- Water Jackets
- Expansion Tank
- Heat Exchanger
- Fresh Water Coolant
- Thermostat Control
- Temperature Gauge

LUBRICATION
- Engine Oil Level
- Oil Pressure Gauge
- Transmission Fluid
- Oil Filter(s)
- Oil Cooler

STARTER
- Battery
- Switches
- Solenoid
- Cables
- Connectors
- CONTROLS

Item	Operation
The battery	Charge the battery(s) fully. Clean the posts and terminals. *Observe* polarity, and connect securely.
Battery mounting	Fasten the battery tightly so pitching and rolling will not move it.
Battery cables	Provide the heaviest possible gauge battery cables to assure minimum voltage drop. Replace worn, acid-eaten cables. Replace weak clamps.
Alternator	Install a fresh V-belt and re-tighten this belt after an hour of operation. Check electrical connections.
Starter	Tighten cable connection and mounting cap screws or bolts.
Lights	Test every light on the boat. Lay in a stock of replacement bulbs.
Fuses	Test every fuse on the boat. Lay in a stock of replacement fuses.
Bilge pump	Test. Be sure switch and fuse are in "hot" ungrounded side of the line.
Windshield wiper	Test. Lubricate if required. Install new blade. Check wiring. Clean commutator.
Ground plate	Trace through and be sure the ground plate is electrically tied to the bonding system and lightning protective system.
Voltage	Measure voltage drop at the terminals of accessories such as blowers. When motor is energized, voltage must not drop more than 10% (only 3% for electronic gear).
Aux. AC generator	Give engine same check as inboard engine. Tighten all connections.

MAINTENANCE

Item	Operation
AC System	As far as practical, inspect the wiring. See that all white wires tie to other whites, blacks to blacks, and green to green.
Electronics	Perform voltage drop checks as cited under "voltage." Increase wire conductor size where voltage sags.

SAILS AND RIGGING

Sails: Sails should be washed in mild detergent and cool water by hand—and scrubbing brush.

After washing they should be inspected thoroughly for rips, tears. Stitching in Dacron sails is the point of most weakness so inspect each seam with care. Most experienced sailors make a practice of having their sailmaker examine and re-stitch each sail as needed every year. It is cheap and worth every penny. Home repairs are possible but usually not as satisfactory.

Spars: Anodized spars can be merely washed. Non-anodized spars should be cleaned up with an abrasive (scouring powder, scouring pads or fine wet sandpaper) and then coated with one of the clear coatings formulated for this purpose. If you want a really shiny spar, buff with rubbing compound before coating. While you're cleaning check spars for straightness, check fittings for looseness and defects (cracks in castings) and oil all sheaves.

Lights and Instruments: Test all circuits and replace components as needed. Better, summarily replace all bulbs.

Noise Abatement: Aluminum spars are noisy, particularly with internal halliards and wiring. Wiring can be enclosed in a plastic tube(s) or it can be seized to the after side of the spar. To do this, lay the spar aft side down, drill pairs of holes about six feet apart each side of the sail track and seize the wires through the holes with stainless seizing wire. Finish holes with epoxy.

Standing Rigging: All standing rigging should be examined with great care. Particular attention should be paid to all swage fittings. Examine these with a magnifying device which will show any hairline cracks present. Cracked swage fittings are unreliable and should be discarded.

All hardware should be examined with a jaundiced eye. Clevis pins in particular should be replaced if they show wear, and all cotter pins should be replaced as a matter of course. Lock nuts aloft should be drilled and pinned if they haven't been already.

Running Rigging: Check for wear and chafe. Replace as indicated. Sometimes sheet life can be extended by shifting them end for end. Additionally, a long sheet with one worn section may be useful in another function requiring a shorter length. Finally, fenders always need lines.

Wire running rigging should also be examined for wear, indicated by short barbs sticking out at the point of chafe or wear. Remove damaged section, end for end the wire or replace entire wire as indicated. If flexible wire running rigging is fitted with swage fittings pay particular attention to junctions which are points of particular sensitivity. Consider replacing swage fittings with more flexible splices or Nicopress fittings.

Oil: Be liberal with the oil can throughout the rig. Shackles should snap, pole fittings should open easily, sheaves should revolve without strain and track cars should move without having to be forced.

Tape: White rigging tape is a rigger's best friend. Everything that can possibly get near a sail should be taped to eliminate tearing. Additionally, when a wire is to be seized to another wire or to a piece of hardware (spreaders) tape the wire first, then seize it and follow with more tape. The first taping will effectively prevent slipping.

PLUMBING

Fuel System

__ *Filler.* Make sure cap assembly is secure to deck. Inspect hose, ground wire from filler cap to tank. Tighten or replace hose clamps as necessary.

___ *Tank vent.* Inspect and clean.

___ *Tank.* Inspect for leaks. Make sure hold-downs or straps are tight and secure. Check operation of tank shut-off valve. Drain, refill with fresh gasoline or diesel fuel.

___ *Fuel lines.* Inspect for cracks, abrasions, leaks at fittings.

Cooling System

___ *Intakes.* Check, tighten, replace clamshell fastenings as required. Clean clamshells, sediment screens.

___ *Through-hull fittings, valves.* Check operation. These should open and close with hand pressure alone. Clean, lubricate, replace units as necessary. Check bedding blocks and caulking.

___ *Pumps.* Clean, check packing and washers.

___ *Hoses.* Inspect; replace any that are worn, abraded, or weak. Tighten, replace clamps as necessary.

___ *Raw (sea) water cooling.* Drain and flush. Inspect for leaks.

___ *Fresh water cooling.* Drain and flush raw water side of system. Drain, flush, and refill fresh water side. Use rust inhibitor, other additives as specified by engine or cooling system manufacturer. Check intake, screens of keel coolers; disassemble if necessary to clear obstructions in keel cooler unit.

Exhaust system

___ *Transom flanges.* Inspect fastenings; replace as necessary.

___ *Hoses, piping.* Inspect, replace if necessary. Tighten or replace clamps.

___ *Standpipe.* Inspect, clean expansion chamber.

___ *Manifold water jackets.* Inspect for leaks. Drain and flush.

___ *Wet mufflers.* Check thermostat operation, if one is present, at engine side of feed to muffler. Clean, inspect muffler. Paint with heat-resistant finish, if necessary.

Potable (Fresh Water) System

___ *Tanks.* Drain, refill. Add purifying tablets as required. Check and adjust tanks hold-downs.

__ *Hoses.* Inspect, replace as required. Tighten or replace clamps as needed.

__ *Pumps.* Inspect packing, washers. Clean screens. Check float valves, polarity of connections to electrical pumps. Switches must be in "hot" wire from battery.

__ *Heater.* Clean, check operation, thermostat settings.

__ *Vents, drains.* Clean, inspect. Check through-hull fittings, valves. Seacocks and valves should open and close by hand pressure alone. Lubricate or replace units as necessary.

Toilets

__ *Pumps.* Inspect and clear joker or check valves of hand pumps. Check connections, operation of electrical units.

__ *Hoses.* Clean inside and out. Inspect, replace as necessary. Tighten or replace hose clamps as required.

__ *Bowl.* Clean. Inspect for cracks, chips. Check hold-down fastenings. Lubricate lid hinges.

__ *Chlorinators, other chemical units.* Clean, inspect; replace chlorine or other chemical according to manufacturer's specifications.

__ *Holding tanks.* Should be drained when boat is hauled. Clean and inspect for cracks, leaks, including hoses and pump-out fittings.

__ *Through-hull fittings, seacocks, valves.* Check bedding blocks and caulking. Seacocks and valves should open and close with hand pressure alone. Lubricate, replace units as required.

Miscellaneous

__ Clear dirt and debris from scuppers, self-bailing ducts, limber holes and similar passages through which water must pass.

TRAILER MAINTENANCE

A well-built boat trailer should remain in excellent condition indefinitely with a minimum of maintenance. In addition to peri-

MAINTENANCE

odic inspections and lubrication, the most important ingredient is a thorough wash-down after each use. Wash with soap and water, just as for your car, to remove road tars and soil.

Trailer Frame

Use a stiff wire brush to remove rust scale. Paint as necessary with a rust-inhibiting coating. Inspect and lubricate tilt lock and hinge mechanism, if trailer is so equipped. Lubricate rollers, several times each season, and use strips of old carpeting to replace torn or rotted bunker covers.

Winch

Inspect and lubricate winch gears, handle and lock mechanism. Wipe metal cable with an oily rag to prevent rust; if cable is worn or frayed, replace with new cable. If fiber winch line is used, inspect and replace if necessary.

Springs

Wash well after each trip. Use a paint brush to coat springs with motor oil, or spray on a commercial rust preventive.

Wheel Bearings

Remove hub and grease seals, and wipe axle spindle clean. Inspect bearings and bearing cups for pitting, then check grease seals for undue wear. Coat inside bearing with grease, and put it in position. Press on the grease seal. Put additional grease on the open area of the hub, and install the hub on the spindle. Grease the outer bearing and install it. Replace the nut on the spindle and tighten as far as it will go. Then back it off until the wheel spins freely. Replace the cotter pin to hold the nut in place. Replace hub caps.

Lights & Wiring

If lights have been submerged accidentally, remove glass or plastic cover, drain water, and dry insides with cloth or paper towels. If you can't remove lights and it's necessary to submerge them, cover the entire light housing with a plastic bag secured with rubber bands. It's better than no protection. Check wiring for cracks and breaks; replace as necessary. Be sure connectors are clean.

Tire Size and Ply Rating	Load Capacity at Various Inflations (Lbs. of Air)					
	30	35	40	50	60	70
4.80/4.00 x 8 (2)	380					
4.80/4.00 x 8 (4)	380	420	450	515	575	
5.70/5.00 x 8 (4)	–	575	625	710		
6.90/6.00 x 9 (6)	–	785	850	970	1080	
4.80/4.00 x 12 (4)	545	550	595	680	755	790
5.30/4.50 x 12 (4)	640	700	760	865	915	

Inboard Engine Troubleshooting

How to use this chart: (1) find below situation matching trouble;
(2) note treatment key; (3) refer to treatment on reverse side in order of key.

Breakdown

Breakdown	Treatment
Motor stops suddenly after period of proper operation.	A,E,B,C,D,K,F
Motor stops suddenly, no spark to spark plugs.	A,E,G
Motor stops, has good spark, won't restart.	A,D,J,K,S
Motor stops, restarts when cool, stops again when hot.	F
Motor stops suddenly, will not turn through full revolution. (Do not restart after inspection and repair.)	Q
Motor stops "frying hot," won't turn over when cool.	OVERHAUL
Motor stops after period of rough, uneven operation.	A,B,C,D,E,G,H,I,S
Motor overheats before stopping, coolant O.K. (Restart only when it has cooled.)	H,L,I
Motor stops hot, low coolant or no coolant flow. (Restart only when it has cooled.)	A,C,LL,L,M
Motor runs by spurts, stops, fuel filters clean.	D,E,H,I,J
Motor runs by spurts, stops, water in fuel filters.	S,R
*Motor stops with heavy black smoke from exhaust pipe.	O
*Motor stops with loud clatter.	A,Z,ZZ,P,Q

Restart and operate motor before prescribed repairs only in an emergency.

Malfunctions

Malfunctions	Treatment
Motor misses, gallops, spits, backfires, loses power.	A,R,E,I,S,J
Motor runs rough, idles poorly, overheats. (Do not run at full power until overheating is corrected.)	L,H,I,J
Motor starts hard, especially in cold weather.	G,I,E,Y,GG
Motor "pops" and "pungs" in exhaust pipe at all speeds, loss of power and compression, hard starting.	Y,Z
*Lube oil level rises, oil looks and feels gummy.	M
*Lube oil level rises, oil feels very thin.	N
Motor idles poorly, indicates ice in carburetor throat, loses top rpm's after a change in brand or type of fuel.	V
Motor "pings" at full load, starts hard.	H,V
Starter motor spins without engaging flywheel gear.	T
Starter motor turns engine, engine won't operate.	D,E,F,H,I,K
Starter motor jams against flywheel gear, won't turn. Solenoid clicks when starter button is pushed. Battery up.	U
*Motor runs rough, noisy, one or more cylinders not giving power as shown by shorting spark plugs with insulated screw driver.	P
*Motor runs rough, loses power, water on spark plug electrodes.	W
*Hot water in the bilges.	X
Motor "eats" lube oil, low compression and power.	Z,B
*Motor runs with thumping or knocking noise.	ZZ

Continue to operate motor at low power only in emergency before correcting condition.

IMPORTANT! ALWAYS CHECK YOUR ENGINE MANUAL FOR PROPER REPAIR AND ADJUSTMENT PROCEDURES!

DANGER! ALWAYS MOP UP SPILLED FUEL AND VENTILATE ENGINE COMPARTMENT BEFORE RESTARTING A MARINE ENGINE!

SAFETY FIRST! DISCONNECT AND COVER BATTERIES BEFORE WORKING ON STARTER, GENERATOR, OR WHERE TOOLS CAN FALL ON TERMINALS, CAUSING ELECTRICAL SHORT!

Inboard Engine Treatment

Key

A Inspect motor for obvious damage, excessive heat, leaking fuel, oil or coolant, loose or disconnected wires, control parts, fuel and water lines.

B Check lube oil level and quality on dip stick, add oil if needed, if level too high, refer to Treatment M and N.

C Check for leaks in coolant system, leaky pump shaft seal, defective circulating pump. Check exhaust cooling water.

D Check to see if fuel tank is empty or shut off.

E Check ignition system for: loose, broken or disconnected wires; cracked distributor cap; broken breaker point spring; shorted condenser; disconnected battery "hot" line; broken rotor; ignition switch "off."

F Replace defective ignition coil that shorts out when hot.

G Battery voltage low. Bad cell, generator not charging, generator not big enough to carry electrical load, poor battery hot and ground connections.

GG Change to lighter lubrication oil for cold weather operation.

H *Spark timing incorrect; have readjusted with timing light.

I *Ignition points burned and/or spark plug electrodes eroded. Replace, adjust. Inspect high-tension ignition wires for insulation breaks.

J *Look for and repair break or leak in fuel line.

K *Replace fuel pump and/or pump diaphragm.

L *Replace worn or broken circulating pump impellers, check thermostat.

LL Raw (sea) water suction plugged or shut off. Remove obstruction.

M *Coolant leaking into lube oil in base. Check for internal gasket leaks, cracked head or block, do not operate until overhauled.

N *Fuel leaking into oil in crankcase. Use Treatment K.

Key

O Carburetor needle valve stuck open. STOP MOTOR INSTANTLY if still running. Drain raw gas from carburetor throat, mop up spilled fuel. Ventilate motor compartment thoroughly. Re-seat valve by tapping carburetor lightly on side with hammer. Have mechanic replace valve as soon as possible.

P *Valve springs broken, motor probably running too cold. Overhaul.

Q *Broken-off valve head is on top of piston, hits cylinder head at top of piston stroke. Remove cylinder head, replace broken valve, look for further internal damage.

R *Dirt or water in carburetor jets and bowl. Remove, clean, readjust.

S Clean fuel filter more often. Remove water and dirt from fuel tank.

T *Disconnect battery, remove starter, clean drive shaft with kerosene and steel wool, look for and replace broken Bendix spring.

U Starter gear is jammed against flywheel gear teeth. Disconnect battery, loosen starter holding bolts until starter is free from block, turn motor over in reverse rotation with wrench applied to "V"-belt wheel or shaft at front end to unjam gears. Tighten starter bolts, reconnect battery.

V Fuel octane rating wrong for your motor. Change to proper fuel.

W *Coolant is leaking into intake manifold or cylinders. Remove head, look for leaky gasket or crack in head or motor block. Have repaired before operating.

X Exhaust pipe or hot raw water discharge is leaking into bilges. Repair.

Y *Exhaust valves burned. Motor needs overhaul.

Z *Worn or broken piston rings and/or worn valve guides. Overhaul.

ZZ *Burned main or connecting rod bearings. Overhaul.

*Should be done by a competent mechanic familiar with your model of motor.

Basic Repair Tools

Ignition
Ignition wrench set.
Ignition point file.
Feeler gauge.
Low-voltage test bulb.
Neon test bulb.
Spark plug wrench.
Timing light.

Mechanical
Combination box, end wrenches.
Stillson and monkey wrenches.
Set of Allen wrenches.
Visegrip and regular pliers.
Machinist's hammer.
Hack saw and blades.
Screwdriver set.
Jackknife.
Ratchet, sockets, extension bar.

Special
Oil squirt gun.
Hand oil-pan pump.
Hydrometer.
Flashlight, troublelight.

Basic Spare Parts

Ignition
2 sets breaker points.
2 sets point condensers.
1 set of spark plugs.
Distributor cap, rotor.
Ignition coil.

Mechanical
Pump impellers, saft seals.
Fuel pump or diaphragm.
Head, valve cover gaskets.
Thermostat.
"V" belts to fit.
Flexible hose to fit.
Assorted hose clamps.
Mixed bolts, nuts, washers.
Plastic and common tape.
Sheet gasket material.
Fuel and lube filter elements.

Fluid, etc.
Extra lubricating oil.
Pump and gear grease.
Hydraulic clutch fluid.
Penetrating oil.
Gasket shellac.

MAINTENANCE

STOWAGE PLAN

Sketch location of lockers and cabinets. Label "A," "B," "C," etc., and list
contents below.

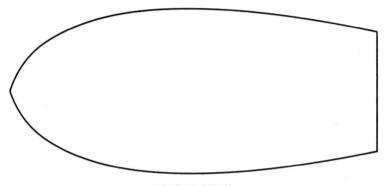

BELOW DECK

ABOVE DECK

WIRING DIAGRAMS

Sketch in location of battery, running lights, other electrical accessories, and the run of the wiring to each. Note wiring color code, and other distinguishing characteristics.

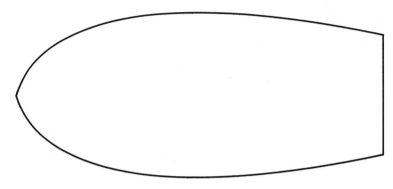

BATTERY SYSTEM

Sketch location of items served by the 110 volt AC system, location of generator, service panel, shore connectors, and run of the wiring.

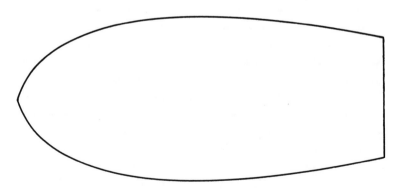

110 VOLT AC SYSTEM

GENERAL INFORMATION

Boat Name_____Manufacturer_____

Year Built_____Designer_____

Length Overall_____Waterline Length_____Beam_____

Draft_____Sail Area_____Displacement_____

State Registration Number_____

Engine(s) Make_____Horsepower_____Year_____

INSURANCE

Firm Name_____Agent Name_____

Address_____Address_____

_____   _____

Phone_____Phone, Office_____Home_____

BOATYARD   MECHANIC

Name_____Name_____

Address_____Address_____

_____   _____

Phone_____Phone, Office_____Home_____

Manager's Home Phone_____

Licensed Radio Technician   Radio Call Sign_____

Name_____   Frequencies_____

Address_____   _____

Phone, Office_____Home_____   _____

NUMBERS AND SIZES

Engine(s) Make_____Serial Number(s)_____

Spark Plug Size_____Gap_____Firing Order_____

Distributor Point Gap_____

Timing Mark Location_____Setting_____

Oil Grade_____Oil Capacity_____

Transmission Lube Grade_____Capacity_____

ELECTRONIC EQUIPMENT

Radiotelephone Make _____ Serial Number_____

Radio Direction Finder Make _____ Serial Number_____

Depth Indicator Make _____ Serial Number_____

Other Electronic Gear

      Make—Item _____ Serial Number_____

      Make—Item _____ Serial Number_____

      Make—Item _____ Serial Number_____

FRESH WATER COOLING SYSTEM CAPACITY _____

SAIL INVENTORY

SAIL	MAKER	YEAR	REMARKS

BULB SIZES

Running Lights _____   Masthead _____

    Starboard* _____   Stern _____

    Port _____   Others _____

*Starboard light usually requires brighter bulb than port light to meet United States Coast Guard visibility requirements.

Cabin Light(s) _____   _____

    _____   _____

Searchlight _____

Instrument Panel _____

Others _____

FUSES, CIRCUIT BREAKER SIZES (Amps)

Main_____   Radiotelephone_____

Running Lights_____   Appliances_____

General Lighting_____   _____

Receptacle Outlets_____   _____

Bilge Pump_____   Other Electronic Gear_____

    _____

    _____

NOTES

NOTES

NOTES

NOTES

The Compass

The *compass course* which you must follow in order to maintain a given heading in relation to true north (true course) is determined by correcting the true heading, plotted on a chart, by the amount of variation for the area shown on that chart, to arrive at the *magnetic course*. This in turn is corrected for *deviation* caused by magnetic influences within the boat.

Note that in any given area, the amount and direction of *variation* will not change from that shown on the chart, with any change in the boat's heading. *Deviation*, being the sum of influences of the earth's magnetic field and the boat's magnetic field, will change with every heading.

The amount and direction of variation are shown on the chart. To correct a true course to a magnetic course, *add* westerly variation, subtract easterly variation.

Deviation must be determined for each boat, as described below. Again, *add westerly*.

To change a magnetic course to a compass course, *add* westerly deviation, subtract easterly deviation. To determine a true heading based on a compass course, reverse the process: *add easterly* deviation and variation, *subtract westerly* deviation and variation.

To prepare a deviation table for your boat, you should

be able to sight over your compass on various headings as you pass a range, and get accurate readings. Use of a pelorus or hand-held compass may be a help, provided that any differences between the boat's compass and hand-held compass readings are taken into account when bearings are recorded.

Two visible objects, preferably ashore or fixed to the bottom, both accurately charted, are selected. From the chart the magnetic range (the magnetic course between the objects) is recorded. A series of runs is made past this range, noting the compass bearing of the two marks on each run when they are in alignment. Each run is made on a new heading, usually in 15 degree increments as shown by the boat's compass. The difference between the plotted magnetic range, and the compass bearing, is the deviation for each run. The listing of deviations for each 15 degrees of compass course provides a deviation table for your boat.

Now for each 15-degree compass heading, draw a line from the *inner* compass rose to the *outer* compass rose, applying the deviation as determined above. You can now use the compass deviation card to find a compass course for a given magnetic course, or the reverse, as shown on the card. An example of a deviation table, and the resulting card, is shown below.

Determining the Deviations

Ship's Head Compass	Range bears Compass	Range bears Magnetic	Deviation
000°	082°	087°	5°E
015°	086°	087°	1°E
030°	091°	087°	4°W
045°	096°	087°	9°W
060°	100°	087°	13°W
075°	104°	087°	17°W
090°	106°	087°	19°W
105°	106°	087°	19°W
120°	104°	087°	17°W
135°	101°	087°	14°W
150°	097°	087°	10°W
165°	093°	087°	6°W
180°	089°	087°	2°W
195°	085°	087°	2°E
210°	082°	087°	5°E
225°	079°	087°	8°E
240°	076°	087°	11°E
255°	073°	087°	14°E
270°	070°	087°	17°E
285°	069°	087°	18°E
300°	070°	087°	17°E
315°	072°	087°	15°E
330°	075°	087°	12°E
345°	078°	087°	9°E

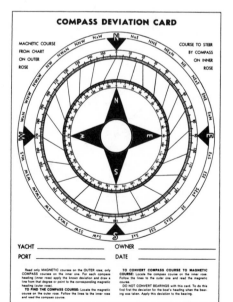

COMPASS DEVIATION CARD

YACHT _____ OWNER _____
PORT _____ DATE _____

Read only MAGNETIC courses on the OUTER rose; only COMPASS courses on the inner one. For each compass heading (inner rose) apply the known deviation and draw a line from that degree or point to the corresponding magnetic heading (outer rose).
TO FIND THE COMPASS COURSE: Locate the magnetic course on the outer rose. Follow the lines to the inner rose and read the compass course.

TO CONVERT COMPASS COURSE TO MAGNETIC COURSE: Locate the compass course on the inner rose. Follow the lines to the outer one and read the magnetic course.
DO NOT CONVERT BEARINGS with this card. To do this find first the deviation for the boat's heading when the bearing was taken. Apply this deviation to the bearing.

Compass
Deviation Card

MAGNETIC COURSE
FROM CHART
ON OUTER
ROSE

COURSE TO STEER
BY COMPASS
ON INNER
ROSE

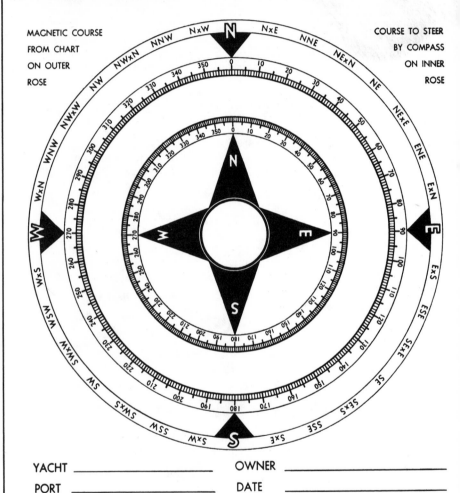

YACHT _____   OWNER _____

PORT _____   DATE _____

Read only MAGNETIC courses on the OUTER rose; only COMPASS courses on the inner one. For each compass heading (inner rose) apply the known deviation and draw a line from that degree or point to the corresponding magnetic heading (outer rose).

TO FIND THE COMPASS COURSE: Locate the magnetic course on the outer rose. Follow the lines to the inner rose and read the compass course.

TO CONVERT COMPASS COURSE TO MAGNETIC COURSE: Locate the compass course on the inner rose. Follow the lines to the outer one and read the magnetic course.

DO NOT CONVERT BEARINGS with this card. To do this find first the deviation for the boat's heading when the bearing was taken. Apply this deviation to the bearing.